BARK, SKIN AND CEDAR

BARK, SKIN AND CEDAR

EXPLORING THE CANOE
IN CANADIAN EXPERIENCE

JAMES RAFFAN

A Phyllis Bruce Book
HarperCollins*PublishersLtd*

http://www.harpercanada.com

HarperCollins books may be purchased for educational, business, or sales promotional use. For
information please write: Special Markets Department, HarperCollins Canada, 55 Avenue Road,
Suite 2900, Toronto, Ontario, Canada M5R 3L2.

First HarperCollins hardcover ed. ISBN 0-00-255730-4
First HarperCollins trade paper ed. ISBN 0-00-638653-9

Permission to quote from writings and broadcasts in copyright has been granted as follows:

Ella Elizabeth Clark, from *Indian Legends of Canada* (1960),
by permission of McClelland & Stewart, The Canadian Publishers.
Daniel Francis, from *National Dreams: Myth, Memory and Canadian History* (1997)
by permission of Arsenal Pulp Press.
Stephen Greenlees, from "Indian Canoe Makers" (1954),
by permission of the publishers of *The Beaver*.
George James Grinnell, from *A Death on the Barrens* (1996),
by permission of Northern Books and the author.
George James Grinnell, from a transcript of the series "Perfect Machines:
The Canoe," Seth Feldman, producer (Toronto: Canadian Broadcasting Corporation, 1995,
ID 9536). Used with permission of the author.
Timothy J. Kent, from *Birchbark Canoes of the Fur Trade* (1997),
by permission of Silver Fox Enterprises and the author.
Eric W. Morse, from *Freshwater Saga: Memoirs of a Lifetime of Wilderness
Canoeing in Canada* (1987), by permission of University of Toronto Press.
Stan Rogers, lyrics from "Northwest Passage" by Stan Rogers © 1980
used by permission of Fogarty's Cove Music and Ariel Rogers.
Gary Saunders, from *Rattles and Steadies: Memoirs of a Gander River Man* (1986),
by permission of Breakwater Books; copyright the author.

Text illustrations by Don Kilby

Canadian Cataloguing in Publication Data

Raffan, James
Bark, skin and cedar: exploring the canoe in Canadian experience

A Phyllis Bruce book.
ISBN 0-00-255730-4

1.Canoes and canoeing – Canada. 2. Canada – Description and travel.
3. Canoeists – Canada – Biography I. Title.
GV776.15.A2R33 1999   797.1'22'0971   C99-930451-8

99 00 01 02 03 04 HC 6 5 4 3 2 1

Printed and bound in the United States

To Gail Cole Simmons
navigator, teacher,
partner

CONTENTS

PROLOGUE

AT A FANCY DINNER IN OTTAWA not so long ago, I happened to sit next to woman from Montreal who, in the polite chatter over preprandial drinks, learned that I was writing a book about canoes. With that, she told me a story about a Danish friend of hers who was mad about birchbark canoes. This chap had studied canoes from his Scandinavian home, he had corresponded with paddlers around the world, he had plied interest into obsession, found his way to Canada and actually purchased a bark canoe to take home. "One day the doorbell rang," my dinner mate explained with a twinkle in her eye, "and there was Sven [we'll call him Sven] at the door with a birchbark canoe under his arm. I hadn't seen him in years, and we had a great visit, but I wasn't so fussy about having to store his birchbark canoe in my living room for weeks until he could figure out a way to ship it home."

Canada, it seems, has an interminable supply of such tales. Travel by train from Kingston to Toronto, turn to the end of the car and one sees an artfully rendered poster of blue lake and rocky shore joined by empty canoe with paddle akimbo, as if waiting for a weary traveller to pick it up and take an imaginary voyage into the wilderness fantasy that is Canada. Look out the window, passing through Napanee, Belleville, Trenton, Cobourg, and even Toronto, and between the rusted backsides of industry there are backyards and porches, and many a faded canoe awaiting the next family venture. Talk to the porter, the conductor, one's seatmate and there are canoe stories of one kind or another. Open the VIA Rail magazine and see an ad for CANOE (Canadian On-Line Explore) an Internet service provider. Look up to the ceiling and see tiles painted sky blue with fluffs of white, more hints of the great beyond as it might have looked to the explorers themselves.

At one end of the spectrum, canoes are cliché, they're everywhere. At the other extreme, canoes are invisible, they're everywhere. Like the railway, the mountains or Hudson Bay, they're part of who we are, an immutable fact of Canadian life. But if one were to pick up any canoe in any part of Canada, hold it up to the light, turn it lovingly over and admire its curves and imperfections, ask of its experiences on the waters nearby, stories will flow, stories that speak something of the essence of its paddlers and the place it calls home. These stories, many of them known only to the people who built or paddled the craft, deserve to be told to a wider audience, because they sum to a generative tracing of a northern nation. And that is more or less what I set out to do in this book.

A year into the writing, however, I made the mistake of attending a dance with a voyageur theme, and therein lies a canoe story to get things under way. It sounded harmless enough, and a decidedly Canadian thing to do, a dance with a voyageur theme. The band for the costumed occasion was called "Rubaboo," after pemmican soup, and included a line-up of musicians who, in their real lives, were about as close to modern-day voyageurs as one could get. There was Peter Labor, who runs an outfitting and tour firm on Lake Superior; Jeremy Ward, a birchbark-canoe builder; and a third troubador who, by association with the other two and in his *ceinture fléchée*, was voyageur enough for me. With my spouse, Gail, dressed in the fine tradition of marriage *à la façon du pays*, and me in an assemblage of raw cotton and buckskin, we headed for the dance floor. Things were going splendidly until midway through the first jig, when my left Achilles tendon broke with a unappetizing snap.

In those first moments of shock and disbelief, while the pain took a moment to register, my main concern was that some keen paramedic would cut off my prized deerhide pants with those penny-cutting shears they all carry. A quick trip to the washroom saw to it that the trousers were replaced with a pair of shorts. Off we trundled to Kingston General Hospital emergency department, where heads turned in bemused disbelief to see a wounded voyageur arrive, in Bermuda shorts and buckskin, draped like a third lumpy braid on his colourful country wife.

In due course, the tendon was stitched back together, a full leg cast applied, and I was shipped home with a packet of painkillers and a twenty-seventh-generation photocopy of instructions on the proper use of crutches. Through analgesic haze over the next few days, lessons from the incident started to register: (a) helplessness is frustrating; (b) frustration accomplishes nothing; (c) it is difficult to perch at a word processor with a bent leg cast extending from crotch to the tip of outstretched toes; (d) it is impossible to do anything with an attention span of thirty seconds; and (e) casts and canoes are not supposed to be mixed. No canoeing. No canoeing!

With the help of my willing partner, who had some sense of how devastating was this last realization, we tried anyway. Getting into the canoe was a trick, but we managed. Paddling, by comparison, was a restorative breeze, as long as one did not dwell unduly on the prospect of swimming in the event of upset. But we canoed on the sparkling waters of Cranberry Lake and all was right with the world.

Encouraged by the success of this outing, I started getting around our split-level home on the crutches with some facility until, a day or so later, I lost concentration and fell down six stairs, fracturing my left arm. The problem with falling down stairs with crutches, one learns, is that they act as a movable fulcrum that in effect launches a person into a high arc before gravity prevails and the floor rushes up with crunching velocity. At that point, I had to concede, canoeing was definitely off the agenda.

It was the sudden loss of freedom that was most disconcerting. I had no idea the extent to which canoeing defined me, and the gratuitous way in which I had taken this mobility for granted. Thinking back on the many days in my workaday life, prior to these accidents, I saw how deeply satisfying it had been to know that I *could* canoe, if the spirit moved, even if I chose *not* to canoe. But, for a while, that possibility was gone. Canoeing was out. And I felt claustrophobia that was even more constricting than the plaster casts. Ruptured, if only for twelve weeks, was the sustaining, if utterly romantic, notion that I could get in a canoe outside the back door and paddle to Lachine or Moose Jaw or Tuktoyaktuk. It was a difficult time, but, as with all meaningful experiences, good came from bad, not least of which was a new appreciation for the centrality of canoeing in its many dimensions in a Canadian life.

And that, wrapped up in plaster, is more or less what this book is about. From the outset, it was my goal to write stories about canoes for people who would never likely buy a book about canoes—a book that would leave out the how-to and where-to aspects of paddling and focus instead on other ways that this craft has informed Canadian experience. At the very least I hoped to explain how it is that a Canadian can finish a hot drink from a Group of Seven coffee mug, place it on a glass-topped mini-canoe coffee table, dress in a spiffy Roots outfit, splash on Canoe cologne, head out in a Plymouth Voyager or Land Rover Discovery (which 1997 advertisements declared came with a "free" 15.8-foot wooden canoe) along the Voyageur Highway to Toronto for a scoff of foie gras, pickled indigenous mushrooms, wild rice, and skin-roasted Arctic char on a warm salad of cooked spinach and ripened Quebec goat's cheese—washed down with any one of five or six beers with canoes on their labels, and served up hot and pricey at a fancy restaurant on the top of the Toronto Dominion Centre called ... what else? ... Canoe.

In the spirit of a craft defined in some dictionaries as "a vessel without decks" or, as Ottawa Valley poet and paddler Phil Chester likes to call it, "the un-cola of boats," it may help to explain what this canoe book is not about. It is not a comprehensive history of the craft. It is not a manual of how to canoe, or a compendium of the best canoe routes in Canada. It is not a study or an anthropological treatise. All of these angles on the topic have been worthily covered already, leaving plenty of room for future research, scholarship and writing of all kinds. This book is meant to be a song, a celebration, an invocation to adventure, an exploration, an assemblage of stories about canoes, written to inform and entertain anyone who might have wondered about the place of this craft in Canadian experience. It is a book about canoes. It is a book about Canada.

The organizing principle for the book is a journey from east to west, following the way in which the country was first explored by canoe, stopping along the way to hear a little about the boats, paddlers and canoe lore that arise in each place. It is a journey to demonstrate that scratching the shore of any river in the country from Gander Bay, Newfoundland, to Masset, British Columbia, hearing from the people who live there, examining the boats one finds there, is an exercise that reveals canoe narratives that speak to the essence of what it means to live in a country such as this.

Having made such a journey, bit by bit, river by river, in the years leading up to the writing of this book, drawing from experiences across the country, I have learned a great deal—although I have yet to find out what happened to the mysteriously disappearing dies for the Canadian one-dollar coin that featured some kind of voyageur image. Maybe it is fitting that we have instead a loonie and not a "crony, paddlie or canotie." But try as I might to include the best of this learning in these pages, it was impossible to fit in the fact that "ocean" is an anagram for "canoe," that singer Anne Murray has a 17-foot Grumman aluminum canoe full of geraniums beside her Nova Scotia cottage, that the original big surf outrigger canoe from the American television program *Hawaii Five-0* is in the Canadian Canoe Museum in Peterborough, or that it is impossible to make Love in a canoe because this small Saskatchewan town is not on a navigable waterway. What is here, one hopes, is a tasty amalgam of voices, all part of the rich Canadian canoeing tradition.

But having spent the better part of two years on this project, I'm a bit restless. It snowed last night and the waters of Cranberry Lake look black and quite delicious against a white shore in the silver shine of morning. It's off to paddle for the last time this season.

JR, Seeley's Bay, Ontario, 1998

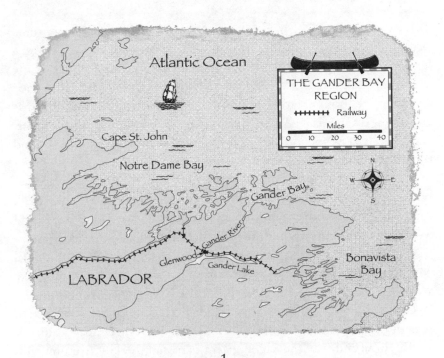

1
—

WHERE CANOES ARE BORN

Though we ordinarily think that rivers run from the heights of
land and mountains to eventually vanish in the sea, when you
approach a river from the ocean it becomes much more enlight-
ening to recognize that rivers are the gnarled fresh fingers of the
sea reaching for the mountains.

—Rudy Wiebe, *Playing Dead: A Contemplation
Concerning the Arctic*[1]

THIS COUNTRY IS A NATION OF RIVERS. By virtue of having three oceans fed by rivers and lakes throughout the country, Canada is also a land of canoes. Veteran Canadian paddler Bill Mason, maker of the legendary film *Paddle to the Sea,* mused, "It is as if God made the canoe and then set about creating a country in which it could flourish. That country was Canada."[2] And, for each river, each watershed, each waterway, there is a people or layers of people through time who are bound to the land and to the water by a canoe.

From the Maritimes to the Mackenzie River delta and places in between, there are dugouts and bark canoes—craft great and small, each made of local materials by local builders to meet local needs and each following more or less the same design principles: broader amidships, pointed at bow and stern, round-bottomed—sleek, economical curves in three planes: side to side, front to back, top to bottom, like an athlete's calf. The use may vary, but the basic principles endure.

Canoe designer John Winters stands before an audience of North American canoeists in Toronto,[3] in January 1998, endeavouring to explain how and why the canoe, having crossed the gulf from individual, aboriginal construction to mass industrial manufacture, has endured as a boat design. He produces a sheaf of wooden battens and proceeds to bend them in a variety of ways to demonstrate. First, he takes two of the flat sticks that are taped together at their ends, top and bottom. Holding these roughly in the middle, orienting vertically in front of his body, he pulls them apart, making the characteristic elongated lemon shape of a canoe as viewed from above. "Look familiar?" he asks. Then he takes just one batten, grasping it at either end and bringing his hands together, making the characteristic "U" shape of a canoe cross-section. Forcing the batten even more by twisting his wrists, Winters emulates a canoe with flared sides, with straight sides, and a canoe rib that curves back on itself, in the manner of a boat with beautifully rounded sides. "Seen these shapes before?" He grins. Then, taking several battens together, hands one above the other in front of him, he bends the sheaf together, stopping at various positions, making a variety of classic canoe-end shapes. "It's more complicated than I'm letting on, but basically what I've shown you holds true. As long as you work with the bends the natural materials allow, you will end up with a reasonable canoe every

2

time." It seems so simple, so straightforward, but so wonderfully rich and complex. Tight curves beget smooth pirouettes on the surface of time, sweeping curves add purpose and elegance in the dance from here to there, the builder and the boat, the tree and the river together in form and function limited only by a maker's imagination.

Later, I visit John Winters at his home near Burks Falls, Ontario. He's an engaging college drop-out and sailor, with lots of savvy and raw boat sense, who got interested in naval architecture and never looked back. He came to Canada from the United States and was doing fine with a firm that was building racing sailboats, until he entered hospital for knee surgery. It was there, and during subsequent convalescence, that canoes caught his designer's fancy:

> It started with Canadian history. I asked my wife to go to the library and just keep bringing me books. The books I enjoyed most were the journals of David Thompson and Samuel Hearne and people like that. I loved that stuff. I kept sending her back to get as much of that as she could get. The boats, at that point ... I felt that any damn fool could make those things, and it didn't seem to be a great challenge or anything particularly interesting. I didn't get interested in the boats until I couldn't find something that I liked.
>
> I had a fibreglass copy of a Peterborough that I had built when I was nineteen, but I felt that there must be better boats than this. So I just started going around bugging canoe shops, test-paddling canoes, paddling other people's boats. And just never got turned on ... So I started designing my own and making them—"strippers"— right here on the front porch.[4]

And what he learned in the process of his own designing and building on his front porch was that as long as one stayed within the bending limitations of the woods being used, no matter what was done in the way of construction, a workable canoe was the result. Canoes, somehow, had a natural symmetry. Winters put it this way:

I think the Indians had the same situation: "We need a boat. The last one we made was too tippy, so we'll make this one wider." That doesn't require an extraordinary amount of design knowledge to do that. And that's the neat thing about canoe design. If you pinch the ends of the boat, it's hard to screw it up. You will get a decent boat as long as you don't do too much to it. It doesn't matter whether you use PVC pipe, or wood. Just let rigid materials bend in more or less a natural way, and do the least you can to control it, and you'll get a boat that somebody will think is the best thing since sliced bread. I can guarantee it, especially if it's a pretty colour. The only bad boats that I have found were the boats where somebody tried too hard to manipulate the shape without knowing what they were doing.[5]

Before long, Winters moves the discussion from the deceptive simplicity of wood battens, pinched ends and gentle curves to hull geometry, mechanical similitude, Froude numbers, ratios, symmetry, and coefficients of design. It seems you can build a faster, stronger, bigger, more efficient canoe but, strangely, it will always retain the essential look of a canoe. Sitting in front of his colour computer screen with its flowing lines of canoes in side-section, cross-section and top-section—artwork unto itself—he laughingly relates the story of being disqualified from a cross–Lake Ontario voyageur canoe race. Using fibreglass on wood, he was able to stray from the classic lines defined by bending battens, and put a high-performance hull below the water-line, retaining the traditional canoe shape and aesthetic above. The result was a canoe that looked like the others in the pack but had nearly twice the hull speed with the same number of paddlers. And although the canoe technically met race specifications, Winters' crew were disqualified because their craft, by virtue of its lines, was in a different league from all of the other entries.

Throughout our conversation there persisted the notion of *canoe*: a river boat, a vessel without decks, a design that has endured and persevered. And, leaving John Winters' high-tech log home in the woods near Burks Falls, I was struck by the notion that while some of the canoes engendered by North America's rivers may have been used on the oceans themselves—indeed some may have been used to cross the great oceans—it is the land, the lakes and the rivers that give these canoes their essential character. Kayaks, though similar in many ways, are not canoes. Kayaks are ocean boats. It is when the ocean meets the land that a canoe is born.

Nowhere, I've learned, is this point better illustrated than where the great Atlantic Ocean meets the principal river of northeast Newfoundland, the Gander, named after its abundance of geese. The boat in question at this junction of river and sea is a canoe, to be sure, but in local parlance it's called the "Gander Bay boat": open top, pointed ends, broad amidships, originally 16 or 17 feet long and, so say the lads of Gander Bay, modelled after the canvas-covered cedar canoes the Micmac of Newfoundland brought up from Nova Scotia or perhaps Maine. And the reason the Gander Bay boat came to be was simple: it was too damn hard to row a dory or a fishing skiff upriver.

Until the late nineteenth century, the principal focus for the people of Gander Bay was the sea. This was where they fished inshore for groundfish such as cod, grey sole, flounder, redfish and turbot; for surface-dwelling fish like caplin, squid, herring and mackerel. At the mouth of the river itself, they set lines or nets in season for migrating Atlantic salmon as they headed upstream or out to open ocean. And it was from the sea, on coastal steamers, that supplies came from larger ports like St. John's. Like the Beothuk before them, they went upriver occasionally, but never very far.

In the 1890s, however, reason to travel up the river changed quite dramatically. To facilitate communication and movement of goods between St. John's and Port aux Basques, the Newfoundland railway was constructed. Gander Bay was too shallow to be a port of any consequence, so the engineers opted to route the track inland, crossing the Gander River at Glenwood, on the north shore of Gander Lake, before heading north to Lewisporte and west, up the Exploits River to Grand Falls and beyond.

In the early days of the railway, people at the coast would laboriously pole, push and row their fishing skiffs upstream to Glenwood for many of the staples and supplies—from cows to washing machines—that used to come by steamer. Two people working long hours could muscle up to Glenwood in three days. The trip back down, with the current, took only one day, but had its moments when it came time to negotiate "rattles," or rapids, with plump little boats that wallowed with a load. Before long, some enterprising person in Gander Bay took it upon himself to copy one of the cedar canoes used by the Micmac inland, and the "double-ender," or "Gander Bay boat," was born.

It was a hybrid boat, originally about 16 feet long, built with the lines of a canoe and the construction techniques of a Newfoundland rowing skiff. On a stout straight keel made of black spruce, with a curving stem head and stern post scarf jointed to either end with dowels, the builder tacked three bulkheads—two more or less the same size near bow and stern, and a wider one in the middle, making the widest part of the boat just ahead of amidships. Giving the canoe its shape were six long battens that were tacked to the stem, stern and bulkheads, three per side: one at gunwale height, one along the keel and one halfway between. The trick then was to split out juniper (larch) ribs that were bent to the curve of the battens after being heated in an old boiler tub half-filled with water and one can of Gillett's lye. When the boat was completely ribbed, the builder then planked it with copper nails as they came through the ribs, starting at the keel, working up the curve of the side, removing battens *en route*, installing inwales and outwales at the top of the outer walls, trimming the ribs flush. All that remained to do was add seats and floorboards; caulk with oakum between planks; and paint, inside and out.

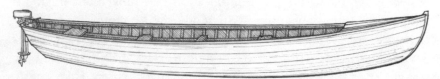

Gander Bay boat, carvel-hulled juniper, 22 feet

The Gander Bay boat was much sleeker and lighter than the skiffs, but it was still a bit too heavy to paddle—as the Micmac paddled their canoes on Gander Lake—so it was fitted with thole-pins fore and aft for rowing on the steadies; in the rattles, or anywhere on the river where current prevailed, the boats were poled. Recalling the early days of the twentieth century on the Gander River in a 1973 television program, "The River Man,"[6] seventy-year-old boatman Brett Saunders drew attention to the central role the Gander Bay boat played in the lives of the people of this remote area of Newfoundland. "The river was our road," he said.

It was left to the wits and ingenuity of any man with a boat to find ways to make money on the river. By degrees, attention of the coastal people turned inland, partly because the river was the only conduit to the railway but also because of growing interest in the rich spruce forests in the Gander River valley. Brett Saunders took all manner of cargo upriver and down, and wasn't beyond having a bit of fun at the expense of his neighbours who weren't so familiar with the freshwater environment. Speaking on camera to the producers of "The River Man," he told the story of taking three fishermen upriver in his Gander Bay boat:

> They were going in looking for work on the pulpwood drive. And halfway up one of the lakes ... this fellow asked me for a drink. I told him, "Oh well, when we get up here a ways, there's a little brook. When we get up there, we'll go ashore and we'll get you a drink."
>
> So when we got there, I landed just upstream. He says, "Skipper, where's the brook?" I said, "Just down around the shore there, a hundred yards or so." And I said, "Bring back a kettle of water too, after you've had your drink, because we're going to have lunch here."
>
> All the time we were passing through fresh water for miles. But he was a saltwater fisherman. He didn't realize the water was fresh!

Lest they get too cocky, the river had lessons for the Gander Bay boatmen as well. An interesting affirmation about the wisdom of the original Gander Bay boat design emerged in the mid-1920s when outboard motors came on the scene. The first of these was a 4.4-horse-power Evinrude Elto, a noisy, heavy-propellered invention that made a lot of sense to people who had spent much of their lives running up and down the Gander River in canoes. In a book about life on the Gander River written by his son Gary, Brett Saunders recalled what happened when these combustion engines were first attached to the gunwales of the original double-ended Gander Bay boats. Apparently the Elto was quite a thing when it arrived in Gander Bay. Although as heavy as a child, it could be clamped to the back of a canoe, propelling it faster than one strong oarsman could make ever make it go by hand. As they did with most technological innovations, the old timers who had always rowed their Gander Bay boats shook their heads in bemused disbelief when the Elto sensation took hold, muttering about what the younger generation was up to *now*.

Boat builders in the Gander Bay area soon realized that clamping a motor to the side of a boat was not the most efficient way to transfer the force of the propeller to the motion of the boat. The motor had to be at the stern. Brett Saunders was not sure what happened in the first instance—whether they just cut the stern off an old double-ender or whether someone actually designed a Gander Bay boat with a transom and square stern—but when they ran this boat with the Elto against a 5- or 6-knot tide in the river mouth, "she would pull a wave along behind and couldn't get any speed."[7]

Of course, canoe designer John Winters would have two explanations for why this would be the case. The first would be wave-making resistance. A canoe-design primer written by Winters for dyed-in-the-wood canoe enthusiasts describes this well:

> Waves created by the canoe's passage are the visible evidence of energy lost in pushing water out of the way at the bow and reduced pressure letting it flow back to its original level at the stern ... As the hull pushes through the water, it creates two sets of waves originating at both bow and stern. The first, called divergent waves, are less significant than their appearance suggests. The second set, the transverse

waves, is also created at the bow and stern and lies perpen-
dicular to the hull's course. These waves travel at the same
speed as the hull and are constantly being created and left
behind. [William] Froude [nineteenth-century boat builder
and naval architect] recognized that the speed and size of
transverse waves varied with the speed and size of the hull
and correctly concluded that they were significant indicators
of resistance. He also discovered that, when the transverse
waves reached the same length as the hull, extraordinary
amounts of energy were required to gain additional speed.[8]

In our conversation at his log home, Winters explained that of all the
factors affecting the wave-making resistance of a canoe, like the Gander
Bay boat, the effect of length in relationship to displacement (the total
weight of the boat and contents when in use) is most significant. If one
takes a boat that is designed to go slowly and somehow suddenly speeds
it up in the water by, say, adding a motor, a doubling of the speed can
sometimes increase the size of the wave following the boat by sixteen
times. Or, to put it in lay terms, artificially speeding up a canoe can
create a following wave that changes the energy required for forward
motion from pushing a wagon on flat ground to pushing a loaded
wagon up a mountain. Winters' second explanation for the lack of
speed on a square-backed canoe goes back to his batten theory.
Chopping the end off a canoe and nailing on a square transom offends
the natural bends of the wood from which the boat is made and is,
therefore, a recipe for hydrodynamic disaster.

The response to this problem in Gander Bay, after much chin-
stroking and pipe-smoking around various hearths and wood stoves on
the coast, was to leave the below-waterline design of the double-ender
alone. The wetted surface of the Gander Bay boat would begin with
and end on the lines of the natural curvature of the wood. To accommodate the motor, they would simply add a small Y-shaped transom
above the waterline on the stern, to which could be clamped in fine
style the red and silver cast-iron Evinrude Elto, with no deleterious
wave effect or decrease in performance. Below the waterline, at least,
the classic canoe design prevailed. The only other modification made

to the original Gander Bay boat was to lengthen the craft from 16 to about 23 feet, which, staying with the original proportions, favoured a beam of nearly 4 feet and depth sufficient to accept all kinds of cargo—from bales of hay for horses used in the logging industry, to logging chains, passengers, kegs of nails, and lumber. Recalling these times, Brett Saunders remembers his younger brother Harold bringing out 50 feet of boom chain and a Holstein cow and her calf, charging a penny and a half per pound for the trip.

Some twenty years after the advent of the outboard motor, the Gander Bay boat would once again prove its adaptability. The most unusual cargo Saunders remembers being borne on the river by Gander Bay boats was a Hurricane fighter aircraft that crashed in February 1943, in a bog beside the river about halfway between the railway and the coast. In his son's book, we pick up the story there:

> [Hurricanes] were being used as an advanced trainer that was flown solo by pilots who had graduated from the dual cockpit *Harvard Trainer* and were getting ready to fly the faster and more heavily armed *Spitfire* overseas. The impact of the crash wrecked the engine, but the fuselage and wings were usable so the RCAF wired for somebody to bring them out to the Bay where they could ship them to Lewisporte via the SS *Glencoe* and thence by rail to Gander. Already the river ice was too thin for horse and sleigh, but I figured it could be done by boat. The distance was just under fifteen miles.
>
> I wired the RCAF in Gander that I would bring her out for $300. They sent out a Sergeant King to supervise the operation and to sign the contract. Although a nice enough fellow, he just didn't believe I could do it by canoe, and said so. I said, "Give me the contract and I'll deliver your plane, guaranteed." I wouldn't let on how I planned to do it, see, until the contract was signed. My plan was to bring it out in three trips on two canoes lashed together catamaran-style. And that's what I did. I hired Harold and another man and we brought out the two wings, the easiest load, first. The canoes held steady by two poles across the gunwales fore and

aft, and a tarpaulin kept the waves from swamping us on the rattles.

With the wings safely unloaded, the sergeant told me he strongly advised against bringing the cockpit and fuselage the same way. "Look here, ol' man," I said, "it's me that has the contract and me that's paying the wages and the gas, so let me get on with it." He declared it would be impossible and announced he would wire his CO for permission to destroy the plane. "Well," I said, "if you people don't want it, let me have it to put in the meadow for the youngsters to play in."[9]

As events unfolded, there wasn't room for the military man on the canoe catamaran anyway. In two trips in one day, Saunders and his two helpers brought out the Hurricane, first the wings, then the fuselage. The wings turned out to be the easiest load. The fuselage, with its armour plate, however, was more of a challenge. Using a tripod, the three of them got the fuselage wrestled onto the two canoes, but the only vantage point remaining from which a man could see ahead was standing in the cockpit of the plane, looking out of the segmented glass canopy.

So there he was, Brett Saunders, perched in the cockpit of a Hurricane Mark I fighter on the shimmering waters of Third Pond, playing the possibilities for upset in mind's-eye images of the river ahead: Weir's Pond, Bellman's Brook, First Pond, Second Rattle, First Rattle, Bread and Cheeze Steady, The Works, The Gut, and around George's Point to the tidewater wharf at Gander Bay. Perhaps, in his imagination, he was Billy Bishop, Ray Collishaw, or one of the other World War I air aces, as he directed his helpers with hand signals and voice. Or perhaps it was just something that they did to make a few bucks and to have a laugh in attempting the impossible. But underlying this spectacular canoe cargo-carrying feat was a knowledge of the boat and its potential, and of the river and its myriad twists and currents, a celebration indeed of the relationship between people and place shaped by the planks in a homemade canoe. The Gander Bay boat was, and is, of the people and of the place—of Gander Bay and of the Gander River.

What is even more fascinating is that the double-ender was not the first canoe to find its genesis in the junction of ocean and river in the

Gander Bay area. On the same coast, in the valley and estuary of the Exploits River, some 40 kilometres north, long before the railway, long before the first settlers came to Newfoundland, there lived a group of aboriginal people of Algonquin linguistic origin, the Beothuk, and they, too, had a unique canoe made from local materials, by local people, to meet local needs on the northeast coast of Newfoundland.

Linked most closely to their Naskapi and Montagnais neighbours across the Strait of Belle Isle, the Beothuk crossed to the island of Newfoundland either on the winter ice or, a less likely prospect according to ethnologists, by boat. Whatever the case, the idea of a bark canoe that came with these people to the Exploits River valley some time around 50 B.C. was one that would change, as they interacted with the rugged island landscape, into a canoe shaped like no other in North America, or the world.

What is perhaps most interesting about the Beothuk canoe is that not one of these original moustache-shaped boats survives to the present day. This seems to support John Winters' notion that surviving canoe designs are those that stay within the bending and other structural limits of the natural materials from which they are made. According to ethnologist Ingeborg Marshall, the only one of these canoes to be destined for possible museum preservation in England was one that caught the fancy of British naturalist Joseph Banks, who requested in 1766 of Captain Wilkinson that it be shipped home on the deck of the HMS *Grenville*. Unfortunately, or prophetically, the frail bark boat was washed overboard and lost on the transatlantic crossing.

The feature of the Beothuk canoe that distinguishes it from every other bark canoe is its profile, the gunwale being swept up, or "hogged," to a sharp point amidships. Like other bark canoes, elsewhere in North America, the Beothuk canoe had markedly upturned ends, and like the Micmac canoe, with its smoothly hogged gunwale, the side profile of the Beothuk, with its abrupt middle corner in the gunwales, required that the battens of wood be cut and somehow affixed with hide or spruce root to accommodate the design. With none of these canoes surviving the passage of history from European contact to the present day, why this canoe was shaped the way it was is a matter largely left to speculation. What is known about the design and performance of the

Beothuk canoe comes from examination and analysis of a small number of model canoes that have been found in Beothuk burial ruins. And, because the last of this race of people died in the early nineteenth century, all of this study of the canoe models must be done without even the oral narrative history that might have been passed up through the generations.

The story of the Beothuk's demise is really, in microcosm, the story of just about every aboriginal group in North America, only in this case depopulation from disease and conflict following European contact was absolute. They were known for their liberal use of ochre as a dye for skin and a paint for wood products, believed to have served practical purposes, like repelling insects and preserving wood, as well as spiritual ends, the colour linking them to the Tartars of Asia, for whom red had religious significance. The Beothuk were likely the first North American aboriginals to have been seen by European fishermen and, as such, are thought to have inspired the term "Red Indian" that has been used to describe all New World tribes. In 1501 the Portuguese adventurer Gaspar Corte-Real captured and transported home fifty Beothuk "man slaves."[10] Like seven unsuspecting aboriginals brought back to France by Norman fishermen in 1507, they soon met the unfortunate ends often suffered by live museum exhibits epidemiologically, culturally and socially unprepared for residence in new and strange locales. Over the next 300 years, as the European foothold in Newfoundland strengthened, the Beothuk population slowly dwindled. In spite of efforts by enlightened Europeans like John Guy and John Cartwright, who attempted to trade with the Beothuk, the group enjoyed none of the benefits and suffered all of the hazards of cohabitation with people who came by sea.[11] Along the way, however, as Beothuk people were laid to rest in burial caves along the coast of Notre Dame Bay, and inland up the Exploits River, day-to-day items were buried with them that have provided insights into who these people were and how they had worked out a life for themselves in the landscape of Newfoundland.

One such grave site was a burial cave on Big Island in Pilley's Tickle, Notre Dame Bay, in 1869. A boy's grave, found among adult interments, contained a wooden image of a boy; toy bow and arrows; packages of food; a quantity of ochre; and three toy canoes, two whole, one in fragments. Author and anthropologist James Howley reports the dimensions of one of these canoes as being 32 inches long, height of ends 8 inches, height of side amidships, 6 inches, straight portion of keel 26 inches and beam 7 inches.[12] Another model canoe of similar dimension was discovered earlier, in 1827, by W.E. Cormack in the burial hut of a Beothuk named Nonosabasut near the site of the main deposit of ochre at Red Indian Lake, the source of the Exploits River. Both of these model canoes, while offering few clues about the actual construction details or technique, give clear indication of the relative dimensions of this canoe and, by inference, of its prominence in Beothuk culture.

The most detailed of all surviving model Beothuk canoes is one made by the last Beothuk, a woman in her twenties, who spent the final six years of her life in the custody or care of a series of English households in Newfoundland before dying of tuberculosis in 1829. Shanawdithit was found in 1823, with two other young, sick and starving women, by fur trappers roaming inland from settlements on Notre Dame Bay. Living for a time with the Peyton family on the Exploits Islands, she fashioned a replica of the canoes she had paddled as a girl. This valuable artifact was presented by the Peytons to Captain William H. Jones of HMS *Orestes* from whose hands it eventually passed to the National Maritime Museum in London, England. Unlike the burial models, which showed no internal structural detail, Shanawdithit's 54-centimetre canoe had ribs and planks and was constructed in a way that showed rich and illuminating detail of how seams, stems and keelson were incorporated into the overall design.

From examination of these models and related historical texts, according to Edwin Tappan Adney,[13] it seems certain that the entire framework of the Beothuk canoe was of spruce (white cedar, apparently, is not found on the island of Newfoundland) but that the construction technique of the Beothuk canoe was very similar to that of other bark canoes elsewhere on the continent. Like the Gander Bay boat, however, it had a distinctive stiff piece of spruce running from stem to stern along the centre line, but where the Gander Bay boat set this plank as a keel on the outside of the hull, the Beothuk design included this stiff member on the inside of the hull as a keelson, leaving a continuous wrap of bark across the bottom of the boat. According to Roberts and Shackleton, in their marker canoe reference work, *The Canoe*,[14] the Beothuk was the only canoe in North America to have a keelson. They suggest that this design feature stiffened the boat and made it better able to withstand periods of coastal travel.

As for the "strongly hogged sheer" (in the parlance of canoe designer John Winters, and technophiles like Edwin Adney), canoe scholars speculate that this adapted the boat for use in wavey conditions and accommodated the marked heeling-over of a canoe that would be necessary to haul in a net laden with fat fish or a harpoon line loaded with seal or porpoise. This modification to the side of the canoe would allow it to be heeled over as much as 35 degrees from horizontal without fear of capsize. Ballast rocks, which were thought to have been carried underneath the floor planks in the larger Beothuk canoe models, would have aided this feature of the boat. As for the uncharacteristically high bow and stern (remembering that the Pilley's Tickle canoe was only four times longer than it was high), Adney suggests that, while this feature might have caused steering problems in a stout breeze, it would also have provided the boat's occupants with shelter when the boat was drawn onto land and pitched on its side. They estimate that a 15-foot Beothuk canoe with 42-inch beam, when turned on its side, would provide 3 feet of headroom for those sleeping under it, whereas a canoe without this feature would have only half that clearance for camping.

To date, the most complete consideration of the Beothuk canoe comes from scholar and anthropologist Ingeborg Marshall in a 1996 work in which she devotes an entire chapter to Beothuk canoes and other means of transportation. In it she confirms the Beothuk canoe had to serve a dual purpose, that of a vessel for the open sea as well as one suited to a river with rapids up and down. She writes:

> The Beothuk, like other North American Indians, built birchbark canoes, which had an excellent carrying capacity and were reputed to be swifter than a ten-oared boat. These canoes were the Beothuk's most important means of transportation, enabling them to travel long distances at speed

15

and to portage with ease. A small canoe could be carried by one man on his head or shoulders and a larger one by two or three. Portage paths on the Exploits River circumvented rapids and the waterfall at Grand Falls ... The Beothuk travelled in their canoes not only on lakes and river systems but also on the ocean. By sea they went as far as Funk Island ... which lies about sixty kilometres out into the Atlantic, well out of sight of the coast. To travel such distances on the open sea, the Beothuk must have been skilled canoeists and excellent navigators.[15]

Marshall goes on to speculate that, to meet the differing demands of ocean and river travel, the Beothuk had, in fact, two major canoe types, "one with a straight bottom line, well suited for travel on rivers, lakes, and the ocean; the other with a strongly curved bottom probably designed specifically for ocean navigation."[16] There have been two attempts to re-create a Beothuk canoe. The first was in the early 1990s, when Grand Falls resident Scott James attempted to make a curve-bottomed Beothuk canoe out of plywood.[17] But this was not a particularly instructive escapade in historical re-creation. When weighed down with rocks for ballast, as the historical record indicates the Beothuk canoe was used on the open ocean, a canoe with a V-shaped cross section and pronounced curve from stem to stern (called "rocker" in canoe-design parlance) could be more stable than anyone ever expected, James learned, but without the bark skin and spruce planking the plywood replica could go little further in illuminating the qualities of an original Beothuk canoe.

In 1996, fascinating experiential research conducted by Lloyd Seaward, a master canoe builder from Bishop's Falls on the Exploits River, suggested that Ingeborg Marshall may have been wrong. While there may have been design variants to meet the demands of river and ocean paddling conditions, Seaward's experiment showed that there was very likely really only one principal style of Beothuk canoe. Seaward was a long-time canoe builder and, although he had never actually made a canoe out of bark and spruce, he knew canoe shapes and design parameters in his hands and in his bones, likewise the properties of these

16

natural building materials. Hoping to turn to the material legacy of the last Beothuk, Seaward found he couldn't get access to Shanawdithit's model, but he was able to use detailed photographs from the National Maritime Museum to help him in his unusual quest:

> This was the first time I'd built a birchbark canoe. I just saw the picture and I got interested in it, since I was used to building canoes. If I'm going to build a canoe, then I decide on the style of canoe. So I'll just go out in my workshop and I'll just draft the thing out. I don't want to see pictures. I can just visualize what I'm going to do because I'm used to it. I just go out and take a couple of strips, battens, and put them on the floor, mark it off, take it off, and make up the molds and go on ahead with the canoe ... When I saw the pictures of the Beothuk canoe, I could visualize how the thing had to be done. I got no measurements from the pictures. So I had to build it according to what I thought would be right.[18]

Seaward built three canoes in all, each 15 feet in length, more or less, and each with a straight bottom (i.e., no rocker) to emulate the shape of Shanawdithit's and the other model canoes. The first was for practice, and on this one the bark was sewn together with strips of caribou hide, handy but not too authentic or durable (although Seaward contends that this material was available to the Beothuk and may have been used if split spruce root was in short supply). For the seams he mixed spruce pitch boiled with bear fat and applied this using strips of old blue jeans as a sort of tape binding on the inside.

The second canoe was actually made of two separate sheets of birchbark sewn together with split spruce roots under the keelson and protected by a strip keel of spruce along the bottom of the boat. This one had quite a severely V-ed bottom. "The one in the sea didn't have a round bottom on it," he said. "It had sides that go almost straight up. When you put some ballast in that, it was a pretty stable canoe. It could carry a lot of weight. She wouldn't be good in the rivers though, with that V-bottom because she'd draw too much water."[19]

Lloyd Seaward's third canoe, still with a straight keel line, had a much more rounded bottom in cross-section. This one he called a "river canoe," and it was from this canoe that he learned valuable lessons about the virtues and versatility of the original Beothuk canoes:

> We used it in windy conditions to see how it would handle because with the high bows we figured it was up the wind and she'd be hard to handle. That wasn't the case at all. Then we used it in a heavy tide in the river. It was far ahead of our canoes. Far ahead. That's because the way it was built on the sides and everything and the way the bow was raked out for shootin' rapids, it paddled so much easier than our type of canoe. It was stiffer. It was harder to tip over. When you turn it over on its side you could pass over on a shallow maybe four inches deep. Then when you get back in the centre again, she'd come back in place. Paddling the river, I would see a shallow ahead, and just change the centre of gravity and pass over the shallows. And this was without rocks, without ballast.[20]

Whether the Beothuk had one round-bottomed canoe for river work and another, larger V-bottomed canoe for trips out on the open ocean to hunt for marine mammals or to gather seabird eggs from some of the outlying islands, it is clear that this canoe supported an aboriginal way of life that involved movement inland up and down the Exploits River and coastal travel. And, in the absence of people to speak about this now-extinct nation, the Beothuk canoe holds in its lines and strange curves tell-tale clues and instructive lessons about a relationship between people, land and water at a place where the ocean meets the river.

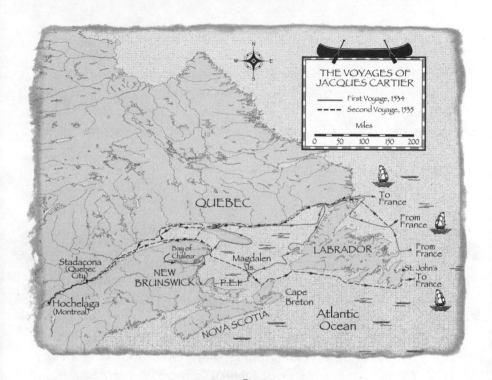

2

CRADLED BY THE WAVES

This commonplace experience of most canoe-trippers is, regrettably, lost on many contemporary constitutional law theorists. Apart from its formality, a constitution is, after all, not unlike the pre-trip organizational meeting. It is a constitutive process which allocates authority between levels of government, among branches of government, and between citizen and state ... Just as the canoe and its myths have characterized our past as a people, the lessons to be drawn from these tales ought to characterize our future.

—Roderick A. Macdonald, *Canexus: The Canoe in Canadian Culture*[1]

AT CLOSEST APPROACH, the gap between Prince Edward Island and the mainland of New Brunswick is about 14 kilometres, red-sand shore to red-rock shore, across warm, shallow water. Elsewhere along the Northumberland Strait, especially along the Gulf Shore of Nova Scotia, the interstice is wider, but on clear days the island is always there, glinting invitingly green on the near horizon. As the Micmac story goes, the great trickster Glooscap tired himself out one day and needed a rest, so he lay down across Nova Scotia and used Prince Edward Island as a pillow, naming it "Abegweit," meaning "cradled on the waves." Perhaps Glooscap fated the canoe-shaped island, Abegweit, to be the site of first contact between the Micmac and the Europeans and later the place that would be called the "cradle of Confederation."

Having likely been in the vicinity of the Gulf of St. Lawrence as a young navigator with Giovanni da Verrazano in 1524 and 1528, and charged by King Françis I to look for gold and passage to the Orient, Jacques Cartier sailed straight to the north end of Baie des Châteaux, now Strait of Belle Isle, before turning south toward PEI. On June 26, 1534, Cartier's two ships made landfall at the Magdalen Islands, at which point he headed south for three days to an encounter that put canoes and sailing ships, Europeans and Micmacs, on the same horizon. On June 29, 1534, the native of St. Malo, France, "discovered" Prince Edward Island, and the next day the Micmac and their elegant and seaworthy bark canoes.

Calling this first encounter a "clumsy, rather comical affair," historian Arthur Ray writes:

> On the last day of June 1534, while Cartier and his crew were sailing along the northeastern shore of Prince Edward Island, they saw boatloads of people crossing a river, but sea and wind conditions prevented them from making contact. The next day the explorer reported seeing a Micmac man "running behind our boats, which were coasting the shore, and making signs to us to turn back." When the French wheeled about, though, the anonymous man "took to his heels." Intent on demonstrating his good intentions, Cartier "landed, and laid ... a knife and woolen belt on a stick, and

thereupon returned to our vessels." With these tentative steps, contact began.[2]

The river being crossed in those first days of summer 1534 may have been either what is now known as St. Peters Bay, into which the Morell, Marie and Midgell rivers flow, or the split in the winding, red-sand spit, protecting Tracadie Bay from the Gulf of St. Lawrence, into which the Winter River flows. Anything west of there cannot in good conscience be considered part of the northeast shore of Abegweit. But, contrary to legend which suggests it was Glooscap himself, napping on Nova Scotia, and using Prince Edward Island as a pillow, who saw the first European visitors to the island, it was families of Micmac who witnessed Cartier's discovery of their island home.

Although the Micmac fashioned frame boats covered with scraped moosehide, as did other First Nations people elsewhere in North America, historians seem to agree that the boats in these first contact scenes were likely elegant bark canoes made to accommodate the exigencies of both river and open-ocean paddling conditions. Sketches and paintings from later periods show Micmac bark canoes with noticeably hogged sheers, like the Beothuk canoes on Newfoundland, with ample recurve in the cross-section, or tumble-home, to allow them to be heeled over to accommodate heavy fish or sea mammals being hauled over the side, and to stop cresting waves from rolling in amidships. But these sheers were smooth, unlike the Beothuk gunwales with the distinctive mid-sheer corner and break in the gunwale wood. And instead of decks or small thwarts connecting gunwales at bow and stern, the ends were sewn together with split spruce root for some distance into the main cargo cavity of the boat to allow them to cut through ocean waves without shipping too much water.

A stiff on-shore breeze would have prevented Cartier and his land party from meeting up with the Micmac on the day of this first sighting, because a prudent sailor (a long way from home) would not be tempted to move too close to an unknown shore with uncertain anchorage, lest his boat be driven onto a sandy shoal. The Micmac had the advantage, in any case. Conditions unfavourable to sailing a ship close to shore, such as high winds and confounding currents and tides, were not of sufficient difficulty to stop them from crossing the mouth of a gap like St. Peters Bay in their birchbark canoes.

What the Micmac were doing on this day of discovery is, of course, a matter for speculation. They might have been fishing, or cruising the shore in canoes, hunting seals. Cartier might have observed a land-based party, perhaps collecting seabird eggs during the June nesting season, or hunting birds for meat or for oil, or perhaps in teams with wooden implements working the red-sand flats for clams or quahaugs. They might have been checking among the fucus, dulse and plants in the tidal zone for blue mussels to fill their bark pots, being ferried across a river mouth to expedite gathering food on a new section of beach. Whatever the situation, the canoes of the Micmac enter the historical record from a sighting on the northeast shore of what is now Prince Edward Island and appear to be ideally suited to both the river and the sea conditions of the Maritimes.

Micmac canoe, birch bark and cedar, 15 feet

It wasn't until several days later that Cartier and his crew actually met a group of Micmac on the coast of New Brunswick at the Baie des Chaleurs. This time the wind and seas were much calmer. Cartier was out in one of the small rowing craft from his ship, the *Emérillon*, exploring the shoreline close in, and was surprised by a large party of Micmac travelling in about four dozen canoes. Apparently familiar with the notion of trading (indicating earlier, though undocumented, contact with the Portuguese fishing crews), the Micmac frightened

Cartier, asking him to land and holding up a bounty of furs on the end of sticks. Unsure of the situation, Cartier apparently got a bit crowded in the encounter and finally fired his musket twice in the air to help clear a way for him back to the safety of his ship. The next day, the Micmac returned to the side of the *Emérillon* and indicated interest in further trade. Arthur Ray recounts the meeting:

> A much-relieved Cartier "likewise made signs to them that we wished them no harm, and in sign of this two of our men landed to approach them, and bring them knives and other ironware, with a red hat to give their chief." The Micmac readily understood this diplomatic gesture and a brisk trade ensued. Cartier said the Micmac showed "great and marvelous joy to possess this ironware and other said articles, dancing continually and going through various ceremonies ... [They] gave us all they had, keeping nothing back, and were compelled to go away stark naked, making signs to us that they would return on the next day with more skins." When Cartier met another group of nearly three hundred Micmac several days later, everyone knew what to do. The Micmac sent the Europeans a present of cooked seal meat; the French replied with gifts of mittens, knives, necklaces, and other miscellaneous items. With this traditional peace offering out of the way, the two groups got down to business, bartering until the Micmac once again had parted with all their furs, including the clothing off their backs.[3]

Relations between Cartier and the First Nations did not go quite so well further up the coast. At Gaspé, Cartier met a group of Iroquois at a summer mackerel fishing camp; their leader, Donnacona, was unimpressed by the large wooden cross the Europeans erected on his land. He was even less impressed when Cartier, in dubious circumstances, continued his journey, and returned to France with two of Donnacona's sons on board the *Emérillon*. Cartier returned the following year, in 1535, and with the assistance of Donnacona's sons "found" the St. Lawrence River and sailed to Stadacona, the Iroquois village at the present-day site of

Quebec City, where the young men were reunited with their family. Not wanting Cartier to proceed any farther upriver, Donnacona orchestrated the arrival in canoes of fierce-looking Iroquois dressed in dog skins, with long horns strapped to their heads, emissaries from the god Cudougny, who danced and sang songs about the evils that were sure to befall the sailors upstream. Undaunted, and still intent on finding a route to the Orient, Cartier continued on up the "Rivière du Canada" to Hochelaga, where he was stopped by swift, shallow water at Lachine Rapids. It was here he was first to make the observation about the essential relationship between North American travel and the canoes of the Micmac and Iroquois he had encountered. To go inland, one needed a boat light enough to be carried around rapids when going upstream, yet manoeuvrable enough to negotiate the whitewater when coming back down a river, strong enough to carry a good load and seaworthy enough to ply big lakes or coastal waters when required. To go inland into Canada, Cartier realized he needed the boat derived of the landscape realities of the New World. Cartier realized he needed a canoe.

As might be expected in a situation between peoples where one group is in need of something belonging to the other, the ensuing relationship between European and First Nations, as it was with Cartier and his hosts, was never completely without tension, as it is to this day. The European attempt to enslave North American First Peoples was a practice more common than the popular historical record would allow, and did nothing to build an enduring sense of trust. Different alliances also mitigated against smooth relations with the tribes of the New World. Samuel de Champlain, for example, allied himself with the Algonquin Nation and, by association and deed, alienated his party from the five member nations of the Iroquois Confederacy,[4] who, in turn, became staunch allies of the British. Henry Hudson and Dutch traders who entered North America via the Hudson River gave their allegiance to the Mohicans who, like the Algonquin, were at odds with the Iroquois. Dutch arms may have slowed the bolstered aboriginal defences, but guns did not stop the ultimate demise of the Mohicans; this alliance and defeat had other historic implications. According to Mohawk historian Zoltan E. Szabo:

> The Dutch decision to help the Mohicans puzzled the Kanien'kehake. They had done nothing to disrupt the previously prevailing peace with the Dutch. Due to this experience, the Kanien'kehake Nation realized the fact that Europeans, represented by the Dutch, did not understand the Turtle Island (North American) People's way of life. As the result of this realization and to exhibit friendly and peaceful intentions towards the Europeans and restore peace with them, the idea of the Kahswentha (Two Row Wampum) was introduced.[5]

Wampumpeag (diminutive "wampum") is actually a compound word of Narragansett Indian origin that translates as "shiny strings of beads," and refers to a practice of stringing and weaving beautiful iridescent beads made from the inner spiral of quahaug shells found on the Atlantic coast. Once cut, ground, polished and drilled, the finished beads were actually cylindrical in shape, measuring about a half centimetre in length and about half that in width. Very rarely, bead makers would find dark, sometimes purple, quahaug shells which would be especially prized because of their scarcity. Although the coast Algonquin, like the Delaware and the Narragansett, were likely the first producers of wampum beads, through trade, inland nations also came to value this commodity and, in fact, made wampum tantamount to an early form of currency among the First Nations of North America.

By the time European colonial settlements were being set up in the seventeenth century, wampum was a well-established currency base among First Nations. Although these valued beads were used as special or sacred jewellery, as ornamentation and in economic exchange with the settlers, wampum was put to the more significant purpose of creating belts. These contained patterns and combinations of white and purple beads that told the stories of various agreements and binding

25

truths between First Nations groups and eventually with colonials and governments.

Significant among these was a sacred text of purple and white beads carefully woven by Iroquois hands into a belt called "Kahswentha," the "Two-Row" or "Covenant" wampum. Still extant and housed in the Museum of the American Indian in New York, the Two-Row Wampum is 33.5 inches long by 2.5 inches (eight beads) wide and shows two parallel rows of richly luminous purple beads set against a white backdrop.[6] Why this is interesting to anyone with a paddler's view of history is that Kahswentha employed the *sea craft* of the parties in the peace agreement—in this case the Dutch and the Iroquois—in particular, the sailing ship and the canoe as emblematic of the cultures from which they arose. Because of the tradition of these covenants being supported by stories in the oral tradition, the actual description of what the Two-Row Wampum means varies, depending on who is telling the story. Usually, however, the meaning of this belt is interpreted along the lines of "two paths or two vessels, traveling down the same river side by side. One, a birch bark canoe, for the Indian People, their laws, their customs and their ways. The other, a ship, for the white people and their laws, their customs and their ways."[7]

Over time, the Two-Row Wampum became part of a body of wampum belts that held the teachings of the many North American Indian peoples, including the Iroquois, whose wampum record remembers the mythological "Heavenly Messenger," Dekanahwideh, "who brought peace to the Haudenosaunee. Said to be born of Huron parents, Dekanahwideh reached out with love to his neighbours, while travelling in a white stone canoe, giving the Iroquois the Tree of Peace, the white pine, whose roots grow out in four sacred directions to symbolize peace and charity and to lead other peoples to its truth. In the wampum record are teachings about east, south, west and north, along with the earth, sky, and the centre that lies in the heart of every human; these seven directions symbolize connection, completion and balance in the sacred hoop or circle. Dekanahwideh's most important legacy is the Hiawatha Wampum Belt. Unifying lessons of the Great Law of Peace—Gayanashagowa—the belt brought the five warring Iroquois nations together in one democratic confederacy.

Even today, when chiefs decide that people need to be reminded of the Great Law of Peace, the Hiawatha Belt is taken from the longhouse and a reading of the belt takes place. When a reading took place at the Kahonsesne Longhouse of the Mohawk Nation in 1996, it took from August 12 to August 17 for elder Jake Thomas to remind people of the tenets of the Great Law. The reason why it might take six days to recite one teaching, recorded in finite patterning of shell beads, is that the Great Law is broken into sections, each one dealing with an aspect of the Iroquois world—the water, sky, plants, animals, birds, fish, world above the earth, world below the earth, myriad worlds on the earth—each element being described and appreciated in minute detail, and each member of the assembly being provided with the opportunity, from time to time through the recitation, to affirm that it is on these basic principles that common Iroquois purpose is founded. It is significant that these lessons were borne to the land of the Haudenosaunee in a sacred canoe. It is also ironic that, unlike the Hiawatha Belt, which remains in the Iroquois longhouse and is available for such ceremonial reminders of the principles it represents, the Two-Row Wampum is tucked away in the Museum of the American Indian, with provenance that reads "Specimen No. 17/5205, purchased through William L. Bryant from William D. Loft, presented by Blair S. Williams."[8]

But Dekanahwideh's Great Law—the teaching of the white stone canoe, as it were—remains a living document for the First Nations, echoing not only seventeenth-century history but reflecting 150 years of constitutional attempts to bring about peace, from the constitution of the United States to the charter of the United Nations.

History shows that Benjamin Franklin became very knowledgeable about wampum as a proximal record of agreements between peoples through his close friend Conrad Weiser, who had been adopted by the Haudenosaunee. Weiser attended a great many council meetings at which various wampum belts were read and discussed, and took to documenting these encounters and passing them on to Franklin and others. When it came time for the Pennsylvania Commissioners, a group of which Franklin was a member, to finalize their land arrangements with the Iroquois, the Americans presented the Indians with a wampum belt of white origin to bind their agreement, indicating significant knowledge and sensitivity to the value and historic role of this recording medium in aboriginal culture. The Haudenosaunee like to argue that in a similar way teachings of the Great Law influenced the spirit, wording, and intent of the U.S. Constitution, mentioning always the presence of Iroquois elders at the 1787 Constitutional Convention, during which the Great Law was discussed at length. Often, comparison between these two documents begins with the similarities in intent (if not in imagery) between the opening of the Great Law and the Preamble to the U.S. Constitution. As transcribed from the original wampum teaching, the first two sections of the Great Law read:

> 1. I am Dekanahwideh and with the Five Nations' Confederate Lords I plant the Tree of Great Peace. I plant it in your territory, Adordarhoh, and the Onondaga Nation, in the territory of you who are Firekeepers.
>
> I name the Tree of the Great Long Leaves. Under the shade of this Tree of the Great Peace we spread the soft white feathery down of the globe thistle as seats for you, Adordarhoh, and your cousin Lords.
>
> We place you upon those seats, spread soft with the feathery down of the globe thistle, there beneath the shade of the spreading branches of the Tree of Peace. There shall you sit and watch the Council Fire of the Confederacy of the Five Nations, and all the affairs of the Five Nations shall be transacted at this place before you, Adordarhoh, and your cousin Lords, by the Confederate Lords of the Five Nations.
>
> 2. Roots have spread out from the Tree of the Great Peace, one to the north, one to the east, one to the south and one to the west. The name of these roots is The Great White Roots and their nature is Peace and Strength.

If any man or any nation outside the Five Nations shall obey the laws of the Great Peace and make known their disposition to the Lords of the Confederacy, they may trace the Roots to the Tree and if their minds are clean and they are obedient and promise to obey the wishes of the Confederate Council, they shall be welcomed to take shelter beneath the Tree of the Long Leaves.

We place at the top of the Tree of the Long Leaves an Eagle who is able to see afar. If he sees in the distance any evil approaching or any danger threatening he will at once warn the people of the Confederacy.[9]

The Preamble of the United States Constitution reads as follows:

PREAMBLE: We, the people of the United States, in order to form a more perfect Union, establish justice, insure domestic tranquility, provide for the common defense, promote the general welfare, and secure the blessings of liberty to ourselves and our posterity, do ordain and establish this Constitution for the United States of America.

Scholars have made similar comparisons with the Preamble to the Charter of the United Nations.

In addition to arguable thematic congruence among these three documents, especially the Great Law and the U.S. Constitution, researchers like Kanatiyosh, a Mohawk lawyer from Akwesasne, go on to draw comparisons between the recommended number of lawmakers, place of executive power and the role of women in matters of the state. These accounts often conclude with the observation that the Haudenosaunee use the symbol of five bound arrows to describe their unity and the strength of the Five Nations, which is strikingly similar to the Great Seal of the United States, designed by Charles Thomson in 1782, and showing an eagle clutching in its talons a bundle of arrows. Kanatiyosh noted that Thomson originally proposed the use of five or six arrows, but Congress preferred thirteen. Says the young Mohawk, "While the language is not exact, the symbolism and ideas are similar enough to see the influence."[10]

In Canada, by contrast, there is no similar congruence between the teachings of Dekanahwideh and the Canadian Constitution. In fact, in March 1987, delegates at a final First Ministers' Conference on Aboriginal Constitutional Matters in Ottawa were flummoxed when elders from the Algonquin communities of River Desert and Barrière Lake, Quebec, gave a reading of their wampum belts, testifying to the sacredness of historic compacts between aboriginal and European nations, linking back through time to the spirit of Kahswentha with its parallel lines of purple "canoes" and "ships" in a river of white beads. Writes University of British Columbia anthropologist Pauline Joly de Lotbinière, "Amidst the ornate glass windows and plush carpets, surrounded by politicians and bureaucrats in business suits and silk ties, the elders struck a curious note."[11]

The Keeper of the Belts who stood before the baffled premiers this day was William Commanda, a resident of Maniwaki, Quebec. Intrigued by the event, Pauline Joly de Lotbinière later travelled to the Wampum Keeper's home to document "a tradition about which there is little mention in the literature on Algonquin culture."[12] In the classic style of his forebears, perhaps with a little bit of trickster thrown in for good measure, William Commanda answered the anthropologist's question with a story about an encounter between one of his ancestors, Peter Tenesco, and the Little People, who appear in the Micmac legends of Glooscap. Why would he answer her question with a story? De Lotbinière tried again to understand by visiting Commanda a second time, only to hear the story of the Little People again. But she persisted.

In time, de Lotbinière was able to show that there was, in fact, a compelling link between the version of history recited from the wampum belts in the glare of chrome and bright lights at the Ottawa Conference Centre and the notion of aboriginal self-government. She argued that the wampum record is inextricably linked to the Algonquin oral tradition and to a people's relationship with the land of their ancestral birth. Through their association with historic treaties, the

Algonquin wampum belts implicitly affirm a way of order, democracy and a well-established tradition of self-government.

What does any of this have to do with canoes, you might ask. As it turns out, the Keeper of the Algonquin wampum belts for First Nations of the Ottawa Valley, William Commanda, is also a keeper and builder of another sacred text, the Algonquin birchbark canoe.[13] Commanda is one of the pre-eminent bark-canoe makers in the world, having built canoes in many places—Washington, DC, during the U.S. bicentennial celebrations; Toronto for the Canadian National Exhibition; and in Montreal at Expo 67—that have ended up in museum collections in Canada, the United States, Japan, Poland, Denmark, Germany and France. His boats are much-coveted works of aboriginal art, but, like the lessons of the wampum belts which have also been objectified and commodified for the tourist trade, the enduring significance of Commanda's bark canoes and their messages about people and place are often lost in the blur of modern-day commerce. Just ask Calgary paddler and historian David Finch.

Perusing classifieds in the weekly *Bargain Finder* in the autumn of 1997, he spied an ad, "Ontario birchbark canoe. One owner." Intrigued—owning a bark canoe being the dream of most Canadian canoeists— but skeptical, Finch dialled the number and spoke to a recently widowed woman whose husband had purchased the canoe in question from an aboriginal canoe builder and his wife who had built the canoe at an outdoor exhibit at the Canadian National Exhibition in Toronto in the summer of 1980. "It needs some work," she said. Beyond that, the woman was unable to provide detail about the craft. "You'll have to come and have a look."

Without a moment's hestitation, David Finch made his way to the Calgary address. What he found was a 15½-foot, 50-pound Algonquin-style canoe made from one large sheet of birch-bark, 33 inches across the beam, 11 inches deep, with three hand-carved thwarts on which the careful cuts of the maker's crooked knife could be plainly seen. The "work" the widow had mentioned on the phone concerned an unfortunate split through the centre bark of the craft, from one side of the centre thwart to the other, as if the bark skin had shrunk and split through dessication in storage without the natural humidity of the outdoors. Finch's hungry eyes moved slowly from the tear, across the undulating golden surface, toward the stern, where a burl in the satin bark, with its darker concentric circles, had been strategically placed during construction to provide natural ornamentation to the rising curve of the stem. But there on the *wulegessis*, the rounded flap of bark along the gunwale end, was dark filigree that looked like writing. Hunching down, Finch saw it was printing in what seemed to be permanent fine-point marker: "William and Mary Commanda."

Almost unable to contain his enthusiasm for this unlikely find, Finch negotiated a price and headed home with the boat of his dreams atop the rattley family van. Days later, he had fixed the split by removing the centre-section ribs and planking and, with a special mixture of natural adhesives, carefully patching in a ribbon of fresh western birch bark along the inside of the hull to make the boat watertight once again. Shortly after that, he was out on the Bow River west of Calgary, living the dream by paddling his Canadian bark treasure in its new Western home. Speaking about the Commanda canoe, Finch says:

> I love the way the patina of age accentuates the character of all the materials. Everything fits. And I'm always overcome by its craftsmanship. I've had to replace some of the little wooden pegs that hold the top gunwale piece on. I'm always just thrilled to be working on and then paddling a craft that has such integrity with thousands of years of travel on this continent. Nothing here was touched by a saw or a motor. I like that.[14]

One widow's *Bargain Finder* item is another man's treasure, just as one politician's pretty beaded belt is the story of another person's whole nation. Bark canoes and wampum belts, lost, or misunderstood, in the glare of progress.

I visit David Finch and we head out to paddle the Commanda canoe, on a sunny weekday morning, marching from the parking lot to meet a company of busy mallards in a backwater of the Bow River beside the Eau Claire Market in downtown Calgary. Getting in—Finch has graciously let me paddle the boat first, while he gets in a second canoe—I notice a group of Japanese tourists who have gathered to have a look at what we're doing. Their guide speaks and points at the bark canoe, after which there is a collective sigh and chorus of enthusiastic nods. After Banff and Jasper, they have touched another part of Canada.

Kneeling in stocking feet, I find that the boat feels ultra-responsive, improbably light, and much too frail to shoulder the full weight of its history. I'm paddling, ever so gently, watching the hand-hewn cedar gunwale slide past stiff-curled yellow birch and poplar leaves that sit, as if suspended, on the still surface of the pond. An Archibald Lampman line of verse bubbles up from school days long repressed: "Softly as a cloud we go, sky above and sky below."[15]

Focusing on the interior of the canoe, I can see now what Finch means about the patina of age and how, without so much as a lick of varnish, linseed oil or preservative of any kind, the grey-gold cedar interior has its own sheen and hand-wrought charm. The ribs are so evenly spaced and unique, each one fuller in the curve than the one before, each one symmetrically chamfered on its sides, each one tapered on the chine, just so, to rise perfectly to inwale joinery. The ribs closer to the shadowed stem follow the U-shaped bottom of the boat, but they also corkscrew ever so slightly to accommodate complex curves. The canoe seems a living, whole entity, accepting and distributing the pull of gravity, the buoyancy of the pond and the resistance of the water, as it is absorbed by my paddle and transferred through pins-and-needled knees into liquid forward motion. A sweet creaking sound accompanies each stroke. Water soaking through my socks reminds me to ask Finch about the New Age, no-dryout pitch recipe he used to repair—well, almost repair—the big crack.

Flying home, I think of naked Micmac traders, William Commanda, the First Ministers, wampum and found bargains. I think of bark canoes and constitutions. Following this experience in Calgary, I have a better idea about the nature of a bark canoe. But what might be a constitution? My *Pocket Oxford* says:

> constitution *n*. ... form in which a State is organized; body of fundamental principles according to which a State etc. is governed [16]

What might happen if our constitution makers paid more attention to the teachings of the bark canoe to ground and freshen the principles on which our confederation is founded? The canoe has form and function, but then again so do the British North America Act and DIY rental agreements and divorce kits from Wal-Mart. But the canoe's form and function are set by the parameters of the natural materials from which it is made and derived from the essence of the Canadian landscape and its First Nations. The canoe has been an integral part of the experience of both French- and English-speaking peoples who followed Cabot and Cartier—three founding peoples, one sacred text. Canoes have balance and symmetry. They are fragile but can be repaired with available materials. In practised hands a canoe can negotiate stormy seas and cranky whitewater with ease, with grace if it is done right.

Canoeing is a journey on which one must ask, "Who are my partners?" "Where are we going?" and "What is our burden?" A canoe ties its paddlers to the water and to the landscape, but it also ties them to each other in significant ways. To move forward, a stroke in the bow requires complementary action in the stern, and vice versa, sort of Newton's third law of motion, Dekanahwideh-style. A canoe invites its occupants to ponder what's ahead, what's behind, what's beside us, what's above, what's below—a canoe invites awareness, a canoe nurtures situated knowing. And the only way to learn these teachings is to paddle. An annual First Ministers' canoe trip. What a concept! We could call the venture "Abegweit."

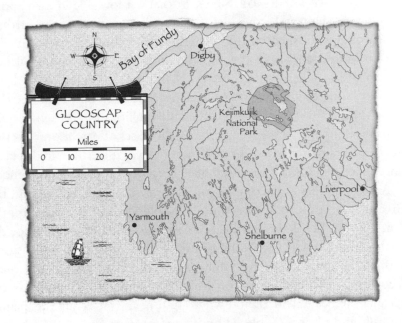

3

MAGICAL CANOES

Myeengun, Shingwauk, and the other educated men dreamed about people, that they never saw before, coming to Canada. White People. Sure enough, a few years after that, Shingwauk dreamed about a boat full of strange people. Ojibwa men went down the lakes until they hit the St. Lawrence River, they went to these big rocks. Shingwauk placed his men up on steep rocks. It's pretty well flat country down there with an occasional bluff. And that's where they signalled each other. They watched for the ship. When the Indians knew it was near, Shingwauk performed a miracle. He made fog settle down so the boat could not land.

—Fred Pine, in *Spirits on Stone: The Agawa Pictographs*[1]

WALKING THE SHORE OF NOVA SCOTIA at low tide in early spring conjures an elemental atmosphere. The red sand, flesh of the earth, is bathed and nourished by the tides that come and go, each day, like seasons in the daily arc of the sun. The birds have yet to come. Silence. The smell is of salt, sand and the sea. Landward, in the morning light, the soft stone that begets these flats. Seaward, the thin blue line that ripples these flats. Ahead, the endless possibilities of a beach ramble: walking, thinking, wondering. Behind, a lone set of bare footprints that will be gone before the day is out. This is the way it has been in this place since time began, since Glooscap plied these shores in his stone canoe.

As the Micmac story of creation goes, first there was Gisoolg, the Great Spirit, who made everything. Gisoolg's helper was Nisgam, the sun, giver of life, light and heat. Then, there was Ootsitgamoo, the earth, placed by Gisoolg in the centre of the circular path of Nisgam, with all its abundant plants, animals and places to travel. And then, according to legend, after the Mi'kmaq world was created (as the Micmac are called in their own tongue), and after all the plants, animals, and birds were placed on its surface, Gisoolg caused a bolt of lightning to strike Ootsitgamoo's surface and from this came an image of a human body, shaped from sand. This was Glooscap. Gisoolg unleashed another lightning bolt, which gave life to Glooscap, but he could not yet move. He was stuck to the beach on his back, only to watch Nisgam travel across the sky every day. His head was facing in the direction of the rising sun, east, or Oetjibanoog, where the summer weather comes from. His feet pointed west, in the direction of the setting sun, or Etgesnoog, where the cold winds originate. His right hand pointed to the north, Oatnoog. His left hand pointed south, Opgoetasnoog. Glooscap watched the animals, the birds and the plants grow and pass around him, but in time he got restless. He asked Nisgam to give him freedom to move about the Micmac world. And so it was that a third crack of lightning freed Glooscap and enabled him to stand on the surface of the Earth.

Unfortunately, this is where the story becomes vague. Some versions have him travelling in the direction of the setting sun until he comes to a great ocean, then travelling south until the land narrows to a point where he can see great oceans on either side, at which stage he walks north to the land of ice and snow before returning home, to the East, the place he was created. Here, on his return, wondering what the purpose of his existence might be, Gisoolg introduces him to Nogami, his grandmother; Netaoansom, his nephew; and Geganogonim-gosseesgo, his mother, who completes the first family. And so it was, according to legend, that life in what we now call Nova Scotia began.[2]

Other versions of Glooscap are lighter on details of his original conception and his family tree, as it were, and concentrate more on how he moved about and where he settled when he finally made landfall back on the east coast. These renderings of the story, as might be found in school texts or tourist literature, seem to agree that when Glooscap came from afar in the very early days he did so in a stone canoe, and that he landed near Digby, perhaps seeking shelter or fresh water in the Annapolis Basin, or perhaps swooshing up St. Mary's Bay, between Digby Neck and the mainland, riding the rip of the Fundy tide.

If you move inland from Digby to the highlands of Kejimkujik National Park, on an expanse of vertical, cool, smooth, fine-grained Cambrian slate (much like one would have found in early school-houses) you can see a series of small-scale, fine-lined petroglyphs. These provide physical evidence of Glooscap's passing, thought to be drawn by some of the early Micmac to record this important part of their history. Colonel Garrick Mallery from the Smithsonian Institution in Washington, DC, was the first person of European stock to locate these drawings, in the latter days of the nineteenth century, and he was struck by their allure: "The faces of the rocks were immense soft and polished drawing-slates, presenting to any person who had ever drawn or writ-ten before an irresistible temptation to draw or to write."[3] Col. Mallery, like everyone else who has visited these rocks, was impressed by the number and instructive quality of these images. Many of them depicted people in canoes, often fishing, perhaps Glooscap in his various travails in the legendary stone canoe.

What is not evident in the petroglyphs, but is suggested in Micmac legends, is Glooscap's role in giving bark canoes to the Micmac. It may be that after a few epochs in the stone canoe, Glooscap had iden-tified a few features of the craft that he thought should be modified for common use by his friends the Micmac. For starters, he scrapped the notion of stone as a building material and turned to the durable and abundant Nova Scotia birch bark and to the strong flexible woods of spruce and cedar. According to one version of the story, perhaps thinking of lightness, he took his design inspiration from the strong yet light breastbone of a bird. Anthropologists Wilson and Ruth Wallis write:

> He procured the bird by killing it with a stone. From its flesh he had a good dinner. While he was picking the meat off the bird's breast, he thought, "If something of this shape were made, it would float on the water." He went into the woods to procure some bark. "If I should kill anything out on the water, I could go for it in this, and would not have to swim.[4]

Folklorist John Murray Gibbon relayed another version of how Glooscap's stone-canoe experience was parlayed into bark boats for the Micmac. Drawing from Cyrus Macmillan's *Canadian Wonder Tales*, he writes:

> Glooscap is said to have come overseas from the hunting-grounds of his ghostly forefathers and landed near Digby on the coast of Nova Scotia in a stone canoe which he plumped into the waves alongside the shore where he slept, and woke up to find it overgrown with trees, so that it looked like a rock-garden. Glooscap appointed partridge to be the master-builder of canoes for the world that flies, and it was the partridge who designed a canoe of rainbow colours for the hummingbird, together with a paddle no bigger than a little pin.[5]

Still another version of the Micmac canoe's origin comes from Michael Francis at Big Cover Reserve in New Brunswick, posted with legends and various illustrations on the World Wide Web, which suggests that it wasn't Glooscap at all, but the Little People who created the canoe:

However, the Little People have always demanded a small gift every time our canoes passed their home at Little People's Point. If we failed to do this they might cause great storms to rage about us, or horrible dreams to visit us in our sleep.

The Micmac Indians today have great respect for their Little People.[6]

Interestingly, it is the Little People who are often credited with the rock art at places like Kejimkujik National Park. Ethnologist Ella Elizabeth Clark describes their contribution:

A belief in dwarfs, "the Little People," was held by most North American tribes. There are scattered references to them in many myths and legends: the Little People are often said to have done the picture-writing and painting on the rocks, and to keep the paint fresh: they were thought, by some tribes, to have strong spirit power and so were greatly desired as guardian spirits.

The Little People who lived in the early world left their carvings to beautify rocks and cliffs and caves. And they helped the early Indians. Small though they were, the Little People were so strong that they killed many of the monster animals that were dangerous to man. "Our mission is to help you," a pigmy once told an Indian hunter. The bones of extinct animals found in their travels, the Indians believed, were the bones of monsters that had been destroyed by the Little People.[7]

Leave it to the Celts from Northern Scotland to claim that Glooscap was not a supernatural being but in fact none other than one Henry Sinclair, Earl of Orkney, a Templar descended from Henri de Saint-Clair who fought beside Godfrey of Bouillon at the taking of Jerusalem. In 1398, he sailed to Nova Scotia accompanied by the Zeno brothers of Genoa, perhaps in search of the Holy Grail. Historian Michael Bradley claims that by 1390 Henry had a number of ships, including "two undecked oared galleys of Mediterranean type useful for manoeuvring the narrow channels of Orkney [at the time a vassal of Norway] ... and one decked longship for battle, based on the old Viking lines."[8] According to many sources, Henry Sinclair built some kind of castle on the high ground due east of the Annapolis Basin in the headwaters of the Gaspereau River (which flows north) and the Gold River (which flows south). Adding to the mystery, at the mouth of both of these rivers, one in Fundy waters, one in Atlantic waters, are the only two small islands in Nova Scotia supporting populations of oak trees, even more curious because oak seeds—acorns—don't float. After years of speculation about Sinclair and Glooscap, author Frederick Pohl in his book, *Prince Henry Sinclair*, identified seventeen specific similarities between Glooscap and Sinclair, including the fact that each had three daughters.[9]

Skeptic Timothy C. Green goes even further with this theory imputing malice and cover-up by later visitors to Nova Scotia, coming down most harshly on the early French explorer Champlain. Green's contention is that Champlain was in on the Sinclair conspiracy and, when he arrived in Nova Scotia 200 years later, deliberately falsified his maps and reports to discourage settlement because of some mysterious allegiance to the Sinclairs.[10]

Other scholars point to historical underpinnings for the Glooscap legend. Michael Bradley explores the time Glooscap left Nova Scotia to carry on his great works elsewhere, knowing the Micmac had learned what they needed to know from him to live, pointing out that, in memory of this parting, the Micmac traditionally chanted "Nemajeeck, Numeedich," which Bradley believes sounds suspiciously like the words of an old Norse sea shanty sung when weighing anchor: "Nu mo jag, nu mo deg." Or consider the Micmac story called "The Water Fairies," published in Ella Clark's book, which has striking parallels with the old Danish folktale recounted in Matthew Arnold's poem "A Forsaken Merman." The story does nothing to discount the contention that Glooscap was really an aging Templar-cum-Earl and that the "stone canoe" was really nothing more than a large Mediterranean galley or Viking longship. One is left to wonder.[11]

There are other accounts of stone canoes in the legends of other

Native peoples, elsewhere in North America. It is said that "the Heavenly Messenger," Dekanahwideh, who was born among the Huron people of a virgin mother, was sent to bring peace and power to his people. According to story, Dekanahwideh's first miracle was the creation of a stone canoe in which he travelled to the Onondaga, where he made his first convert, the equally legendary figure Hiawatha. Those who weren't initially convinced of Dekanahwideh's great power were shown how he could defy death and darken the sun at will. As he travelled in the lands of the warring Mohawk, Oneida, Cayuga and Seneca, he spoke a message of peace from his stone canoe and, as the story goes, through the efforts of Dekanahwideh a Great Peace was achieved and the Six Nations Confederacy was born. Dekanahwideh's gift of the great white pine tree provided the Iroquois with a symbol of unity that reminds them of common bonds to this day. Before leaving the lands of the Iroquois Confederacy, Dekanahwideh appointed fifty chiefs, and then disappeared into the Great Lakes in his stone canoe, promising to return if this great peace among nations was ever compromised.

Moving northwest, the Ottawa First Nation of the upper Great Lakes region, in the vicinity of Michilimackinac and the junction of lakes Michigan, Huron and Superior, also had a lithic vessel in their lore, this time a white stone canoe committed to paper by James D. Edgar, who, in 1885, wrote a long narrative verse in which the following apocalyptic scene testifies to the power of the white stone canoe to save the innocent:

> All around them in the waters,
> Old and young were struggling, sinking
> Men and maidens without number,
> Of all nations, tribes, and kindreds.
> Ancient chiefs and famous warriors,
> Came with shouts of hope and triumph,
> Dashed their paddles through the surges,
> Laughing at the foaming billows.
>
> Slowly each canoe was filling,
> Sinking lower, sinking surely,

Unless hidden hands of Spirits
Smoothed its pathway through the waters
...

On this passage to the Island
There were some canoes of White Stone
Bearing only little children—
Happy, smiling little children—
And the waters never harmed them,
As they glided gently onwards,
To the island of the Blessed.[12]

And, according to John Murray Gibbon (probably drawing from the work of Henry Schoolcraft), a stone canoe emerges in the legends of the Chipewyan Indians north of Lake Athabasca in the southern Northwest Territories:

> They believe that at death they pass immediately to another world where there is a large river of water to cross. They must embark in a stone canoe, and are borne along into a wide lake which has an island in its centre. This is the island of the blest, and the object of the disembodied soul is to reach it. If their lives have been good, they will be fortunate and make it.[13]

These stone-canoe stories have a universal ring to them, especially the notion of the canoe as liminal vehicle bearing the human essence from one world to another. They echo the soul ships, or *uramon*, of the Asmat of Irian Jaya in Melanesia, people known for their graceful canoes and for their belief in an analogous notion of souls being transported over water by canoe to a place of everlasting. Similarly, an 1850 sketch by Samuel Bard[14] shows Mosquito Indians on the Caribbean coast of Nicaragua using a dragged canoe as transport for a body during a traditional funeral.

As one heads west across Canada there are many other examples of canoes drawn on stone that evoke tales of conquest, crossing over from the mortal world into the next, and guardian spirits. In a dissertation on the subject of the canoe in Canadian art,[15] Donald Burry, artist and historian, details some of the other sites of canoe petroglyphs and pictographs across the country: in Quebec at Bromptonville; in Ontario near Peterborough, on the French River, at Agawa Rock on Lake Superior, at Darky Lake in Quetico, on Pictured Lake near Thunder Bay; in Manitoba on the Bloodvein River; in Saskatchewan along the Churchill River; and in British Columbia, possible petroglyph sites at Sproat Lake on Vancouver Island and Jump-Across Creek on Dean Channel near Bella Coola, and pictographs near Port John and in the Hedley region of the Similkameen River valley. Each of these renderings of canoes in prehistoric aboriginal art on stone radiates a story about the centrality of canoes in the early cultures of North America.

Of these sites, the one I know best is Agawa Rock, north of Sault Ste. Marie, Ontario. The strawberry-blond rock with its contrasting ochre images was never more magisterial than on a gut-cold winter day in the early 1980s when, having snowshoed across Lake Superior Provincial from a point on the Algoma Northland Railway to the ice of Gitchigumi at Agawa Bay, a group of us tromped our way down through drifts of deep snow on a crevice trail leading to this ancient spiritual place. No one spoke as our eyes crossed faded images of snakes, animals, Michipeshu, the mythical lake-dwelling cat, and canoes. Another time, another season, I travelled back to Agawa from a camp at Beaver Rock, to the south, with archaeologist Thor Conway,[16] who, to a group gathered in canoes floating at the base of Agawa, told of the Ojibway artists and storytellers who painted these striking images and of the stories they represent. The canoe images, he related, are among the oldest well-dated rock painting in Ontario and actually are a pictorial account of war between the resident Huron and bands of Iroquois from present-day Quebec and New York State who came north in an attempt to meet the growing seventeenth-century hunger for fur. Of the snakes and big cats, denizens of the underworld, he wasn't so sure.

Other Indian legends, not so well illustrated, speak to the symbolic and often spiritual power of the canoe. In many instances, the canoe is central to legends surrounding large cataracts where all worlds seem to converge: Grand Falls on the St. John River in New Brunswick, Iroquois Falls on the Abitibi River in northeastern Ontario, Kakabeka Falls on the Kaministikwia River, west of Thunder Bay, Parry Falls on the Lockhart River in the Northwest Territories and of course Niagara Falls between Lakes Erie and Huron, to name a few sites.

Ella Clark attributes the following story about the origin of Niagara Falls to the Seneca, the westernmost people of the Iroquois Confederacy:

Long ago, a beautiful girl of the Seneca Indians was betrothed by her family to an old and ugly man. She did not want to marry him, but her father insisted. Knowing no other escape, she one day jumped into her canoe and pushed off into the swift-flowing Niagara River. It would be far better, she thought, to seek death in its angry waters than to marry a man she hated.

In a cave behind the rushing waters of the Niagara lived the Thunderer, the great chief of clouds and rain, and the guardian of the harvest. As friend and protector of the Seneca people, he noticed the girl's canoe approaching and saw her unhappy face. He knew that in a few minutes her boat would be dashed against the rocks. So he spread out his wings, flew to rescue the girl, and caught her just before her boat crashed to pieces.

For many weeks, she lived with the Thunderer in his cave. He taught her many things. For one thing, she learned why so many of her people had been dying, why the fever-sickness was always busy among them.

"A snake monster lies coiled under the ground beneath your village," the Thunderer told her. "He creeps out and poisons the springs, because he lives on human beings. The more people he devours, the more he wants. So he can never get enough if he waits for them to die from natural causes."

"What should we do?" asked the girl. "How can we escape from the deadly snake?"

"Your people must leave their village," replied the

Thunderer. "They must move nearer the great lake."

The Thunderer kept the girl with him in his cave until the death of the ugly old man among her people.

"Now you may return home," he said to her. "And tell your people all you have learned from the Thunderer."

The girl remembered all his teachings, and the people listened to her words. They broke up their homes and made a new village near the great lake. For a while all was well. No sickness entered the new village.

But after a while the old fever-sickness returned, and the Indians began to die from it. The huge serpent had dragged himself after the people and hoped to kill as many in the new village as he had killed in the old. The Thunderer saw him creeping along the ground. One night as the serpent neared the creek beside the village, the Thunderer hurled a thunderbolt at him. The noise woke up all the people, but the bolt only injured the serpent. It did not kill him.

The Thunderer hurled another thunderbolt. And another. And another. At last he killed the serpent, the poisoner of the water.

The dead snake was so huge that when the Indians uncoiled it, it lay stretched out for a distance of greater than twenty arrow-flights. They pushed it into the Niagara River, and watched it float down the stream.

"It looks as big as a mountain," they said to each other. "Can it get through the narrow place between the rocks?"

When the huge body reached the narrows, it could go no farther. It was wedged between the rocks. The water was forced to rise above it and to fall over it in a giant cascade. As the weight of the serpent monster pressed on the rocks, the rocks were pushed back, bent like a giant bow.

Never again did the Senecas have the fever-sickness in their village. And the giant waterfall, in the shape of a great bow that is bent, remains in the Niagara River to remind Indians of their friend and protector, the Thunderbird.[17]

Prior to being driven away from land in the Niagara region by the Seneca in the late seventeenth century, the Chonnonton, or "people of the deer"—so-called Neutral Indians, or "la Nation Neutre," by Champlain because, when he encountered them, they were at peace with both the Huron and the (then) five nations of the Iroquois Confederacy—had rich, storied lives that included very similar tales associated with Onguiaahra, the great river. Like the Seneca, they regarded the river with a feeling of awe and reverence, and considered the Great Spirit of Niagara as the embodiment of supernatural power. J.B. Mansfield recounts another more familiar story, of Neutral origin, from the falls: "The Maid of the Mist," which demonstrates this reverence:

> They heard in the thunder of the falls the voice of the Great Spirit, which they were taught to believe existed over all, and they regularly contributed part of their crops and the fruits of the chase to him, and even went so far as to offer human sacrifice on their return from wars waged upon them. As an annual offering of good will and gratitude for the blessings they had received during the year, and for their deliverance from many evils which had threatened them, it is related that they offered up each spring the fairest maiden of their tribe, sending her over the falls in a canoe filled with fruits and flowers, the canoe being guided by her own hand.
>
> The honor of being selected for this sacrifice was eagerly sought after by the young women of the tribe, and that clan, which happened to be the one possessing the maiden selected, took great pride to itself for the honor thus conferred. What terminated this superstitious practice is said to have been the selection one spring of the daughter of the principal chief of the nation. Upon the day fixed for the sacrifice the father was perfectly self-composed and stoical, as became an Indian chief, and did nothing to show that he preferred the sacrifice should not be made; but as the canoe containing the maiden and the fruits and the flowers moved out over the rapids above the falls, another canoe containing the father shot rapidly out from the shore, and both

disappeared over the great cataract almost at the same moment. The loss of their beloved chief was too great, and it is said from this time on the sacrifice in the spring of the fairest of the flock was discontinued.[18]

Two illustrations from this book depict events in the story. "The Maiden's Sacrifice" shows the young woman standing in a bark canoe as it crests the brink of the falls with another canoe in silhouette close behind, and "The Maid of the Mist" shows the same young woman rising from the base of the falls, *sans* canoe, with angel wings on her back.

Ella Clark's rendition of the story, which she attributes to the Seneca origin, places the date of this last sacrifice at 1679, when the daughter of Chief Eagle was selected for sacrifice. Clark contends that this was despite protest from the French explorer René-Robert Cavelier, Sieur de La Salle, who, records show, was involved that spring with the construction of a blockhouse at the mouth of the Niagara River, just downstream from the falls. Whatever the origin of this story, be it Neutral or Seneca, or both, what is significant is that in Clark's version of the tale both the girl and her father paddled white canoes. The quick conclusion here is that the adjective denotes canoes of birch bark, but these canoes, because they were always built with the red/gold inner bark of the tree on the outside of the hull, with similarly coloured cedar ribs and planking on the inside, were never white. A more accurate conclusion perhaps is to link the white coloration of the Onguiaahra canoes in the Maid of the Mist story to the white stone canoes of myth and legend, the vessels to convey souls to the island of the blest.

Of all the stories of canoes crossing between worlds, there is none better than the venerable French-Canadian folk tale "La chasse-galerie" translated as "The Flying Canoe" or, more ominously, "The Witch Canoe." The name of this story is derived from the French *chasse*, meaning "hunt," and *galerie* from "Sire de Gallery," a condemned hunter. Folklorists contend that the tale is a variant of a universal legend called "The Wild Hunt," which interprets strange noises in the air as belonging to a hunter condemned to hunt throughout eternity. But it is the image of a magic, flying canoe that endears this story to North American sensibilities.

"La chasse-galerie"—the flying canoe

"La chasse-galerie" is set in the time of early days of logging in Canada. The date is nearing Hogmanay and a group of lonely lumber-jacks in the wilds of *le pays d'en haut*, north of the St. Lawrence River, is approached by a stranger who offers to convey them to their loved ones (in some versions to their girlfriends, and in tamer versions to see their "old folk") for New Year's Eve and to have them back in time for work at dawn the following morning. Edith Fowke conveys a lively sense of what one lumberjack was experiencing in the cookhouse that night:

> It was an evening like this, the last day of the year, when I was thirty-four or thirty-five. Gathered with my friends around the cookhouse, we took a little drink: but if little streams make great rivers, the little glasses ended by empty-ing great jugs, and in those days we were thirstier and drank more often than today, and it wasn't unusual to see the cele-brations end with fist-fights and hair-pulling. The rum was good—not better than this evening—but it was good. I assure you.
>
> I had indeed imbibed a dozen little glasses myself, and by eleven o'clock, I tell you frankly, my head was spinning and I fell on my sleigh-rug for a little sleep while waiting for the hour to dance around the boar's head from the old year into the new, as we are going to do tonight at midnight before

going to sing in the new year and offer best wishes to the men of the neighbouring shanty.

I was sleeping then for some time, when I felt myself rudely shaken by the boss of the lumberjacks who says to me, "Joe! Midnight has come and you're late for the square dance. The fellows are leaving for their trip, and me, I'm going to Lavaltrie to see my blonde. Do you want to come with me?"

"To Lavaltrie!" I replied. "Are you crazy? We're more than a hundred leagues from there, and besides, if you have two months to make the trip, there's no way to go in the snow. And there's work the day after New Year's."

"Dumbbell!" replied my friend. "Don't worry about that. We'll make the trip by rowing a bark canoe and tomorrow morning at six o'clock we'll be back in the shanty."[19]

The only catch to this wonderful opportunity as the friend, Baptiste Durand, explains, is that the men in the canoe have to make a promise to the Devil not to speak about God or to carry any religious symbols with them on the journey, lest their souls be forfeit. Off they go to town, narrowly missing steeples of the various French hamlets on the way to meet up with their sweethearts in Lavaltrie. As might be expected, Baptiste has a few too many drinks at the dance (on top of the few they were having prior to midnight in the shanty) and the trip back ends with the canoe crashing into a tall pine tree, tipping the revellers into a branch, whereby they tumble into the snow, unconscious, but with souls intact, to be rescued by shanty mates with a moral lesson to tell their grandchildren:

> All I can tell you, friends, is that it isn't as funny as one thinks to go to see your girl in a bark canoe in the depth of winter, riding in the chasse-galerie, especially if you have a wild drunkard who interferes with the steering. If you believe me, wait till next summer to kiss your sweethearts. Then you won't run the risk of travelling with the Devil as helmsman.[20]

This wonderful piece of canoe legendry has made its way into just about every book of French-Canadian folktales; it has been the subject of various drawings, paintings and woodcuts by artists, including George Pepper, Henri Julien (painting entitled *La dégringolade*), and F.S. Coburn (painting entitled *V'la l'bon vent V'la l'joli vent*, 1899); it even caught the attention of nineteenth-century physician William Henry Drummond, who established quite a reputation writing narrative verse in the English idiom of the French-Canadian farmer. In his first book of poetry is a lyric, "Phil-o-rum Juneau," inspired by "La chasse-galerie":

> An' up up above t'roo de storm and snow, she's comin',
>   wan beeg canoe,
> But I know on de way canoe she go, dat de crowd he mus'
>   be dead man,
> Was come from de Grande Rivière du Nord, come
>   from Saskatchewan,
> Come too from all de place is lie on de Hudson Bay Contree,
> An de t'ing I was see day New Year night is le fantôme
>   Chasse Gal'rie.[21]

Today, there is no end to the incarnations of "La chasse-galerie." The story has been revived and given new profile as the subject of a forty-cent stamp from the Philatelic Services of Canada Post, released on October 1, 1991. The image of the flying canoe has made it onto "Maudit," an overproof (8 per cent alcohol) ale from the Quebec brewing company Unibroue, based in Chambly, Quebec. (Maudit's sister brew, brought onto the market around the same time, is called, in translation, "End of the World" beer.) And, in a surprising design gesture, mounted on the World Wide Web by the Ontario Ministry of Natural Resources, is a much less sinister evocation of "La chasse-galerie" entitled "Magic Canoe." Visitors to this website are invited to get in the magic canoe and, through the magic of computer video, whisk over the parks of Northern Ontario, viewing the blue lakes and rocky shores from above, over the prow of their flying canoe. Even the Rheostatics' album *The Blue Hysteria*[22] has on its cover a strange image of flying monkeys making their way through a night sky in a magical red canoe, drawing, however subtly, on the long folk tradition of "La chasse-galerie."

From the legend of Glooscap and his stone canoe to "La chasse-galerie" and its various modern derivatives, the archetypal canoe crossing the universal threshold from here to eternity is a constant. Whether it is the original stone canoe, or the white stone canoe, or a flying canoe, this impossible notion, this deliciously improbable idea, has captured the human imagination.

Nothing seems more antithetical to Glooscap's stone canoe, though the weight of materials might be comparable, than a concrete canoe. Surely, in reality, such a boat would simply sink. Not true. The first boat made of concrete, a rowboat, was built by one Joseph Louis Lambot for use on his estate in France in 1848. Seventy years later, at the end of World War I, when all available plate steel was needed for war effort, industry turned to concrete to build boats, creating the "Selma," the largest concrete boat ever made, 427 feet long and tipping the scale at a grand 4,185 tons. The same situation emerged during World War II as well, largely because of the success of earlier efforts, but with less favourable results.

After the war, the American Concrete Institute teamed up with the American Society of Civil Engineers and came up with a contest: a concrete-canoe race meant as a challenge to civil-engineering students, and to aid in the professional development of young civil engineers, as well as to increase awareness of concrete's versatility, durability, strength and flexibility as a building material. Some thought it a ludicrous idea. But it was one that really played yet again on the notion of canoe as connection of worlds. In this case the building of a concrete canoe was set up as sort of an outrageous rite of passage for young engineers to see them from the puerility and naïveté of youth to the maturity and experience of the adult world of professional engineers.

The idea was brought to fruition in Canada at Ontario universities, including the University of Toronto and McMaster University in Hamilton, in the early 1970s by a team of enthusiastic young civil engineers. The early attempts were big and cumbersome, but by all accounts, everyone involved learned a lot about canoe design, about concrete, and about the process of innovation. In the 1974 Ontario race, for example, McMaster's canoe weighed in at a back-breaking 500 pounds, an entry that ended up on the bottom of Grenadier Pond in Toronto's High Park (where it may be still). The following year, the contest had expanded, and at Lake Seneca, in King City, north of Toronto, teams from seventeen universities and community colleges competed. This year the boats were sleeker, and lighter, and events in both the men's and women's divisions were taken by U of T teams using the same 14-foot blue canoe with the name of their alma mater emblazoned in brushed white paint on both sides. This time, the winning U of T team moved on as the only Canadian entry in the North American Concrete Canoe Championships in Columbus, Ohio—the so-called Indianapolis 500 for concrete canoes. Following this event, U of T civil-engineering student, and concrete-canoe team member Nora Stewart was quoted as saying:

> We completely psyched out the opposition before the race even started. The other teams were unloading their equipment, and teams were carrying their canoes down to the water. The University of Toronto canoe was picked up by one man, casually carried down to the water and tossed in. It was like driving a modern Porsche up to the starting line against a group of Ford Model T's.[23]

U of T won the race hands down, against all comers. "I think we could have stopped for coffee and still won it," crowed Ms. Stewart. U of T won the men's, ladies' and faculty members' races for 14-foot canoes that year. The day of the race, the local paper in Columbus is reported to have run the sports section heading "St. Louis Comes Second in the Concrete Canoe Race," with a note in much smaller print, toward the bottom of the page, that the race was won by a team from the University of Toronto.

What the reportage did not reveal was that the U of T team had a couple of aces in the hole in their faculty complement. Civil- and mining-engineering advisors knowledgeable about concrete as a building material helped the team add latex to the concrete and reinforce the boat with fibreglass cloth. This mixture was then well smoothed with sandpaper and painted, resulting in a canoe with concrete that was only ⅜ of an inch thick, weighing about 65 pounds, less than a canvas-covered wooden canoe of the same length. And, also in the U of T court was a professor of physical and health education, Kirk A.W. Wipper, a long-time paddler and collector of canoes, who showed them how to take the lines off his favourite (and fastest) canoe, a fine specimen made by the Rice Lake Canoe Company, near Peterborough.

In the intervening years, the American Society of Civil Engineers has teamed up with Master Builders Incorporated, of Cleveland, Ohio, a leading innovator in the development, manufacture and marketing of advanced construction materials and systems. According to a Master Builder's annual report:

> Commitment to excellence is the driving force behind the company's decision to sponsor the National Concrete Canoe Competitions. For ten years, the National Concrete Canoe Competitions have provided a forum to showcase the versatility of concrete and the ingenuity of future engineers. It is with pride that Master Builders contributes to the future of construction and engineering through sponsorship of this event.[24]

The stinging win by U of T at the National Concrete Canoe Competition in 1975 in Columbus was accompanied by a number of rule changes to equalize competition and to make more of a race for spectators. It was decided that teams would have to submit the design of their canoe before the race so that, after the race, lines of winning canoes could be copied and funnelled into the next year's creative processes. This being a competition about specifications and getting as close to allowable limits without going over the line, the published rules for the Cement Canoe Competition by 1999 ran to about a dozen published pages, with caveats, codicils and addenda to close the loopholes opened through cut-throat competition. The call for competitors details a four-part submission: design paper; oral presentation; visual display; and the final product to be raced in sprint, slalom, and distance courses by men's, ladies' and mixed crews. To provide a taste of the rules for this unique North American event, here is a sampling from Section II—"Design and Construction Requirements":

B. The Canoe

1. The canoe shall be built within the current academic year of the national competition. The same canoe shall be used at both the regional and national competitions. In the event that the qualifying canoe is damaged between the regional and national competitions, the Chapter/Club may patch, repair, and refinish the canoe. In the event the qualifying canoe is destroyed, the Chapter/Club may rebuild the canoe. In either case, the resulting canoe shall be of the same design, material, proportions, and performance characteristics, or the Chapter/Club shall forfeit to the designated alternate Chapter or Club within their Regional Conference. No new flotation shall be allowed between the regional and national competitions without point deduction.

2. The dimensions and/or hull configurations of the canoe are not restricted.

3. Use of transverse structural elements shall be permitted as long as they do not prevent paddlers from exiting the canoe ...

4. The gunwale shall be finished in such a way as to prevent injury to the paddlers, i.e. no exposed reinforcing or sharp edges ...

5. Sealed cavities are permitted only at the bow and stern

for flotation. Cavities are subject to inspection by the judges. If sealed cavities are used, evidence shall be produced to show that the cavity or cavities contain flotation material and are not hollow.

6. The canoe shall float horizontally when filled with water. A point within 0.6 m (~2 ft) of the most exterior point of each end shall break the water surface. The canoe shall be certified as such before entering any race.

7. Flotation material is permitted within the first 0.6 m (~2 ft) of either the bow or the stern and shall not total more than 1.2 m (~4 ft) ...

8. Any external protrusion(s) shall be made of the same materials as the hull and shall be permanently attached to the hull.

9. Fixed paddler restraints, such as, straps, seatbelts, Velcro, or any other item that attaches the paddler to the canoe or which interferes with the paddler safely exiting the canoe in the event of capsizing are not permitted ...

10. Movable steering devices are not permitted.

C. Materials
1. A minimum of 75% (by weight of solids) of the binding material shall be Portland cement ...

2. Binding material is defined as the solid portion of the binder(s), i.e., not including mix water, slurry water, or water serving as the dispersing medium of an emulsion.

3. Binders are defined as cementing materials, either hydrated cements or products of cement or lime and

reactive siliceous materials; also materials such as asphalt, resins, and other high molecular-weight polymers and materials forming the matrix of concretes, mortars, and sanded grout ...

4. Pre-packaged or pre-mixed concrete, mortar, or grout is not permitted.[25]

Thanks to the addition of micro balloons that make the cement less dense than water (before racing, canoes must pass a "swamp test" which is nothing more than filling each with water to make sure it won't be renamed *Titanic*), and to shapes that rival any Olympic sprint canoe, the concrete canoe can be quite functional. The limiting factor, amusingly, is not so much construction and design techniques, although these are still critical, as it is finding young engineers who can paddle and who are physically fit. The Cement Canoe Competition continues annually as an unofficial rite of passage for young engineers, their stone boats, as did Glooscap's, taking them from one world to the next.

Closing the subject of threshold-crossing magic canoes, I am drawn to the number of times I have witnessed or heard of canoes being used in wedding ceremonies.[26] Before a discussion about Beothuk canoes and Gander Bay boats with the editor of *Downhomer* magazine in St. John's, Newfoundland, could come to a close, Ron Young had to tell me about a photo he remembered about a couple in full wedding attire—white dress and tuxedo—shooting a rapid in a Gander Bay boat. I think of Bill Mason's daughter, Becky, who was married to her husband in a canoe ceremony on Meech Lake. I think of the Royals, Andrew and Fergie, honeymooning on the Thelon River in the Northwest Territories. I think of outdoor author Cliff Jacobson taking the whole thing to the limit with a full wedding ceremony conducted at the brink of Wilberforce Falls (the bride with "Wellies" under the ruffle of her dress) during an Arctic canoe adventure. I think of my own first date (a seven-week canoe trip)[27] with the woman who is now my wife, and of our subsequent wedding ceremony that involved kilted groom and bride-with-train taking a nuptial paddle during the reception in a backyard pool. It is only after all that, and in light of the rich history of canoes crossing thresholds, that the real symbolic significance of these antics comes to light. The notion of canoe with its own measure of magic has been with us in Canada since time began, as amplified in a verse by turn-of-the-century poet Alan Sullivan:

Oh, gently the ripples will kiss her side,
    And tenderly bear her on;
For she is the wandering phantom bride
    Of the river she rests upon;
She is loved with a love that cannot forget,
    A passion so strong and true
That never a billow has risen yet
    To peril the White Canoe.[28]

4

FROM RIGHT SIDE UP TO UPSIDE DOWN

I am creating the thing that makes the sounds in
the water; it develops like a growing child.

—Song of the Cree canoe-builder Miitaaskoonaanicaa[1]

FROM THE MAINE RIVULETS that become the St. John River in the high country, to tidewater at Reversing Falls, there are pieces of the story scattered throughout the historic St. John River valley. Beneath the long, high-prowed river canoes and other boats that crease the waters below and above hydro-electric dams at Grand Falls and Beechwood are stumps of stout basswood and white pine with cut marks of fire, stone and steel. Preserved by the airless environment inside the river itself, these are the trees that became the early dugout canoes to ferry Micmac and Malecite from one place to another. They called this river Oo-lahs-took, "goodly river," for provisioning their lives: its fish and fresh water; its trees—the paper birch, white cedar, spruce and balsam — whose bark, heartwood, roots and sap gave them canoes with which to move up and down, to the limits of the smallest tributary and overland to places beyond. And the lives of the people who came later, Loyalists mostly, escaping the American Revolution, were underlain by the rich soils of the St. John River valley, nourished by the river. They made canoes for work and pleasure, different canoes from the dugouts and bark-craft of the Indians, but canoes nevertheless that give the St. John River valley a special place in the hearts of people around the world.

The piece of that story I am working on today is a canvas-covered canoe that sorely needs attention. I have been writing the biography of Bill Mason,[2] a man who, when he was alive, was obsessed with canoes in general, Chestnut Canoe Company canoes from the St. John River valley, in particular. As part of the research process, I have met up with Mason's lifelong chum Don Campbell, who has taken me to their old haunts on the rivers of Whiteshell Provincial Park in Manitoba. After our days on the water, Campbell takes me to his home, in Winnipeg. His family has grown. He and his wife, Willy, are retired. The inclination to paddle has largely faded. After tea, and more Bill Mason stories, he invites me into the backyard, where, fixed to the fence with wooden brackets, is the old red family canoe, a Chestnut, from Fredericton via Eaton's or the Hudson's Bay Company store in downtown Winnipeg. "I've talked about this with Willy and the kids," he intones with funereal solemnity. "We would like this canoe to go to another family, people who could fix it up and look after it. If you think you could

59

mend the broken ribs and planks and maybe put new canvas on, we'd like you to have this old canoe."

"Oh" is all I can think to say. "It's red."

The paint is cracked and faded, but that beautiful shape is still there and still evident. There is not one straight line on it; not a flat spot on the bottom. There is a gentle curve, or "rocker," along the keel from end to end. There is a plump round curve, or "chine," where bottom meets side. Farther up the sides, below the worn gunwales, there is a subtle recurve in the wall, or "tumblehome," that gives a certain look of strength and stability to the craft. Walking around, I notice fine, clean Vs, or "entry lines," at bow and stern. And, running my hand over the brittle patina of old paint, I can feel the intersection of thin cedar boards beneath the sun-warmed, taut canvas skin.

We each take an end, turn the boat upright and set it down on the grass. The smell of cedar and old varnish wafts up through spiderwebs and takes me to a place where I've been a million times. There is laughter, there is music, there is pine and water. There are memories of rain and sparkling white light, of tears on portages, of burnt food and cans of peanut butter crushed and oozing in the bottom of aged green canvas packs.

"Do you think you can fix those ends?"

"Pardon?"

"It sat for quite a while on the ground before we got it up onto the fence, and I think both ends are a bit rotten. And we fixed a few broken ribs and planks under the stern seat with fibreglass. I think it may have been dropped once too, by accident."

That smell. Sweet, aromatic white cedar, mixed with turpentine, varnish, earth, water, dry rot and old lace. I'm transfixed by that smell. It takes me back in the twitch of a muscle at the nape of my neck to the Haliburton Highlands, to Algonquin Park, to Temagami, to James Bay, to busses and trailers and trains. Soaping pots and circle trips. Days when it was too hot to think, others when it was too cold to matter. Fresh walleye on sticks by the fire. Growing up. Broken paddles and lost first-aid kits. Canvas and kerosene, rivers and rapids and finding bits of old logging chains. Cuts and blisters, sunburns and rashes. Letters from home in general-delivery boxes behind counters in tiny post offices in out-of-the way places. It's all there, in that intoxicating smell.

I suppose, had camp been a disaster of misfit or homesickness, that this same aroma would have sent me reeling. But camp wasn't like that. It wasn't like that at all, at least not through the filters of time. Camp was about privilege—I was so fortunate to be able to go—but it was also about capability. It was about individual accomplishment in a group context. It was about being outside. It was about wood-smoke and oranges.[3] It was about responsibility and stewardship. It was about building association with nature. It was about love and the capacity to feel. And all of that, magically, inexorably, was infused into the wood and canvas and, I suppose, the idea of canoe, like this one that had come my way on the wind.

"Oh ... yes. I think we can fix that. Once the canvas is off, I'm pretty sure we can either replace the stems, decks and gunwales or splice in new wood as required. It's a fussy job, but it would be fun to do. Otherwise the boat is a beauty."

And so home I came from Winnipeg to Seeley's Bay, with a little piece of New Brunswick on the roof, surprised, sheepish even, with the delight that the gift in its many dimensions has brought. Clearly the Campbell family had loved this canoe. Don had bought it as a young man, when he and Bill Mason worked for the same advertising company in Winnipeg. Before either of them was married, they had paddled it together to their Whiteshell haunts, where Mason had sketched and Don had spent his days with his camera along river and shore. And then, after Mason moved east, Don and Willy were married and, as their family grew, the loads got bigger and bigger until the 16-foot red Chestnut "Pal" could no longer carry them all. The kids used it when they were in their teens, but they moved on into their own lives. Don and Willy used it, but not all that often. And so, eventually, they came to a point where they knew in their hearts that it was wrong to just let it sit. A boat like this needs to be loved, but it also needs to be paddled. It would never do to just put it up for sale. No, a canoe like this, even though it is just an assemblage of tacks, canvas, cedar boards and a bit of paint, a canoe like this needs to be given, like an aging family pet, to a "good home," a circumstance befitting its long service and its substantial meaning. There was a lesson to be learned in refurbishing the old Chestnut.

Removing the canvas was easy enough. Forty-year-old brass screws came easily from the outer white ash gunwales, as they did from the oak keel. Once the tacks were pried loose from holding the canvas at little painted puckers covered by the outwale, the whole canvas skin slid off and sat on the lawn, stretched out with its two hollow symmetrical lobes, like a pair of loved dance slippers. Setting up the wooden shell on a pair of trestles, first upside down, I could see the saw marks and the little dents around each tack connecting me instantly to the hands in that Fredericton workshop that had crafted this boat, post–World War II. Along the centre line, where the keel had been, was a sprinkling of sand glued to bare wood with an amalgam of mud, fish guts and anything else that had filtered between the planks into the space between the canvas and the boat itself. Beneath the stern seat, clearly visible now on the water side of the boat, were the impact marks of a rock on a day when a much heavier person had been in the stern. Planks had been split, ribs had been broken, and the perfect outer curvature of the boat interrupted by a nasty bruise. Turning the boat over, I found fibreglass scar tissue, with its cold resin drips, like jack wax[4] on snow, holding the damaged area together with graceless efficiency. Other cracked ribs and broken planks showed more clearly now as well, with reflected light entering the boat through the planking. And on the points of bow and stern—evidence of the boat sitting for long periods overturned on damp ground—there was rot that crept into the decks and inwales and down into the curling stems to which the delicate side boards were carefully tacked.

The first job was to pry apart the ends of the boat and to remove the rotten stems, making sure to leave a cleanly cut, steeply angled end for gluing carved replacements. Using the same procedure for the inwales— the decks, it turned out, were just darkened from water damage and quite salvageable—cutting past the rot into the sound, original wood, it came time to fashion new pieces to fit, first the stem tip, then the inwales, one at a time. Once all that was glued firmly in place, I was able to reattach the end planks, replacing the rotten ones, making the stems true and firm for a second time in the life of this venerable little boat.

The next job was to cut out the broken and tired planking on the bottom of the boat and contemplate how to repair the broken ribs. The books suggested replacing whole ribs, a massive job to be sure, but on the advice of my neighbour, who happens to be a Dutch shipwright and boat builder *par excellence*, I opted instead to chisel out just the broken portions of the ribs and to fashion new cedar splices to glue in. "As long as your scarf [angled] joints are seven times longer than the width of the boards, you'll be all right," he assured me. "Cut battens the size and shape of the rib stock, steam them to the right curve, shape them to fit, glue them and then hold them in place with battens jammed up under the seat."

It sounded easy enough. And all was going well. Using a big covered pan of water on the barbecue, I steamed the new rib pieces and curved them around pieces of firewood using old cargo straps to hold shape to the curvature of the firewood until the cedar cooled. But in gluing these into place by jamming battens under the seat and down onto the splices, I inadvertently splayed the ends of the original ribs and put a horrible bulge at the stern end of the canoe. Back to the drawing board. Or at least back to square one. Cut out the new splices, make a second set and glue these in. Only this time I removed more planking to enable both ends of the each splice to be clamped to the tapered ends of the old ribs, into order to maintain the "faired" shape of the canoe. With 20-odd feet of new 3-inch wide by ⅛-inch thick cedar planking, cut from an old fence post, the boat was ready for new canvas, the real test of patience.

I had learned to canvas canoes from eighty-year-old Alf Moore, and his friend "Young Bill" (sixty-five years old), who lived just down the road from camp in Minden, Ontario. Moore, like builders in New Brunswick, Newfoundland and elsewhere across the country, had learned to make boats from his father, who had learned from his father before that. His specialty was a 12-foot trapper, a very stable little boat with flat bottom and flared sides, from which, Alf claimed, you could fire both barrels of a twelve-gauge shotgun while standing and not lose your balance. The day I learned about canvassing a canoe, Alf had one of these squat canoes upturned on saw horses in his low, damp basement. He draped heavy cream canvas over the bare back of the canoe, tied one end to a bolt on the floor and then gathered and hooked the other end of the canvas sheet to a block and tackle attached to a floor hook at the other end, and cinched it up tight. "One man can pull ten hundred pound with this," he puffed.

The books said that you achieve the same effect—stretching the canvas onto the various curves of the canoe hull—by pushing the hull of a new canoe into a canvas envelope, slung like a hammock, using boards braced to a ceiling to wrap the body, as it were, into the covering material. With the old Chestnut, I was working outside and had neither floor hooks nor a ceiling to tighten the canvas. "Just stretch the canvas between two trees and weight the canoe down with firewood," my neighbour encouraged. It sounded like an excellent compromise at the time, especially when he suggested that the inside of the boat be lined first with foam camping pads to avoid damaging the hull with the rough firewood.

All was going well, extremely well, until one of the homemade canvas clamps gave way under the strain of the stretching and the weight of the boat, and the four billets of ironwood I'd added for extra weight. Like most devastating accidents, there wasn't much to see or to hear when the damage was done, except an unceremonious crack when the wooden clamp gave way and an ominous crunch, when the boat hit the ground after falling about 6 inches from its position slung between the two trees. The good news was that the newly spliced ribs had held firm. The rebuilt stern was fine. The bad news was that one of the big ironwood logs had crashed through a parallel constellation of planks and ribs at the other end.

There was nothing to be done but fold up the canvas and go back into wood-repair mode, starting with the broken canvas clamp and moving, however reluctantly, back to rib steaming, plank planing, cutting, fitting, cutting again, glueing, clamping and rebuilding. The only consolation was that I was able to spend another three weeks of evenings with my head inside that old canoe, hands busy, head swimming in that nostalgic smell of varnished cedar. In time, the boat and I were back at the canvas stage and, this time with the neighbour's help, I was able to stretch on a new canvas skin, fill it with a slurry of plaster-like material and, after about a six-week drying period, sand it and paint it. I had a thought as the grey undercoating went on to paint the boat green, maybe even with yellow trim like the boats at camp, but this boat had originally been red, Chestnut red, and, in the end, that's what it stayed.

All those hours, all those days, all those weeks that passed, communing with this 16-foot piece of New Brunswick history, afforded ample time to think and to wonder about every aspect of this canoe. So simple. So functional. So elegant. So suited to the Canadian landscape. So similar in so many ways to the bark canoes, even the dugouts, that the Malecite of the St. John River valley would have built long before there were brass tacks, planers, cotton canvas or paint. And even though this boat, in the minutiae of its construction details, was very different from its aboriginal ancestors, its fundamental shape, the way in which that shape was created by the natural bends of local woods, was identical. There had been an evolutionary process that linked the original dugouts and bark canoes to these so-called modern canoes. And, as a little digging in the library revealed, this process is as evident in the evolution of the Chestnut canoe in the St. John River valley as it is in the Otonabee watershed in central Ontario, home of the other famous Canadian canoe, the Peterborough.

Somewhere in the mists of history, the St. John River would have been crossed by early aboriginals, or perhaps even by descendants of the mysterious Earl Sinclair, on rafts or even in rudimentary dugout canoes made from the abundant timber in the area. But when the first European settlers moved into the St. John River valley, the main wave of immigrants being people of British stock who migrated north during the American Revolution, 1783–84, or immediately on its conclusion when they felt the Treaty of Paris failed to make adequate provision for them, they encountered the canoes of the Micmac and Malecite. So durable and well suited to the river, its terrain and the needs of its people were these birchbark canoes that they endured as the craft of choice for river travel until the beginning of the twentieth century.

Thus, the same boats that the Indians made and paddled in pre-contact times conveyed Champlain on the Kennebec River in the early 1600s, the United Empire Loyalists in the 1700s, and the new industrialists of the 1800s.

As the nineteenth century drew to a close, birch bark of sufficient quality for boats was scarce. This shortage turned a perceptive young man from Ohio to a lifelong quest to document what he saw as a dying tradition. Edwin Tappan Adney was nineteen when he first summered in the St. John River valley in 1837. Although born in Ohio, son of

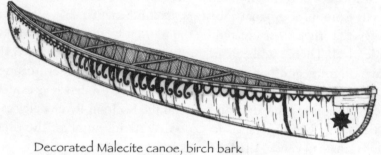

Decorated Malecite canoe, birch bark
and cedar, 14 feet

bright, educated parents, Adney was not much for school and, instead of college or university in his late teens, he opted to spend three years with the Art Students' League in New York, meeting the likes of Ernest Thompson Seton in New York's various museums of natural history. Short of money and unable to afford a return to art school, he ventured to New Brunswick in the spring of 1887 for what was intended to be a short vacation. By chance, he met Malecite Peter Joe, who lived in a temporary camp near Woodstock. Adney got to know Peter Joe quite well and, as the days turned into weeks that extended his stay far beyond original plans, the young artist took increasing interest in the lore and craftsmanship of the Malecite, paying special attention with his sketching to Peter Joe's work with bark canoes. Two years later, Adney returned to Woodstock, where, with Peter Joe's tutelage, he built his first bark canoe, taking time to sketch and record every step along the way, drawings and construction details that were reported in the July 29, 1890, edition of *Harper's Young People* magazine. These efforts would be the opening entry in a body of work that spanned a lifetime and crossed a continent and became the first (and still most authoritative, with the posthumous assistance of Howard I. Chapelle, curator of transportation at the American Museum of History and Technology) accounting of aboriginal canoes and kayaks from coast to coast to coast.

In Adney and Chapelle's remarkable book, *The Bark and Skin Boats of North America*, are sketches and descriptions of not only Peter Joe's boats but of a host of other Malecite canoes as well: the Malecite-Abenaki 2½-fathom ocean canoe, the 3-fathom canoe of the Passamaquoddy porpoise hunters, the Malecite racing canoe, and the 2½-fathom St. John River canoe developed late in the nineteenth century.[5] In exhaustive detail, Adney and Chapelle laid out the sequence of steps for choosing bark, for building canoes from the ground up, for lashing gunwales with split spruce roots; they include insights into the ins and outs of rigging a canoe for sailing, details on paddle construction, and even instruction on the meaning of various decorations scratched by builders into the rind of birch immediately below the gunwales and on the bow and stern faces of the boats. Even before Adney's original article from *Harper's Young People* was republished in *Outing* magazine in May 1900, things were starting to change in the St. John River valley.

For the last few decades of the nineteenth century, during the time Adney and Peter Joe were building their bark canoes in Woodstock, non-aboriginal boat builders in territory just south of the American border, along the Penobscot River at places like Veazie and Old Town, Maine, driven partly by the limited supply of birch bark, and informed by boat-building traditions from England and elsewhere, had been experimenting with other coverings for canoes. They had come up with more or less the same canoe lines described by Adney, to the extent that these new boats were cedar ribbed and planked with hardwood thwarts, decks, stems and gunwales, but instead of outer skins of bark they stretched heavy cotton sail canvas onto the exterior of the hull, tacked it on, and painted it to keep out the water. And it was only a matter of time before these canvas-covered canoes at the hand of American sportsman and adventurers found their way into the waters of the St. John River. Records show that the B.N. Morris Canoe Company of Veazie, Maine, began production of canvas-covered canoes in 1882, followed shortly thereafter by E.M. White, in 1889, and again soon after that by the Old Town Canoe Company.

There is nothing in the East Coast historical record, however, to detail exactly how this innovation occurred. We do get a glimpse of what happened in a parallel process of evolution that transpired at Rupert's House on James Bay at the turn of the century. Writing in the June 1954 issue of *The Beaver* journal, Stephen Greenlees, a visiting ethnographic film-maker with the National Film Board, recounts what happened at the Hudson's Bay Company canoe-building factory in Cree country:

> Originally, the canoes built at the Rupert's House factory were of course birchbarks. They were made for freighting, 30 feet long, strongly constructed and serviceable. These craft could, and did, withstand the rough going of very long trips such as the journey from Rupert's House to Lake Mistassinni and back ... I can testify, from having owned a birchbark canoe and having travelled many hundreds of miles of rough canoe country in it, that the bark craft, properly made, is by no means flimsy or frail. It is not so strong and durable as a good canvas-covered canoe, however, nor so easy to paddle.
>
> Due to the way in which the bark has to be lapped around the canoe frame, the narrow, inch-long indentations characteristic of birchbark are at right angles to the direction of paddling, which slows down the canoeman's speed. Also, even good bark has little knobs and warts which can easily get scraped off when the canoe touches rocks or shale, causing leaks which must be patched with gum. The spruce or pine gum is rendered less prone to drying and cracking by heating it before application and mixing a little lard in with it ... The frequent re-caulking of the joins between the different

sections of bark is a necessity which becomes tedious when the canoe is in constant use ...

The records show that it was in 1902 when John Iserhoff was chief of the Rupert's House band that the first canvas-covered canoe was built there. This was the first canvas-covered craft to appear anywhere in the James Bay country, and was fashioned according to design derived from observation of canoes at points farther south. It was built alongside birchbark canoes in the Hudson's Bay Company canoe factory at the post. This first canvas-covered canoe was constructed exactly like a bark canoe, however, except for the outside covering.

The ribs, the lightweight slats for the bottom and walls, and all the rest of the frame were the same as required for a bark canoe, with canvas for the outside layer instead of birchbark. There were no nails nor screws anywhere in the canoe. The bindings and fastenings were entirely of split spruce roots in the traditional bark canoe style. The experiment revealed to the Indians that canvas made a quite durable outside surface, less prone to crack than bark, with no seams to spring leaks, and offering less resistance to the water when the canoe was moving. For the next eighteen years the factory made both birchbark and canvas-covered canoes, all on the old-time birchbark pattern without nails.[6]

Some similar evolutionary process may well have taken place in Maine a quarter-century earlier but it would likely have gone one critical step farther than the building process at Rupert's House. If a canvas-covered canoe is built in the age-old birchbark building style, it would be constructed from the outside in, meaning the outer shell would be attached to gunwales in a canoe-shaped frame, into which planking would be laid and fixed with hammered-in ribs. But in order for the shift to modern canvas-covered canoes to occur, at some point in the evolutionary process the building sequence had to be reversed because the canvas boats being made in Maine were made from the inside out: ribs steamed and bent around a form (in the first instance, probably an old dugout canoe) and affixed to inwales to which planking was tacked.

69

The last item to go on the canoe in the inside-out protocol was, of course, the canvas which would have been stretched over the canoe, as Alf Moore showed me in Minden, or stretched under the canoe hammock-style, in the manner of my refurbished Chestnut. Outside-in or inside-out, the move to create canvas-covered canoes in Rupert's House and Maine and elsewhere (like Peterborough) was driven first by a shortage of birch trees in sufficient size and number to support an ongoing canoe-building industry.

In *The Wood & Canvas Canoe*, Jerry Stelmok and Rollin Thurlow see influence from Canada and England as possibly building a technological bridge that allowed the Maine builders to shift from from one building technique to another, from outside-in construction in the venerable bark-canoe tradition to inside-out construction in what would become the durable ways of the modern canoe industry. They explained:

> The theory of building upside down over a form with metal straps [for bending over or "clenching" brass tacks that would come through plank and rib], nailing the ribs and planking together, and stretching the canvas over the wood hull must have been a radical idea to the Maine builders. The builders of the all-wood American sailing canoes and the Peterborough canoes had been using canoe forms since the 1860s, and it would seem reasonable that those building methods would eventually be copied by the Maine builders. However, there is no indication that the Maine builders were aware of the other building techniques. The all-wood canoes were not in use in the woods of Maine, and there were no builders using these techniques in the region.[7]

And so it was that in the dying decade of the nineteenth century came flashy new canvas-covered canoes out of Maine and into the St. John River valley. Whether they were paddled or shipped into New Brunswick is unclear, but when one of these revolutionary new boats cruised down the St. John River to Fredericton in the summer of 1897, it caught the eyes of Harry and William Chestnut, sons of the local hardware-store owner. Now their late teens, these two had grown up on the St. John

70

River, spending long hours fishing, camping, and doing what children and young men do when they are captured by play on a river—agreeing fully with Rat, in *Wind in the Willows*, who remarked: "There is nothing, absolutely nothing, half so much worth doing, as simply messing about in boats."[8]

Harry and William Chestnut, like their father, Henry, and their grandfather Robert before them, had paddled on the river in what was available, namely Malecite bark canoes, which, by this time were, as historian Richard Sparkman, noted "generally of poor quality due to the shortage of good birch bark."[9] In his book, *The Story of the Chestnut Canoe*,[10] Kenneth Solway implies in an opening ramble that the Chestnut brothers found their old bark canoes leaky and uncomfortable and were, in their discontent, ripe to try anything new. So shortly after the canvas-covered canoe from Maine turned up at the town wharf in Fredericton, the Chestnut brothers procured one of the new boats (some say they bought it used from an adventurer who'd paddled it downriver from Maine, while others say they purchased it) and, with the help of Fredericton boat builder J.J. Moore, built a copy and in the process worked out a way to manufacture the new style of boat. Their ambitions took their father, Henry, and R. Chestnut and Sons Hardware Store into the canvas-covered canoe business, which became in its heyday one of the most influential canoe manufacturers in the world.

Of the various accounts in the canoeing literature, no two seem to agree on the ethics underpinning the genesis of the Chestnut Canoe Company. In an interview given to *Canadian Forest and Outdoors* magazine some time after the company was in business, Harry Chestnut, who by this time was chief executive officer of the firm, told his public: "We got many tips from the Indian. We used the Indian shape for our first models, and we use the same principle and same kind of wood in construction, but we reverse the process in building."[11] This was all true, but only to a point. In notes accompanying a reprint of the 1950 Chestnut Canoe catalogue, author and historian Roger MacGregor paints a slightly different ethical picture:

> In the summer of 1897, the *Daily Gleaner* [Fredericton newspaper] reported that W.T. Chestnut has imported a

71

canvas canoe from a "leading and renowned boat building house in the United States, it being especially for use at Pine Bluff Camp." The canoe was apparently exhibited that year at R. Chestnut and Sons' store for a few days. Later reports suggest that the canoe originated at the canoe factory of B.N. Morris of Veazie, Maine. The next year "an exact counterpart" of this same canoe was reportedly built by the local boat builder J.J. Moore and pronounced by W.T. Chestnut as "just as pretty and good in every way as his own favourite Pine Bluff Canoe."[12]

Branching out from their affiliation with builder J.J. Moore, the Chestnuts later affiliated with a small sash and door company in Fredericton and continued to expand the line of boats they sold out of the back of their hardware store. In 1905, they published their first canoe catalogue and set up a dedicated canoe shop and, in 1907, incorporated the Chestnut Canoe Company. This is where the tale gets even more complicated.

Decades before the canoe builders in Maine were perfecting the canvas-covered canoe, carpenters, smiths and boat *aficionados* in central Ontario had also been experimenting with alternatives to the aboriginal canoes. In this case, however, the sources of inspiration for the effort (and the canoes used by most of the settlers in the Otonabee River watershed near Peterborough) were dugouts rather than the less durable, more friable, bark boats. As canoe regattas grew in popularity in this water-rich area, efforts to make dugout canoes lighter and faster resulted in boats being constructed from planks held together with ribs, rather than whole logs of pine or basswood. In the space of only a few years, these all-wood boats in the Peterborough area moved from a "hogtrough" aesthetic, a term coined by innovator Samuel Strickland, to sleek (relatively speaking) dugouts with names like "Shooting Star" (built by Strickland's son, George), to flush-batten polished racing craft and pleasure canoes made of thin wooden planks for which Peterborough became known around the world.

Some canoe historians give significance to a comment by one of Samuel Strickland's literary daughters, Susanna Moodie (his other daughter was Catharine Parr Traill). In *Roughing It in the Bush*, Moodie writes: "These were the halcyon days of the bush. My husband had purchased a very light cedar canoe, to which he attached a keel and sail; and most of our leisure hours, directly the snows melted, were spent upon the water."[13] Some readers take "light cedar canoe" to mean that this was a plank canoe. But it may be, at that time in the development of the canoe, that weight was a relative thing. In comparison to a giant dugout canoe of oak, or even pine or basswood, a smallish dugout, made of cedar, with sides heated with water and splayed wide with strong thwarts, weighing, say 100 pounds or thereabouts, could be what Mrs. Moodie was referring to.

The development of the all-wood Peterborough canoe is a bit of a mystery. How, where and at what point in time, space and evolution did dugout canoe-construction change from building outside-in (hollowing logs out) to building inside out (putting ribs and planks over a form)? Some historians suggest that this was a near-spontaneous response by Thomas Gordon of Lakefield and/or John Stevenson of Ashburnham (Peterborough) to the need to build faster, lighter regatta canoes, these two innovators being credited with building the first plank canoes in the Peterborough area around the summer of 1857.[14]

In contrast to this centralist point of view, canoe historian C. Fred Johnston argues that the notion of a plank canoe was a Western idea (driven as well by a paucity of bark), which arose among aboriginal boat builders west of the Rockies, and was brought east by the great mapmaker David Thompson after his Pacific journeys in 1810–11, when he was sent to survey the Muskoka–Madawaska rivers to determine feasibility for a water transportation route through Upper Canada. Sometime between then and 1857, it was introduced to the good folk of the Peterborough area.[15]

Wherever the notion of moving from a solid wood canoe to a plank canoe originated—and this will likely be the source of lively debate for years to come—the fact remains that Canada in general, and

Peterborough in particular, with its network of canoe builders and canoe-building companies that came and went in the latter half of the nineteenth century, became known throughout the world for its open all-wood canoes that were paddled with a single-bladed paddle, so much so that in the evolution of canoe racing, culminating with today's Olympic paddling events, there are two racing classes in the canoeing competition: "K" class, referring to decked kayaks paddled with double-bladed paddles; and "C" class, referring to open canoes paddled with single-bladed paddles, the "C" standing not for "canoe," as many people think, but for "Canadian," which refers back to the early days of the all-wood Peterborough canoe.

In the Peterborough area, all-wood canoe building became an art unto itself. In the early days, planed planks with square edges were simply butted together, nailed (or sewn in the case of David Thompson's Columbia River canoe) to each other or to ribs, and either caulked with oakum (like the Gander Bay boat) or, in the very early days, made waterproof with the same pitch-and-tallow mixture that had been used for centuries to seal the seams of bark canoes. More involved construction techniques included lapstrake construction, which, like in the European rowing skiffs and dories, involved overlapping the edge of one plank on the edge of the next; ship-lap construction, which involved various tongue-and-groove configurations on adjoining planks; and, finally, various types of board-and-batten techniques, in which small strips of wood would be used to cover the cracks between planks. As the board-and-batten building techniques became more sophisticated, builders were able to plane a groove for the small strips, thereby allowing the creation of so-called flush batten canoes with completely smooth outer hulls. It was this technology, with its male moulds and plank construction techniques, that some writers feel might have been adopted by the Maine boat builders in their quest to make a better canvas-covered canoe.

There is very little in the historical record about canvas-covered canoes being built in the Peterborough area prior to 1905. However, there was one exception. South of Peterborough, at Gore's Landing, where people from Toronto would disembark from their carriages at road's end and boat up Rice Lake into the Kawarthas, was a place of innovative canoe building that saw canoe builder Daniel Herald design a double-walled, ribless canoe which employed a sheet of waterproofed canvas in a novel way. This canoe, patented in 1871, used a form, now used through the modern canoe-building world, but instead of applying ribs and then planks to create a new boat, Herald, in a design predating plywood, applied one layer of thin planks, in the manner of ribs, from side to side and then, on top, tacked a second layer of longitudinal planks that became the outer hull of the boat. Between these two layers he bonded a piece of canvas with white lead paint that helped keep the water out.

When, according to old catalogues, the Peterborough Canoe Company started selling canvas-covered canoes around 1905, a row over the Canadian patent broke out. The fledgling Chestnut Canoe Company and the venerable Peterborough Canoe Company came to blows in Canadian courts.

In 1905, prior to the incorporation of their canoe company, the Chestnut family was able to obtain a Canadian patent for canvas canoe construction, having borrowed a good thing from their American neighbours. Four years later, encouraged by brisk sales and the promise of ever-expanding trade, and more wary now than before of domestic competition from central Canada (Chestnut was able to build canoes for about the same cost as their competitors in the United States but consumers who shopped for boats south of the border were forced to pay a tariff of about $10 per boat, which was a substantial increase on an item valued at $35 in Canada), Chestnut filed a lawsuit against Peterborough, alleging violation of its canvas canoe patent. According to Roger MacGregor, Peterborough's reply to these charges was "lengthy, detailed and devastating,"[16] to such an extent that Chestnut made no response in court and the suit died for want of prosecution. Presumably Peterborough was able to show that a variety of canoe builders in the United States and Canada had either been building or at least tinkering with canvas-covered canoes for years.

With that, canvas-covered canoe building was off and running in eastern and central Canada, with shops popping up in Peterborough and New Brunswick. In Nictau, New Brunswick, in 1925, Vic Miller, a lumberman, hunter and guide, started building canoes in a shop in his back yard on the shores of the Tobique River. The impetus for his build-ing project was frustration with the fact that horse-drawn wagons that hauled canoes over portages and tote roads in northern New Brunswick could carry only one boat at a time, so Miller set out to make a narrower boat that could be nested right side up on a wagon. As might be expected, the lines of Miller's canoe looked very similar to the bark canoes the Malecite had perfected for use in this local area, finding the perfect balance between a totally round-bottomed boat that would draw too much water in the shallow rivers and streams, and a completely flat-bottomed boat that would be stable but impossible to manoeuvre in current. And years later, like the descendants of E.M. White and the founders of the Peterborough Canoe Company, Vic Miller's family has a story hinging on ethics and the Chestnut Canoe Company.

Apparently one of the first proud owners of one of Vic Miller's canoes was a Tobique River guide called Ogilvy who had, as one of his spring fishing clients in the late 1920s, a Fredericton businessman and canoe builder himself, Harry Chestnut. Lo and behold, in the late autumn of 1931, the Chestnut Canoe Company came out with a canoe it called the "Ogilvy Special," described this way in the Chestnut catalogs:

> In collaboration with that dean of New Brunswick guides, Mr. David Ogilvy, we produced in the late autumn of 1931 a new 18 foot canoe which we tried out thoroughly and after chang-ing the model slightly four different times through 1932 we find it now approaches in both looks and performance the perfection insisted upon by our manager. Ogilvy Bros. and other guides who have used it say it is "just right" and the "best yet". This model will be known as the Ogilvy Special ...
>
> It is so straight on the bottom and so flat from side to side that it skims over the top of the water rather than through it and has therefore very light draft. It can be poled through the heaviest rapids with the minimum of effort and the flat floor makes it very comfortable for the feet of the poler on an all day's trip. The shape is such that it is probably the steadiest canoe of its size ever built, as indicated by the

photo of a 200 pound man standing well into the bilge without upsetting or even getting the gunwale down near the water.[17]

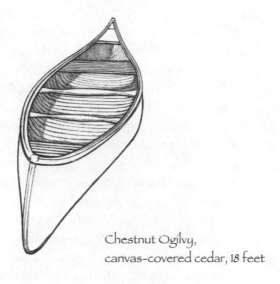

Chestnut Ogilvy,
canvas-covered cedar, 18 feet

Recounting this situation, Vic Miller's daughter-in-law says that the whole Miller family thinks that Harry Chestnut copied the Miller canoe, as he had done with the E.M. White canoe from Maine some years before. According to Wilma Miller, "the [Chestnut] Ogilvy is just a flawed Miller sold under another name."[18] When this was presented to Don Fraser, Chestnut Canoe Company sales manager until it went out of business, he denied it. Fraser is something of an expert on Chestnut canoes, who purchased four of the Ogilvy forms when the firm was dissolved.[19] But in response to Wilma Miller he is not so sure that there was any design pilfering going on on the part of his former employer, saying, "I told her I found that hard to credit—the canoes don't look alike." Completely unmoved by his denial, Wilma Miller retorted: "Of course they don't look alike! Chestnut didn't get it right."[20]

Exact source of the Ogilvy canoe notwithstanding, it is a venerable river craft that came from the woods of New Brunswick for which there was such demand from working rivermen, surveyors and adventurers, that Chestnut eventually produced the shape in five different lengths: from the 16-foot model, telegraph code "Henry," through "Dave, Jock, Alex, and Joe," getting larger in 2-foot increments, all the way up to the 40-inch-wide, 26-foot "Chief" model that weighed a modest 160 pounds (when compared to its payload of nearly a ton of paddlers and gear). The principal virtue of all of these craft was its all-round capability going down river, in rapids or in flatwater, but also, because of its relatively flat bottom and shallow draft, its ability to perform when being poled up river. A big man could stand firm on the ample floor of this canoe and make the canoe shiver laterally or surge through downstream Vs with only minimal risk of losing balance.

What the Chestnut Canoe Company got exactly right was the same thing that the aboriginal boat builders who preceded them did, and that was the general shape and design of the canoe that has persisted from 1850 to the present. Though the dugout canoe underwent the transformation to the all-wood Peterborough canoe, driven largely by the need for faster, lighter canoes for racing, and similarly, though the bark canoe underwent the transformation to the canvas-covered canoe, the basic idea of the canoe lived on, as long as its lines never contravened the natural bending and strength capacities of the natural materials from which it was made.

These early canoe builders were not without market savvy. There were noticeable efforts to create niches in the market for canoes. Peterborough-area canoe companies, for example, in addition to developing various lines of hardy canvas-covered canoes favoured by surveyors, prospectors and outdoor recreationists, continued to build all-wood canoes, and to adapt these for racing and for pleasure, even creating courting boats, with cabinets for libations and Victrola record players, that looked more like furniture than workaday conveyances. Along with the Maine canoe companies, Peterborough-area canoe companies also produced an array of boats and accessories to meet demand for a burgeoning interest in canoe sailing that swelled before the years leading up to World War I. Chestnut made sailing canoes too, and canoes with cork sponsons on the side to allay public fears about the safety of open canoes, but it stayed with a slightly woodsier image than Peterborough, making snowshoes and related products for outdoor living, and trying to appeal to a broad spectrum of needs with its canvas-covered boats. Interestingly, with the arrival on the boat scene of the Evinrude Elto outboard motor, both Peterborough and Chestnut made square-stern canoes and, after much experimentation, came to exactly the same conclusion as the Gander Bay boat builders in Newfoundland had: the best way to put a transom on a canoe is to leave the double-ended waterline as is and to make a "Y" in the stern stem, above the waterline, in a way that won't cause the boat to drag along a wave so big as to render the boat useless.

Of the many ironies in the early rivalry between Chestnut and Peterborough was a significant downturn in the canoe market in the years following World War I and their eventual amalgamation into Canadian Watercraft Limited in 1923, although both companies continued to build under their own trademarks until bankruptcy, for Peterborough, in 1961. According to historian John Jennings, there are many reasons why this happened, most centred on the move away from wood canoes to fibreglass and aluminum construction. Notes Jennings, "Unfortunately, the combination of new designs and new materials in the hands of craftsmen used to wood, appears to have resulted in many inferior craft ... the switch to fibreglass canoes may have come too late, given the rapid expansion of competition in this field."[21] Chestnut continued to make canoes into the 1970s, even after the firm, in serious financial straits, was purchased by the Lock-Wood window company in 1977. According to Ken Solway, the last Chestnut canoe was built in New Brunswick in May 1979.[22] These were ignominious ends to two venerable canoe makers whose legacy is so much a part of Canadian heritage.

One positive effect of the rivalry between Chestnut and Peterborough was to create space for all sort of other outlandish canoe innovations and modifications to reach market. There were, for example, some wonderful innovations to move canoes from place to place, by road, by sea and by air. One of these was a folding canoe designed and patented by Lt. Col. C.M Douglas, M.D., V.C., of Lakefield. During the Northwest Rebellion, Dr. Douglas was assigned to take charge of the military hospital at Saskatoon when the steamer which was taking him up the South Saskatchewan River was stopped by low water.

Undaunted, Douglas unfolded his invention, loaded his medical supplies and paddled the last 320 kilometres, arriving well ahead of the big boat.

There were also nifty innovations to adapt canoes to the aircraft that were being used more and more to access the back country. In 1930, for example, Chestnut modified their 18-foot Labrador model with removable prows that enabled the flat-topped hull to be lashed securely to the underbody of a Fairchild hydroplane.[23] An even more ingenious innovation was implemented by an employee of the Ontario Department of Lands and Forests who saw a need for canoes to be segmented so that they could be carried inside the cabins of small bush planes.

Working in the early 1920s in the Ontario Provincial Air Service hangar, located on the waterfront in Sault Ste. Marie, Ontario, Jack Hyde developed a prototype for a four-part, sectional canvas-covered canoe that could be assembled and disassembled with the twist of a series of "C" brackets at each joint, using a special little wrench he designed. Weighing only 73 pounds, these so-called Hyde Canoes could be transported easily on or in departmental aircraft and, when assembled, were perfectly serviceable craft. Getting canoes quickly into fire locations was essential, and Jack Hyde's canoe expedited this but, when on location at a blaze, fire fighters could break apart the segmented canoe, carry it uphill through heavy bush, reassemble it and use its inner cavity as an intermediate water reservoir for gasoline-powered water pumps that could only lift water a certain distance up a grade.

The most interesting innovations that occurred through the early years of the Chestnut and Peterborough canoe companies, however, were not made in response to strictly functional, work-related needs of people working in the out of doors. The most potent influence on canoe innovation in the twentieth century has been a growing interest in using canoes for leisure and recreation. Writes canoe historian Jamie Benidickson, "The period spanning the 1920s and 1930s was a transitional era of gradual but noticeable development in all aspects of recreational canoeing."[24] The cottage and regatta crowd on Stoney Lake and elsewhere in the Otonabee River watershed, the island-hopping summer families on the St. Lawrence, as well as the landed gentry in the St. John River valley, and elsewhere, were always looking for canoes that were faster, sleeker, more comfortable, more beautiful or more exclusive than their neighbour's or their competition's. This force generated elaborate sailing canoes, giant canoes for racing, canoes with polished inlay and beautiful hand-carved detail, even supposedly non-sinkable canoes with cork-filled sponsons, or air chambers, along their gunwales designed for "ladies and children, for beginners, and for anyone who is the least timid about venturing on the water."[25] Padded seats were added, decks were lengthened to accommodate on-board cabinets for picnics and libations, and one Peterborough model—the Comfort Craft—could be ordered with an special cupboard for a fold-out phonograph.

All-wood Peterborough Comfort Craft, 16 feet

The construction gimmick that comes to mind most often when I'm paddling the (finally) refurbished Chestnut Pal or driving down the St. John River valley past Fredericton, thinking about canoe building as it changed through the years and the forces which shaped that evolution, has to do with the rotted-out ends on the Chestnut that had to be replaced before new life could be breathed into this old boat.

The Rice Lake Canoe Company, started in Gore's Landing by Daniel Herald (of Herald Patent Canoe fame) and later moved to Cobourg, was a firm that seemed to think more about lines and substantial design features of their boats than about cosmetic issues. Rice Lake Canoe had identified the breakdown of canoe stems as a major flaw in modern canoe design. "All too often," an advertisement in the January 1924 edition of *The Beaver* reported, "the result has been a splitting of decks and a spreading of gunwales from the stem joint, resulting in a shortening of the life and service of a canoe." In this two-page advertisement, under the heading, "NOW! A REVOLUTIONARY IDEA THAT DEFINITELY ESTABLISHES SUPERIORITY OF RICE LAKE CANOES," the company pulled out all the stops to garner the favour and attentions of the canoe-buying public:

> Being leaders in the industry, it was but natural, therefore, that the Rice Lake Canoe Company should be the first seriously to attempt to remove these weaknesses. Many experiments were undertaken and many new ideas tried out, with their successful termination in the invention and development of the Rice Lake Crown Plate. As illustrated in Fig. 1, the Crown Plate is of light weight, but strong aluminum alloy construction, and encases the bow and stern stem joint as to make spreading of the gunwale an impossibility, and, since it takes the place of the ever-splitting old type wood deck, all danger of breakage in that direction is eliminated ... While weighing slightly less than the wood and screws which it replaces, this plate is capable of withstanding the strain and jerks of towing. It will safely absorb the shock of collision with docks or with rocks or snags and go bravely through the banging and dragging which generally accompanies portaging, and the Crown Plate will prevent injury to the canoe if it is turned over on rocky shores or allowed to remain overturned for a time on wet beaches or mud banks.[26]

The company that gave us the aluminum crown plate is long since gone, their elegant boats with the novelty decks almost vanished. (One can be seen in the Canadian Canoe Museum in Peterborough—the same one used by the original University of Toronto Concrete Canoe team, under the tutelage of Kirk Wipper, to design their winning stone canoe in the 1970s.) I still prefer boats like Don Morgan's old Chestnut Pal with the terminal design flaw that the Rice Lake crown plate was supposed to rectify, boats that live on into second and third lives in the hands of people like me who can't let go of the canvas-covered canoe idea, and all that it represents.

The greatest irony of all, of course, is that in spite of new technologies—lamination, fibreglass, aluminum, fancy fibres and resins—that have been employed since World War II to make canoes, bigger, heavier, lighter, wider, slower, more portable and on and on, the basic aboriginal design principles described so completely by Adney and Chapelle still prevail. The most meaningful innovations, like the advent of the all-wood canoe in Peterborough, Ontario, where racing and water-based urban recreation were a phenomenon, and the evolution of the canvas-covered canoe, in Rupert's House, in Maine and New Brunswick, and, yes, in Peterborough, were changes made to the craft that were wrought within the limitations of the natural materials and crafted to meet the needs of local people in their home environment. Innovations that contravened these limitations didn't last. Bark canoes and dugouts may have been replaced in the marketplace by more modern technology, but the original spirit of those vessels is present in every voyage, in every boat, even in the nostalgic smell of Reversing Falls or old varnish and cedar.

5

LACHINE

You hesitate. The trees are entangled with menace.
The voyage is perilous to the dark interior.
But then your hands go to the thwarts. You smile. And so
I watch you vanish in a wood of heroes,
Wild Hamlet with the features of Horatio.

—Douglas LePan, "Coureurs de Bois"[1]

FROM HIGH IN THE HILLS above Nipigon, home of *Paddle to the Sea*, to Ottawa, Illinois, just west of Chicago, in a sweeping circle around the Great Lakes that tips east, the St. Lawrence River watershed collects rainfall from more than a million square kilometres of heartland North America. Trickles that make the streams and rivers that fill Lake Superior, the biggest freshwater lake in the world, must fall 180 metres down rapids and cataracts before their energy is spent at Lachine Rapids, at Montreal, Quebec, where they settle for a final, muscled run past Anticosti Island to the Atlantic. For Europeans coming the other way, the journey into the North American heartland, up what Cartier called the "Rivière du Canada," begins with a leisurely sail against a 6-knot current on a wide, expansive river, until Lachine.

At this fabled rapid, still billed as one of the biggest whitewater thrills Canada has to offer,[2] the equivalent of 140 tractor-trailer loads of water seethes and purls past each point on the shore every second of every day, making a barrier to ocean ships that separates even now the lowly sailor and faint-of-heart boatman from the real voyageurs. It is here, 600 kilometres from the Gulf of St. Lawrence, 100 kilometres from the last tidal effect at Trois-Rivières, but a mere 6 metres above sea level, that canoe country begins. It is here at Lachine that Jacques Cartier, and Samuel de Champlain after him, learned that to move up country required boats and boat lessons from the aboriginals. It was here that the European, in search of riches beyond, was forced into canoes. Cartier wrote in his journal:

> The sayd men did moreover certify, unto us, that there was the way and beginning of the great river of Hochelaga and ready way to Canada, which river the further it went, the narrower it came, even into Canada, and that there was fresh water, which went so farre upwards, that they had never heard of any man who had gone to the head of it, and that there is no other passage but with small boates.[3]

And so it was that Lachine became the point of origin and portal into history for what would become the most recognizable North American "small boate," the voyageur canoe. It is fitting, some would say, in the bawdy spirit of the men who paddled these big canoes, that this magnificent gate to Canada would be named as a destination never reached. In the seventeenth century, René-Robert Cavelier, later Sieur de La Salle, was on a mission, destined for China, when he ventured across the Atlantic and hence through the Great Lakes to the mouth of the Mississippi. But China was not to be found. La Salle took a seigneurial management job on the south shore of the St. Lawrence at a place his friends called from then on, in spirited jest, and in honour of his noble intended destination, "Lachine."

Today the rapids themselves look as they did in La Salle's day, as they did when Frances Anne Hopkins and dozens of other artists painted them. Only now, instead of bark canoes with skilled Mohawk and French-Canadian voyageurs guiding well-heeled city patrons smoothly through the menacing green waves from one end of the broad, curving rapid to the other, you see noisy jet boats and personal watercraft—"sea lice"—drowning the shrieks of paid passengers. And on the north side of the river, at the point above the brink, where loaded canoes would have left with trade goods and returned laden with furs from *le pays d'en haut*, the original Hudson's Bay Company warehouse has been preserved and turned into what is now a National Historical Site dedicated to the fur trade and its hardy voyageurs.

Much has been said about the palimpsest of history at Lachine, layers of human enterprise, one on the other, each travail leaving more immutable marks than the one before. The Mohawks and the Algonquins came and went. Cartier caught fish and sought diamonds and gold. Champlain ventured inland, *en canot*, and the French who followed, allied with one First Nations group, and then the other. There were settlers who pulled and burned stumps and, like the Haudenosaunee before them, carved farms up the banks of the St. Lawrence valley. And of course there were traders, Montreal businessmen, who partnered with the Indians to establish an inland network of contacts and depots up country and a river highway of commerce, terminus Lachine, so different in style from the British fur empire based on the shores of James and Hudson bays.

Heraldic imagery on the crests of the two rival fur companies highlights these two approaches to the land and its people, as exemplified by the Montreal traders and the Hudson's Bay Company. There is not a canoe, or a beaver for that matter, to be found on the HBC crest. On the crest of the rival North West Company, formed through an alliance of Montreal traders under an image of a beaver and a tree bearing the motto "perseverance," inside a rather florid, French-looking perimeter, there are two boats. They're separated by a coloured stripe on a common background, one freight canoe heading west and one stylized sailing-ship heading east, strongly reminiscent in spirit, if not in literal meaning and design, of the Two-Row Wampum that sealed the original deal between Indian and European.

The traditional historical viewpoint is that the large freight canoes of the fur trade did not arrive until after 1759 when James Wolfe defeated Louis-Joseph de Montcalm-Gozon, seigneur de Saint-Veran, on the Plains of Abraham. The end of the French and Indian wars in the late eighteenth century (which were waged from 1689 to 1763 in the valley of the St. Lawrence) brought with it a flood of Highland Scots who joined United Empire Loyalists escaping the American Revolution. These hearties set up shop in Montreal in 1779, and began a central trading organization, the North West Company, rival to the imperious Hudson's Bay Company. Instead of relying strictly on the Indians to bring furs to their ships, as the HBC was doing in the north, NWC traders adopted the ways of the French traders in Montreal, utilizing a network of inland depots established by early French traders and Indian bands throughout the Great Lakes, and bolstering an organized transportation system to move trade goods and supplies inland and furs back to port at Montreal. This canoe transportation system thrived during the period 1770 to 1840, with large bark canoes being put to commercial use, although in much reduced numbers, into the early years of the twentieth century.

But in a new and comprehensive examination of the development of voyageur canoes, *Birchbark Canoes of the Fur Trade*, author and historian Timothy Kent shows that the evolution of the freight canoe was gradual, as it had been all along, and that contrary to those who might suggest that the building of fur-trade canoes was limited to yards in the St. Lawrence River valley, at places like Trois-Rivières, there was, in fact, canoe building going on across the full extent of the North America fur-trading realm. Wherever there were birch trees for bark, spruce for root and pitch, white cedar for ribs and planks, and a need, canoes were built—and as European hunger for fur amplified this need, the canoes of the fur trade grew. Timothy Kent traces this evolution:

FUR TRADE CANOE TYPES, WITH SIZES, CREWS AND CARRYING CAPACITIES

Indian Canoe
13-16 feet, 2 paddlers.

Fishing Canoe
15-18 feet (?), 2 paddlers.
Capacity: 10(?) pieces cargo (merchandise and provisions), plus baggage, equipment, and crew.

Bastard 16-Piece canoe or Half-size canoe
18-24 feet, 3-4 paddlers.
Capacity: 16 pieces cargo (merchandise and provisions), plus baggage, equipment, and crew.

Canot du Nord or North Canoe
24-28 feet, 4-6 paddlers.
Capacity: 30-35 pieces of cargo (20-25 pcs. merchandise, plus provisions), plus baggage, equipment and crew. *Grand total* capacity 3,000 pounds, including the crew.

Bastard canoe
29-33 feet, 6-8 paddlers.
Capacity: 35-50 pieces cargo (25-40 pcs. merchandise, plus provisions), plus baggage, equipment, and crew.

Canot du Maître or Montreal canoe, standard 8-place model
33-36 feet, 8-10 paddlers.
Capacity: 70-75 pieces cargo (60-65 pcs. merchandise, plus provisions), plus baggage, equipment, and crew. *Grand total* capacity 7,000-9,000 pounds, including the crew.

Canot du Maître or Montreal canoe, 10-place model
37-40 feet, 14-16 paddlers.
  Capacity: passengers & provisions, plus baggage, equipment, and crew.[4]

These boats, whatever the size, were ideally suited to the Canadian landscape, balancing design with purpose, strength with efficiency, and staying always within limits set by the materials nature could provide. High prows at bow and stern added to seaworthiness in rapid or lake and allowed the boats to be used for shelter when tipped on their sides. A broad, yet gently curving cross-section allowed great weights to be carried without excessive draft, allowing passage over shoals and in even relatively shallow rivers. The undifferentiated interior of the craft allowed cargo, passengers and paddlers to be placed and replaced for maximum advantage, loaded at the bow when travelling against the current or wind, trimmed level for maximum speed on calm water, and loaded stern heavy when travelling down wind or with the current to add a weather-vane effect to assist the steersman. Curve on the longitudinal axis, or "rocker," especially at bow and stern, would facilitate turning, but long clean entry curves at the waterline would allow the loaded boats to pass through the water with a minimum of slowing wave production. Resilient and flexible cedar ribs and planks, sheathed with the miracle woodland fabric from the paper birch, would give on impact with rocks or dropped cargo and, in the event that hulls were broken in the exercise of their duty, repair materials were always close at hand.

Why voyageur canoes were never built larger than the 40-foot, ten-place *canot du maître* ("places" referring to the number of thwarts in the boat at which passengers and/or paddlers could sit), likely supports John Winters' contention that workable canoes never contravene the properties and capabilities of the natural materials from which they were made, the limiting factor on the length axis being the thickness and weight of the gunwale boards needed to impart rigidity to the boat, and the thickness of cedar required to make sturdy ribs versus the ability of that wood to be steamed and bent by the canoe makers. There would come a length, presumably beyond 40 feet, at which one end of a canoe would start acting independently from the other, either bending like a thick dog's tail through the mid-section on the horizontal axis or rotating in corkscrew manner through the vertical axis of the boat. Conversely, because these boats were derived to travel a particular constellation of landscapes and river, there may have been design limitations imposed by the maximum length of boats that could be carried around obstacles on certain portages, or safely beached on treacherous lakes, or effectively manoeuvred, whether on account of draft or turning ability, up and down the various rapids along the way. What is clear from the historical record is that the biggest canoes, the *canot du maître,* or Montreal canoes, were used on the big river and big lake portion of the voyageur highway from Lachine to the Lakehead, where there were few portages, and that the *canot du nord* and smaller boats were used in the smaller waterways outside the St. Lawrence River watershed.

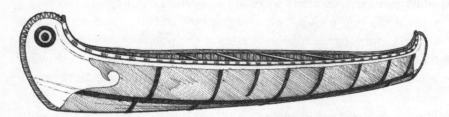

Royal canoe, birch bark and cedar, 28 ¾ feet

A typical journey beginning at Lachine would see fourteen voyageurs, or *engagés,* in a Montreal canoe, or *canot du maître*—one steersman, or *gouvernail,* in the stern, one bowsman, or *avant de canot, devant* or *ducent* in the front of the canoe, and a dozen middlemen, or *milieux*— leaving in a flurry of colour in a brigade of two to thirty canoes in all, under the leadership of a company clerk, or *bourgeois,* carrying several tons of cargo in 90-pound *pièces,* and maybe a passenger or two. More often than not, the expedition would just get under way and would have to stop, either to pray for safe passage at Ste.

Anne's church on the westernmost point of the Island of Montreal or, if the clerk was new, to stop to explain that tradition dictated a "baptizement" (full immersion in the river) unless a load of high wine (brandy) was lightened on the lips of everyone in the canoe. Once under way in earnest, however, crews would make their way up the Ottawa River to the Mattawa, stopping eighteen times either to track their loaded or semi-loaded canoes up rapids or to portage around falls. The Mattawa River was still an upstream struggle but, on reaching Lake Nipissing and the beginning of the downhill run on the French River to Georgian Bay, tracking poles would be heaved into the bushes and the crews of non-swimmers would begin the delicate business of shooting rapids with tons of valuables housed in boats made of fragile cedar and paper birch.

It is difficult to assess what was more dangerous, shooting downstream or portaging back up. Either way, there were untimely deaths from a variety of accidental causes, each marked with a plain wooden cross. This spectre always evoked the removal of hats and usually a word of prayer or a song for the deposed. The deliverance from death, marked by safe arrival at Michilimackinac or Fort William, fortified by a general sense of well-being brought on by the completion of an arduous physical challenge, was one of the driving factors behind the legendary revelry of the up-country voyageurs.

How long it took for *mangers de lard* to get from Lachine to the Lakehead depended on the nature and duration of mishaps along the way. It was about 1,400 kilometres from Lachine to Fort William. Barring any serious accident, a *canot du maître* paddled by a crew of fourteen would have a hull speed of between 6 and 8 miles per hour. This value, however, would be adjusted on rivers by the speed of the current and the length and ruggedness of the portages and, on lakes, would be affected by the number of days when crews would be *degradé*, or windbound. And, depending on what was being carried for freight—Montreal canoes carried blankets, scarlet cloth, stroud, calico, gartering, pins, beads, flour, pork, and occasionally exotic loose items including cast-iron wood stoves and the odd live pig—if precious cargo was ever in danger of getting wet, from upset or from serious leaks in the bark seams, crews would be forced to stop to dry things out.

Writing from the point of view of a *canot du maître* passenger on such an occasion, missionary William T. Boutwell explained in his journal what a campsite looked like when cargo was being dried:

> Our encampment looks not a little like a clothier's establish-
> ment from the rolls of cloth, and pieces of stroud nailed to the
> sides of trees and spread upon bushes. It might, however, be
> mistaken for a laundress establishment in seeing shirts, blan-
> kets, vest. &c. In addition to the 5 bales that were drenched,
> was a box containing sundries, such as knives, forks, siedlitz
> powders, sulphur, starch, saltpeter, snuff, and other numerous
> articles, all of which were soaked. Five or six of us have been
> employed the remainder of the day in hanging out and drying
> wet goods. I have labored in wringing shirts and spreading
> clothes until I am quite tired. We shall not be able to get half
> through today with this unpleasant work.[5]

The hardships notwithstanding, the hard work and monotony of the voyageur's life lent themselves to song. To mention the term "voyageur" is to conjure up distant strains of schoolchildren, campers, or even loads of modern-day canoeists singing "C'est l'aviron" or "En roulant ma boule roulant," accompanied by the hypnotic rhythm of paddle stroke, real or imagined. These two songs are examples of responsive lyrics, sung first by the *gouvernail*, and repeated back in like pitch by the rest of the crew. Voyageurs sang about aspects of life that mattered—love, their church, "obscene versifications" of trail trials and, of course, canoes. The venerable French ballad "Mon canot d' écorce," in a decidedly Canadian mixing of motifs, is a song about the voyageur experience, written in French, and sung to the tune of an old English sea-shanty called "Blow Ye Winds of Morning." The final stanza of this ditty, in translation, gives some idea of the whiskered sentimentality of this sort of paddling song:

> Along the river banks I've wandered, all along St. Lawrence's tide
> I have known the savage races and the tongues that them divide
> (repeat)

—You are my voyageur companion!—
I'll gladly die within my canoe.
And on the grave beside the canyon (repeat)
You'll overturn my canoe. (repeat)

His cart is beloved of the ploughman,
    the hunter loves his gun, his hound;
The musician is a music lover—to my canoe
    I'm bound. (repeat)[6]

Echoing the notion of canoe as liminal vessel, taking its occupants from one world to the next and back again, the *canot du maître* took goods and people from the coastal world to the realm of the Great Lakes. An even more significant threshold was crossed by the smaller *canot du nord*, that being the path at Grand Portage on Lake Superior (in present-day Minnesota) that took voyageurs out of the St. Lawrence watershed, over the divide and into rivers of the arctic basin. This crossing was always marked with a ceremony at the height of land in which adventurers who made it this far would be inducted into an elite fraternity of "winterers." Among other distinctions, as the story goes, they would be entitled to display a *plume noire*, a black feather, in their hats and would have to promise never to kiss another voyageur's wife without first securing her permission. Moving to the smaller North canoe required more skill, fewer paddlers, and a change in diet for many, shifting from the pork and biscuits of the Great Lakes/St. Lawrence route to the pemmican-based menu of the West. Attendant with this status change was a lofty regard for the "winterers" (if only in their own imaginations), the pejorative *mangers de lard*, pork-eater, being reserved for the grunts who shuttled between Grand Portage and Lachine.

    This class distinction was especially acute for the Montreal traders and the partners of the North West Company, who, in the winter of 1785, formed a dining club named after the fur-bearing rodent that had given them their *raison d'être*. Condition of membership in the original Beaver Club of Montreal was status as a "winterer," that is, you had to have paddled, or been paddled in, a North canoe and you had to have spent at least one winter in *le pays d'en haut*. There were nineteen original members of the Beaver Club: eight French-speaking Montreal traders; three (all with the surname "Frobisher") Englishmen; six Scots; and two members from the United States, Alexander Henry and Peter Pond. The proud motto of the club was "Fortitude in Distress," a self-impor-tant slogan that had to be emblazoned on gold medals which each member was obliged to have cast with the name and date of his first visit to Indian country. Of the august group who wore these medals at lavish dinner parties in the latter years of the eighteenth century and into the first decades of the nineteenth century were the most famous Nor'Westers of all, among them William McGillivray, Sir Alexander Mackenzie, Roderick McKenzie, Duncan McGillivray, David Thompson, and Simon Fraser. Aside from the other well-documented accomplishments of these hardy fur traders, the most enduring part of their legacy was perhaps the epicurean debauchery that transpired in the regular dinner meetings of the illustrious Beaver Club.

Besides the orderly minutes of Beaver Club meetings, which made up in financial and attendance details what they lacked in true colour, the only eye-witness account of these raucous goings-on was set to paper (and, apparently, with some storytelling licence) by a young officer in the British army who was assigned to travel west with William McGillivray and fellow Beaver Club member Angus Shaw. Lieutenant Landmann, still only in his late teens, was destined for the garrison on St. Joseph's Island in Lake Huron, and the Nor'Westers were on their way to Grand Portage. Landmann and his canoe party caught up with McGillivray and Shaw at Lachine, just in time for lunch:

> At La Chine we found the two canoes, destined to proceed with us, by the shore opposite to a house belonging to the North-West Company, and wherein an abundant luncheon was waiting our arrival. Several officers in the army, amongst them Colonel Gordon and Lieutenant McArthur of the 60th regiment, and some of the North-West Company, not about to form part of our expedition, had accompanied us, all of them, I believe, natives of the Highlands of Scotland, so that I was the only *foreigner* amongst them. We sat down, and

without loss of time expedited the lunch intended to super-
sede a dinner, during which time the bottle had freely circu-
lated, raising the old Highland drinking propensity so that
there was no stopping it; Highland speeches and sayings,
Highland reminiscences, and Highland farewells, with the
dioch and dorich, over and over again, was kept up with extraordinary energy, so that by six or seven o'clock I had, in
common with many of the others, fallen from my seat.[7]

This connection between paddlers and libational multi-course meals
has echoed its way through history to the present day. Records of the
first recreational canoe clubs, formed in the northeast United States in
the latter decades of the nineteenth century, show elaborately penned
menus that emulate the extravagant and excessive culinary traditions
established by members of the Beaver Club. The menu for the four-
teenth Annual Dinner of the New York Canoe Club, held December
13, 1884, reads as follows:

Oysters in Ice
Clear Soup
Fillet of Bass • Sauce Tartare
Roast Venison • Currant Jam
Sweet Potatoes au Gratin
Irish Potatoes Souffle
Grouse • Bread Sauce • French Peas
Celery Salad • Shellac Dressing
Crackers and Cheese
Pudding
Caramel Ice Cream
Orange Sherbet
Grapes • Oranges • Nuts • Bolts • Screw Eyes • Etc.
Coffee
Smoke[8]

Absent from this menu was any indication of what the revellers
might have used to wash down these fine comestibles. The menu for

the sixth annual dinner of the Knickerbocker Canoe Club, held December 16, 1888, in New York City, however, lists libations as well, along with a meal that would appeal to even the most Mediterranean of voyageurs:

Blue Point Oysters • half shell
Pottage • Gumbo
Striped Bass • Sauce Hollandaise
Pommes de terre Parisienne
CHIANTI
Macaroni à l'Italienne
Filet de Boeuf aux Champignons
Petits pois français
CHAMPAGNE
Quail • Roast • Currant Jelly
Salad • Lettuce
Pudding
Fruit • Fromage
Café Noir[9]

The pages of *Sail and Paddle* magazine also record the festivities of the curiously named "Puritan Canoe Club" which, in their published menu for the January 12, 1889, annual dinner shows fancy fare but, like the New York Canoe Club menu excerpted above, makes no mention of alcoholic beverages of any kind. This organization must surely have been named ironically because by this time the connection between revelry and canoeing was so well established that it would be unthinkable for a group of paddlers to gather with the expectation of everyone staying upright for the duration of the meeting.

Voyageur food, as it happens, has affected the march of North American history in more substantial ways as well. Besides consuming pork and pemmican for food while on the trail, voyageurs often roasted the tail of the animal whose skins they were transporting, a practice that connected them to the high offices of the Roman Catholic Church. Grace Lee Nute, in her definitive 1931 book about voyageur life, marks the significance of this element of the paddler's diet by pointing out how

96

it became the only allowable red meat for consumption during Lent:

> A beaver's tail was considered an especially dainty morsel,
> and the story is that the voyageurs in the French period ate
> it even during Lent. To determine how far they were
> sinning, the matter was referred to the [scholars at the]
> Sorbonne, and, no doubt, because the aquatic habits of the
> beaver so closely resemble those of the fishes, the privilege of
> eating the tail in Lent was permitted.[10]

Beaver tails notwithstanding, keeping voyageurs fed on the trail, especially beyond Fort William in wintering country, was an ongoing problem that brought the rivalry between the Hudson's Bay Company and the North West Company to a nasty head in the so-called Pemmican War of 1812–16 in southern Manitoba. Members of the Peguis Indian Band, who lived in the vicinity of the Red River valley, had always provided nutritious pemmican, buffalo meat and grease to passing canoe brigades in return for trade goods, regardless of company affiliation. But in 1810, when Thomas Douglas, the fifth Earl of Selkirk, persuaded the Hudson's Bay Company, in which he was a major shareholder, to establish an agricultural colony, this upset the politics of the situation.

Worried that there would not be enough food on hand to feed settlers coming to the Earl of Selkirk's land grant, his agent and governor of Assiniboia, Miles Macdonell, issued a proclamation forbidding the export of pemmican from the colony for a year, starting in January 1814. Because of Selkirk's allegiance to the Hudson's Bay Company—although the rule was to apply equally to all traders in the area—members of the North West Company, their *engagés*, and their Métis allies in the area took this as an act of aggression. A subsequent proclamation by Governor Macdonell which prohibited the hunting of buffalo from horseback complicated the situation further, and led to a pitting of the governor, the Earl of Selkirk and his Red River settlers, in alliance with the local Ojibway, against the Nor'Westers and the Manitoba Métis, a pemmican discontent that erupted at a place called Seven Oaks, northwest of the confluence of the Red and Assiniboine rivers in what is now downtown Winnipeg. In the skirmish, Métis fighters, led by Cuthbert Grant, killed Robert Semple, governor of the Selkirk settlement, and twenty of his men, forcing the rest of the settlers to abandon their new prairie home. Six further years of major discontent between the Hudson's Bay Company and the North West Company finally led to their amalgamation in 1821, a turn of events which leads directly back to our point of origin, Lachine.

By 1820, the situation between the two major fur-trading companies in North America had disintegrated to the point that the HBC sent thirty-three-year-old George Simpson—the man who would be called "The Birchbark Napoleon," "The Little Emperor" and "Father of the Fur Trade" (by those who estimate he sired seventy children between the Red River and the Rocky Mountains)—to North America to take charge in the event that the company's governor, William Williams, was arrested and/or killed by the NWC. Arriving via Hudson Bay, Simpson spent his first winter in Athabasca country, but when the two companies merged in 1821, the very able Simpson was promoted and made governor of the whole Northern Department of the HBC. Five years later he was promoted again to become governor of all the company's trading territories in the whole of British North America, shortly thereafter moving his headquarters to Lachine, where he remained based until his death in 1860.

Known for his peripatetic lifestyle, Simpson led by example, and was not afraid to leave people cringing in his wake. Peter C. Newman paints this portrait of the governor's legendary travels:

> During all but three of the thirty-nine years he spent in charge
> of the HBC's northern fur trade, Simpson ranged across the
> continent in furiously paced forays, inspecting his posts,
> hectoring discouraged Factors, preaching the doctrine of cost
> efficiency and loving every minute of it. He was constantly in
> motion. He crossed the Rockies at three latitudes, completed
> twelve transatlantic round trips, eight visits to Boston and
> New York, and three great journeys to forts on the Columbia
> River in the Oregon Country. His most trying trek was by
> snowshoe during the winter of 1822–23, when he went from

Lake Athabasca to Great Slave Lake and back, up the Peace
River to Fort Dunvegan and across Lesser Slave Lake to
Edmonton House. Simpson loved being on the move, wafting through the melodious forests of the great Northwest,
dictating memoranda to his accompanying secretaries and
being treated everywhere like a resplendent emperor on an
imperial progress. "It is strange," Simpson once wrote to his
friend John George McTavish, "that all my ailments vanish as
soon as I seat myself in a canoe."[11]

In spite of his espoused love of the canoe as tonic and conveyance,
one of the first acts Simpson undertook on becoming governor of the
HBC was to replace on many freight routes canoes with Orkney-style
flat-bottomed scows called York boats, after York Factory on Hudson
Bay at the mouth of the Hayes River. These craft could carry three
times the cargo of the *canot du nord* and, although more difficult to
portage, were amenable to river travel, both with and against the
current; they took less skill to manoeuvre, being rowed not paddled,
could be sailed on lakes, and tended to last longer than their faster,
more elegant, and more fragile bark and cedar predecessors.

For his personal travels, however, Simpson retained his own stable of
express canoes, one of which, the "Rob Roy," was fully 42-feet long
and thought to be one of the largest birchbark canoes ever built. In a
1828 journal, kept while accompanying George Simpson on a whirlwind journey from Hudson Bay to the Pacific, Chief Factor Archibald
McDonald describes one of these special canoes:

> Light Canoes—specially made and adapted for speediest
> travel. I saw those, the very ones spoken of, at Norway
> House, on their passage up. The Governor's was the most
> beautiful thing of the kind I ever saw; beautiful in its lines of
> faultless fineness, and in its form and every feature; the bow,
> a magnificent curve of bark, gaudily but tastefully painted,
> that would have made a Roman rostrum of old hide its
> diminished head. The paddles, painted red with vermilion,
> were made to match, and the whole thing in its kind was of

faultless grace and beauty—beauty in the sense of graceful and perfect fitness to its end.[12]

Other accounts of Governor Simpson's impressive cadre of St. Lawrence valley Mohawk boatmen describe usually about a dozen strong, young men paddling their *bourgeois* in his sleek, 33-foot canoe— 60 strokes per minute, 8 miles per hour, often covering 90 to 100 miles a day. Whether Simpson and his "praetorian guard of Iroquois boatmen"[13] could sustain such impressive mileage is unlikely, but there can be little doubt that these feats impressed many people within the fur-trade community. Chief Factor Archie McDonald, for example, boasted that he himself in a small canoe with only three voyageurs had on one occasion paddled 98 miles in one 24-hour period. Knowing Simpson and the way he travelled though, this feat, he was sure, was achieved regularly in the governor's express canoe.

For others in the realm of the fur trade, it was something of an honour to paddle or to be paddled in one of George Simpson's canoes. For example, to the surprise and delight of a company of astronomers from the U.S. Nautical Almanac Office, who wrote to the HBC for permission to proceed to Cumberland House, on the Saskatchewan River, to view a total eclipse of the sun that was to occur in the summer of 1860, Governor Simpson offered one of his express canoes and the services of a crew of his elite voyageurs, suggesting they expedite their journey from Fort Garry via St. Paul, Minnesota. The eclipse viewing was a bust because, after days and hours of slogging to get to Cumberland House, the weather at the moment of truth was cloudy. Expedition naturalist Samuel H. Scudder, in his book, *The Winnipeg Country*, was not impressed, writing: "Three thousand miles of constant travel, occupying five weeks to reach by heroic endeavour the outer edge of the belt of totality; to sit in a marsh, and view the eclipse through clouds ..."[14] The only aspect of the trip that in any way salvaged the effort was the fact that they had been able to paddle in what was later described as "the Cadillac of north canoes," the pride of the Governor Simpson fleet of express canoes.

Besides the express canoes themselves and their impressive voyageur crews, the protocol of Governor Simpson's canoe arrivals became stuff of legend as well. With him on many of his cross-country journeys, helping create the visual and aural effect of entry, was fellow Scotsman Colin Fraser, whose principal claim to fame on Simpson's excursions was neither his navigational or business skills, nor his ability to paddle, but his ability to skirl a tune on the bagpipes. At the least provocation, Fraser would inflate the tartan bag and herald the entrance or exit of the illustrious Mr. Simpson, which, in concert with the *chansons* of the voyageurs, made for quite a spectacle. Sarah Foulds Camsell, who grew up at Norway House, on the Nelson River, recalls a memory of Simpson's first arrival into her world:

> Sir George Simpson used to be called 'the Emperor of the North,' his arrival at Norway house or at any other post of the Company was always a great event. He always traveled swiftly in what we used to call flying express canoes. I can remember the first time I saw him arrive. He and his secretary were in one canoe with eight picked men to paddle it who were French-Canadian voyageurs and Iroquois Indians, the most skillful and daring of all canoe men. Another splendid large canoe followed, also with eight men. The canoes were beautifully painted at each end, and the voyageurs moved their paddles, which sometimes they stained with vermilion, all together with perfect regularity, all singing as they sent the canoes swiftly on their way. A salute was fired and the whole ceremony of Sir George Simpson's arrival was duly carried out every time he came, including the distribution of 'regales,' as they were called, of rum to the canoe men, and there was no less impressive ceremonial when he went away.[15]

It was this aspect of George Simpson's colourful contribution to North American history that makes him the first Canadian on record to realize the symbolic and ceremonial value of canoes. His exploration of this dimension of big bark canoes, long after the last of the real, workaday voyageurs had retired or gone on to York boat service, was never more grand or significant than his final canoe spectacle, orchestrated at Lachine, in honour of Queen Victoria's son and heir to the British throne, Albert Edward, Prince of Wales (later King Edward VII), on Wednesday, August 29, 1860.

By this time, late in his tenure with the HBC, Simpson, seventy-three, spent his days in a splendid country home on Île Dorval, just upstream from Lachine, separated from the bustle of commerce at HBC headquarters. Also resident on the island was his secretary and close friend, E.M. Hopkins, and his wife, Frances, the painter. The official host for the prince's visit was Lieutenant-General Sir Fenwick Williams, but the pageantry was vintage Simpson. The prince, age nineteen, was on his honeymoon, having just married Alexandra, daughter of King Christian IX of Denmark. Upon arrival in Montreal, he officially opened a bridge over the St. Lawrence named after his mother—the original Victoria Bridge was one of the greatest engineering feats of the day—and, following this civic duty, he and his entourage were conveyed by road to a landing on the north shore of the St. Lawrence opposite Île Dorval, at which point His Royal Highness was transferred to a barge from which to view the proceedings. What followed was described the next day in the *Montreal Gazette*:

> A flotilla of nine large birch-bark canoes was drawn up in a line close to the head of the island. Their appearance was very beautiful: the light and graceful craft were fitted up with great taste, each having flags in bow and stern: their crew, composed of one hundred Iroquois Indians from Caughnawaga and the Lake of Two Mountains, being costumed *en sauvage*, gay with feathers, scarlet cloth and paint.
>
> As soon as the barge carrying the Prince pushed off from the mainland, the fleet of canoes darted out from the island to meet him in a line abreast, and to the inspiriting cadences of a voyageur song. On nearing the royal barge, the line

opened in the middle apparently to let it pass, but suddenly wheeling around with a rapidity and precision which took everyone by surprise, they again formed a line with the Prince's barge in the middle, and in that form reached the landing place, when the canoe song ceased, and a cheer burst from the voyageurs, which H.R.H., with face beaming with pleasure, returned by saluting his Indian escort.[16]

The *Gazette* story goes on to detail who was there and what they ate, along with a host of other minutiae for the socially aware in their readership, mentioning in passing that "no ladies were invited, nor were any present, except three immediately connected with Sir George, viz., Mrs. Hopkins, and her sister Miss Beechey, and Mrs. McKenzie."[17] The royal tale continued as the formal portion of the visit came to an end and the prince actually left Île Dorval in a bark canoe:

About 4.30 the party embarked in the canoes and proceeded in great style and at a rapid pace towards Lachine. One, bearing the Royal Standard and carrying the Prince, the Duke of Newcastle, and General Williams, taking the lead, while the remainder in line abreast followed close behind it. About the centre of the brigade we observed Sir George Simpson directing the movements in person.

Passing down close along the north shore, the flotilla at that point (Lachine) again executed the extraordinary evolution of wheeling round in line and then crossed the St. Lawrence to Caughnawaga, where crowds lined the banks.[18]

Pure schmaltz. A photo opportunity before the term had been coined. More significant, however, than the show for the people of Lachine was the effect that this canoe experience had on the Prince of Wales. Simpson made a gift to him of one of the voyageur canoes from the pageant, a light but bulky piece of cargo that followed H.R.H. back to London. Later in his Ontario journey, the prince was presented in Peterborough with a second canoe, this time one of the sleek 18-foot racing dugouts being developed by John Stevenson and colleagues in that part of Canada.[19] With two canoes to paddle on the Thames, the prince's interest in canoes took him to the company of another Scotsman with Canadian canoe experience, one John MacGregor, who the previous year had visited Ontario, where he paddled bark canoes near Ottawa before moving on to Kamchatka (Siberia), where he gained experience with skin kayaks of the northern aboriginals. MacGregor began experimenting with building decked wooden canoes, one of which he called "Rob Roy," perhaps to laud Rob Roy MacGregor, hero of the Highland Clearances, or perhaps to acknowledge the name of the largest of Governor Simpson's express canoes he may well have encountered in some manner during his Ontario visit in 1859. In any case, John MacGregor took his 90-pound, 15-foot decked wooden canoe with its mast, lug and jib sails, and double-bladed paddle on an extended trip on the Continent in 1865 and returned to publish the classic first recreational canoeing tale, *A Thousand Miles in the Rob Roy Canoe on the Lakes and Rivers of Europe.*[20] Whether the name of MacGregor's craft can be linked back to George Simpson is a matter of speculation, but what can certainly be linked back to Canada was the Prince of Wales's enthusiastic endorsement of an organization of canoeists started by MacGregor in July 1866, an outfit that in 1873 became the venerable Royal Canoe Club.

The modern legacy of George Simpson's canoe extravaganzas is substantial. Although it is not known what became of the ten-place, 40-foot voyageur canoe that was shipped to England as a souvenir for the Prince of Wales, there is an eight-place, 28-foot bastard canoe in the National Maritime Museum in Greenwich, England, which canoe historian Timothy Kent feels may have been a second gift to Prince Edward following his zealous response to the Lachine pageant of August 1860. However, another canoe that was surely a part of Simpson's last pageant, the so-called Quebec Canoe, was preserved and, until its destruction in a 1990 fire, one of only a handful of extant original voyageur canoes. Featured on a recent cover of a heritage canoe periodical,[21] the Quebec canoe is 25 feet long and, in contrast to high-prowed voyageur canoes, appears to be simply a larger version, in form and proportion, of an elegant Algonquin canoe from the Great Lakes region. On each end, painted in traditional fashion into the birch bark, are royal, prominent crowns with "V.R." beneath. There is a large maple leaf added to the bow end of the right wall, making this one of the first times in history that this symbol was used to connote a Canadian connection. And below the gunwale in large serif letters are the words "THE QUEBEC," for all the world to see.

Following the prince's departure from Canada, the Quebec canoe was stored at Lachine in anticipation of other visiting dignitaries. In the early years of the twentieth century, however, the canoe was purchased by the head of the McLean Lumber Company of Canada and presented as a gift to the Buffalo Canoe Club, in Buffalo, New York, because of a family connection between the owner of McLean Lumber and the club, where it was put on permanent display. Bark canoes being essentially disposable craft, the Quebec canoe deteriorated in the Buffalo Canoe Club's outer boathouse until 1972, when Henri Vaillancourt of Greenville, New Hampshire (subject of John McPhee's book *The Survival of the Bark Canoe*), and Richard Nash (a bark canoe builder who worked for Kirk Wipper at the Kanawa Canoe Museum in Haliburton, Ontario) were hired to restore the aging craft to its original splendid condition. Unfortunately, a fire in the outer boathouse destroyed the Quebec canoe on Christmas eve, 1990, severing this material link to the heyday of George Simpson's canoe days.

Even more significant than club connections and the remaining physical artifacts from George Simpson's love of pageantry and voyageur canoes are the images that remain. His secretary's wife, Frances Anne Hopkins, in a stirring sketch now housed in the Royal Ontario Museum, documented the flotilla of bark canoes awaiting the Prince of Wales in 1860. The flags are flying, the paddlers are erect in their places, the sense of drama is palpable. At the time, Frances had been in Canada for only two years, but she took much interest in all of the doings at Lachine. Through her husband, who was constantly with George Simpson, the artist gained access to everything that was going on at this busy depot and to the *joie de vivre* of the governor himself. Hopkins' voyageur canoe paintings, most of which were crafted after Simpson had died, have become a priceless historical record of the last days of the fur trade in Canada. Reprinted so often and in so many places, they have become clichés. Yet setting one of these, *Shooting the*

Rapids, in historical context is useful because it conveys much about the general spirit of fun and adventure at Lachine.

Shooting the Rapids depicts sixteen voyageurs paddling four passengers over the brink of what appears to be a precipitous and potentially canoe-eating drop. The craft rides high in the water, as if the human load barely touches its cargo-carrying capacity. Without historical context, the image can lead a viewer to the conclusion that this was the way things were in the days of the fur trade—people being paddled about in empty canoes on a ratio of four paddlers per passenger. In fact what is going on in this painting is exactly what is going on at Lachine to this day. Visitors—in this case Simpson's successor, HBC Governor Dallas, and a Mr. Watkins from the London office of the HBC—along with Frances Hopkins and her husband, Edward, are being given a joy ride on a sunny afternoon on July 25, 1863. Simpson loved a show and there was nothing better for important people passing through Lachine than to be given a run down through the rapids in big, stable, lightly loaded canoes manned by some of his most skilled express canoemen, before settling on the river bank for a picnic or retiring for tea by the fire.

The fact that Frances Hopkins' paintings have become the popular texts for re-creating the fur trade era in the modern imagination, shows the power of the visual image. Many authors—from Grace Lee Nute to Timothy Kent and Eric Morse in his classic books, *Canoe Routes of the Voyageurs*[22] and *Fur Trade Canoe Routes of Canada/Then and Now*[23] —have documented the voyageur's lot of long days, crippling labour, scant job security, and short life span. Yet, somehow the vividly coloured images of ceremonial canoes with flags and pipers and voyageurs—Simpson's express-canoe images—are the ones that persist in text books, re-enactments and historical ephemera. Nowhere was this phenomenon more evident than in an initiative undertaken by the Canadian government to mark the hundredth anniversary of Confederation, the Centennial Voyageur Canoe Pageant.

Government policy documents setting out the centennial plan detail a host of athletic events: the Centennial Athletic Awards Program for schoolchildren; the First Canadian Winter Games in Quebec City; the Pan-American Games in Winnipeg; a cornucopia of world championships (snowshoeing, badminton, motorcycling, lawn bowling, boxing, horse-shoe pitching, water skiing) and special sports events; the Alpine Centennial Expedition in the Yukon; the Calgary-to-Winnipeg Balloon Race; the Centennial Folk Festival and Highland Games; and, the grand-parent of all anniversary celebrations: the Voyageur Canoe Pageant.

The idea of the Voyageur Canoe Pageant was to re-enact the voyageur epoch of Canadian history by bringing to life the original routes of the explorers and fur traders from Rocky Mountain House, Alberta, to Lachine, Quebec. At a time when Canadian heritage was being considered with close scrutiny, organizers felt that it would be a natural and fitting tribute to Canada's early days to position the canoe centrally and experi-entially in Centennial celebrations. It would be a colourful reminder of Canada's past that would raise the profile of the Centennial in each layby and whistlestop on the original cross-Canada communication link:

Description of the Project

Canoemen from all the provinces and the territories have been invited to man a brigade of canoes to make the trip from Rocky Mountain House to Montreal, a distance of 3,283 miles, during the period from May 24 to September 4. These canoemen, who will be dressed in the garb of the voyageurs, will follow a schedule throughout the route that can be closely co-ordinated with the staging of local centen-nial celebrations and aquatic events.

The canoes will bear the name of the provinces and terri-tories, and the names of explorers selected by them as being representative of their past history.

Twenty-six foot canoes, specially made to resemble the early voyageur canoes, will be used. Each canoe will carry a crew of six, plus up to one ton of cargo. The canoes provide sufficient freeboard for running rapids and crossing large lakes.[24]

The summer of 1967 remains a vivid memory of my teenage life. As Bobby Gimby's song reminded us all from every radio station, every Muzak speaker in every dentist's office and every school public-address system, it was the hundredth anniversary of Con-fed-er-ation, and to mark that occasion my parents invited a couple of cousins to come from England. The plan was for us all to travel to "Man and His World, the Universal and International Exhibition," in Montreal. On account of this family adventure to Expo 67, I would have to forgo camp for the summer. But the Centennial Voyageur Canoe Pageant eased the disappointment of not going on a canoe trip that summer.

I never actually saw any of the canoes or any of the paddlers, except in occasional photographs in the newspaper, but it touched my imagination. Because it was an event that spanned the country (more or less, at least from Alberta to Quebec) for four months, perhaps because the image of rugged young men in big canoes once again plying the waters of Canada was so resonant, the Voyageur Canoe Pageant received more than its share of media coverage. It seemed that every week or so there would be another shot of paddlers in headbands over sun-darkened faces, with bandanas on loose cotton shirts, paddling canoes with high prows emblazoned with the stylized maple leaf logo, around which were stencilled the name of their home province or territory and names like Sir Alexander Mackenzie, William McGillivray, bold heroes all.

With them every stroke of the way, if only in my dreams, I followed the pageant from Edmonton to Winnipeg, to Fort William, Sault Ste. Marie and North Bay. By the time they arrived in Montreal on Labour Day weekend, I was on my way back to school, imagining more than ever being part of the triumphant paddle down the Ottawa River to the Lake of Two Mountains, through the turbulent white water of the mighty St. Lawrence at Lachine, and then around the main island of Montreal to the Expo site on Ile Ste-Hélène. The country, or so it seemed, shared with the paddlers of the Centennial Canoe Pageant the vicarious thrill of achievement.

Of course, in the entire hundred-year march of Canada's history as a confederated nation, there had not been anything like a voyageur canoe plying any of its waterways. There had been plenty of people in canoes of all shapes and sizes, paddling hither and yon throughout the century, but the notion of big bark canoes crossing from one side of the country to the other had petered out at least fifty years before Confederation. Still, there was perhaps no more potent way to celebrate the notion of Canada as a nation than to orchestrate a 100-day, 5,600-kilometre canoe trip that, as the brochure that went out to schools said, "will follow the time-honoured routes from the Rockies in the west to Montreal in the east." Or, as our other official language put it:

> Pour rappeler le courage des pionniers qui sillonnèrent notre pays, une armada composée de 12 canoës refera pendant 100 jours, du 24 mai au 2 septembre 1967, la route allant des Rocheuses à Montréal, soit environ 3,500 milles.
>
> Les participants de cette grandiose expédition porteront des costumes d'époque; les canoës auront 25 pieds de long et seront la réplique exacte des premiers canoës canadiens. De plus, ils seront spécialement renforcés pour sauter sans danger les rapides et traverser les grand lacs.[25]

Wherever the idea originated, it was brilliant. It was vintage Simpson. The act of making an east–west river connection from mountain across prairie to shield and riparian lowland was resonant, and the image of a brigade of (simulated) birchbark canoes, when it popped up in North Battleford or The Pas, Kenora or Mattawa, however clichéd and naïve, evoked a strong sense of our history. So what if it never actually happened? The movement of canoes from west to east, from periphery to centre, focused attention on Montreal, a place deeply rooted in Canada and reminded us of the fur trade, which had its genesis just upstream from Expo 67, at Lachine.

The voyageur echoes from this great event continue. Bill Peruniak, the captain of the Ontario boat—named in honour of Nor'Wester and Beaver Club reveller William McGillivray—was so struck by the training and leadership development possibilities in the north canoe experience that he formed a company called Northwest Connexion, dedicated to applying canoe learning to other contexts. In tracing the idea, Peruniak recalled:

I do not remember at which point in 1966 or 1967 my appreciation of the North Canoe reached a level where I began to think of continuing the experience with a band of friends after the Centennial race was over. With great clarity and intensity, I would have images or vision of brigades of North Canoes once again cruising Canada's waterways. Sometimes I would see them heading up choppy Stuart Lake, proudly disdaining the wind and spray, and aiming for the sharp blue mountain peaks many miles away. Sometimes I watched them go flashing down the North Saskatchewan, skillfully following the main current as it piled up along the high cut banks of one river-bend after another. Sometimes I caught them racing through the Boundary Waters, that enchanted land of granite, pine, and blue lakes. Sometimes I would spy their dim forms gliding through the dense fogs off Lake Superior's North Shore.[26]

Bill Peruniak participated in the Voyageur Canoe Pageant at a time when he was switching from his role as principal of Atikokan High School, near the Quetico area of northwestern Ontario (where he founded the first for-credit outers club in a Canadian school) to a teaching appointment at the newly created McArthur College of Education at Queen's University in Kingston. The idea of North-canoe-as-training-vehicle niggled away in his mind until spring of 1980, when he borrowed money to purchase canoes and launch the first "Voyageur Seminar" designed for teachers, administrators, business people—anyone interested in exploring notions of community and leadership on a voyageur canoe trip. Over the years Peruniak has chosen various portions of the voyageur highway from Alberta to Ontario, but settles most often on the French River, a venue which, in addition to being steeped in the voyageur tradition, is accessible and replete with a host of other saleable virtues: clean, warm water; excellent campsites; classic blue-water-rocky-shore scenery; and challenging, but not too challenging, portages and runnable rapids.

One of five week-long French River seminars offered in the summer of 1993 was aimed at educators and business managers on the theme of "leading high-perfomance teams." By now Peruniak had distilled the voyageur to a lofty mix of aims and objectives, so near and explicit, yet so far removed from the unstated character-building aspects of the original Voyageur Canoe Pageant. The objectives for the high-performance team-building River Seminar were laid out in that year's brochure:

1. **Empowerment**
   To go beyond the accepted management functions of arranging, directing, and telling; and to practise such facilitative skills as cheerleading, offering support, removing obstacles, creating opportunities, and nurturing champions;

2. **Consensus**
   To go beyond the pseudo-teamwork of some "management by consensus" operations; and to learn how to ride the turbulence and ambiguity of consensual decision-making that is the real article;

3. **Commitment**
   To go beyond the notion of teamwork as the coordination of routine activities; and to discover a quality of team spirit characterized by spontaneous initiative, bold risk-taking, pride of ownership, and enthusiasm;

4. **Group Dialogue**
   To go beyond the formality of the agenda-driven business meeting; and to practice community-meeting skills, with a view to balancing the needs of the individual, the group, and the task;

5. **Journal-Writing**
   To go beyond the superficiality of unassimilated experiences; and to engage in daily journal-writing in order to clarify and deepen one's experiences.

Recommended reading: (1) Thomas Sergiovanni's
Moral Leadership (Jossey-Bass) and (2) Scott Peck's
The Different Drum (Simon & Schuster).[27]

In the summer of 1998, on the nineteenth annual Voyageur
Seminar, Bill Peruniak chose a constitutional theme, "Revisiting
Canada at the Millennium," this time invoking the voyageur motif in
its myriad dimensions under an epigraph from Sir John A. Macdonald:
"We are a great country, and shall become one of the greatest in the
universe if we preserve it; we shall sink into insignificance and adversity
if we suffer it to be broken."[28] Whether this improves the general
constitution of the country does not really matter. Through the single-
minded, almost single-handed, efforts of one dedicated participant in
the Centennial Voyageur Canoe Pageant, the *idea* of voyageur has been
modernized for a new century. Rooted in the riverine geography of
North America, it has, apparently, as much relevance now as it had in
George Simpson's day; the big canoe experience easily crosses lines of
gender, vocation and ethnicity and can provide a guiding and grounding ethos for human enterprise wherever it might be situated in Canada
or the United States.

Scholars like Harold Innis[29] and his protegés Donald Creighton[30]
and Marshall McLuhan have amply demonstrated that the east–west
axis of commerce from Lachine to the Lakehead, extended west by the
mighty Saskatchewan River, and subsequently the Canadian Pacific
Railway (established with canoes during the fur trade, with its voyageur
agents responsible to a company and government in the East and ultimately across the Atlantic) created a unique pattern of development,
and intercontinental communication. Canadian expansionism differed
from the continentalism and frontier experience, with its cowboys and
free-marketeers, that occurred south of the border. Creighton's writing, for example, establishes the central role of the canoe and its attendant services to the Canadian way of doing business.

The voyageur idea, in fact, pervades much of North American
culture. A quick scan of the World Wide Web reveals all manner of
voyageur connections in North American life: Black Feather Wilderness
Adventures; Voyageur Bus Lines; Voyageur Outfitters; Voyageur Radio

Station; Voyageur Outward Bound School; Voyageur Restaurants; Voyageur hockey teams; Voyageur Highways; a TVOntario series about civic and national culture called *Voyageurs*; a musical group from Peterborough called "Rubaboo" named after pemmican stew; Camp Voyageur for underprivileged children; brand-new Plymouth Voyageur mini-vans; Naturally Superior Adventures, based in Wawa, Ontario, featuring Lake Superior canoe trips in voyageur canoes; voyageur conference themes; voyageur dances; voyageur music ... and on it goes. The most telling sign of all, at least in terms of Canadian culture, is the nomination of folk singer Stan Rogers' classic song "Northwest Passage" as the unofficial Canadian national anthem.[31] Look closely at the lyrics and you find where today's voyageurs are hiding and who they really are—they're truckers, hauling freight as they always did, from one side of North America to the other, still looking for Lachine:

Ah, for just time, I would take the Northwest Passage
To find the hand of Franklin reaching for the Beaufort Sea
Tracing one warm line through a land so wide and savage
And make a Northwest Passage to the sea

And through the night, behind the wheel, the mileage
   clicking west
I think upon Mackenzie, David Thompson and the rest
Who cracked the mountain ramparts, and did show a path for me
To race the roaring Fraser to the sea

How then am I so different from the first men through this way?
Like them I left a settled life, I threw it all away
To seek a Northwest Passage at the call of many men
To find there but the road back home again.[32]

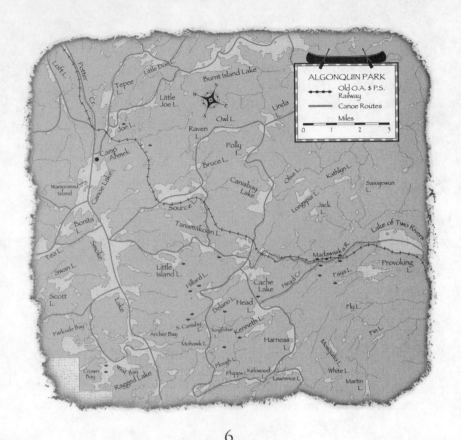

6

CHILDREN OF NATURE

We don't have the cathedrals of Europe, or the art of Italy, or the ancient treasures of Egypt, but we do have an aboriginal and historical collection of watercraft that is unmatched in the world.

—Ken Roberts, *Maclean's*[1]

IN JUNE 1921, fourteen-year-old Dorothy McMichael left her friends at a central Toronto high school and headed home, uncertain about what this summer would hold. Her parents were never much for Muskoka in the warm months—cottages, boats, matching their neighbours' leisure choices—so for the past few years they had been loading their only daughter in their McLaughlin touring car and heading east for the bumpy two- or three-day drive to the coast of Maine for some R and R by the sea. But of late, young Dorothy's attention was drifting, turning to boys, much more than her mother would have liked. So Mother McMichael asked her friends about other options that might channel her daughter's attentions in these pivotal teen years. The choice she settled on did not sit well with Dorothy, at least not initially, but it was one that would change her daughter's life. Dorothy would go to camp, a girls-only installation called Northway Lodge on Cache Lake in the heart of Algonquin Provincial Park.

Fortunately, with the recommendation came an old camp uniform from the recommender's daughter, who had outgrown the outfit and the desire to attend Northway another summer, and a list of clothes to bring, headed by the observation from camp director and founder, Miss Case, that "cutting down to necessities is in itself an attractive experience." The list went on:

- Camp uniform (olive woollen suit, middy and knickers made at Wright & Ditson, Boston).
- Second suit of old woollen bloomers or knickers and flannel shirt or khaki suit.
- Four middies, two white and two coloured, for morning wear, middy ties; (grey shirt may make one of the four).
- One pair Keds or moccasins for about camp and for canoes—rubber soled.
- One pair low-heeled shoes for hiking.
- One pair high canvas leggings or putties.
- Heavy outside sweater, dark colour, soft cloth hat.
- Raincoat, sou'wester hat.
- Swimming suit, one-piece wool jersey, and cap.

- Three cotton union suits underwear. One woollen gauze suit underwear. Three pairs ribbed cotton stockings. Three pairs woollen stockings. Two pairs pajamas, flannelette. Heavy bath robe. Four small bath towels. Four face towels. Laundry bag. Wash cloths. Small work bag fitted out.
- For the cot: Two pairs of heavy dark blankets, weighing 12 pounds total. Two pairs outing flannel sheets. One small pillow. Two small pillow cases.
- All articles should be marked with owner's name.
- Two small or one large duffel bag, containing the entire outfit, is an established requirement, no *trunks* being used. Chests are provided at camp.

As embroidered name labels were sewn onto each of the items on this list, Dorothy started getting used to the idea (a) that she was leaving home to be on her own, or at least away from the family, for the first time and (b) that she was actually going to have to wear the hand-me-down bloomers that had come from her mother's friend. Leaving was all quite traumatic, especially in the olive drab bloomers.

Sitting in her Guelph, Ontario, condominium overlooking Riverside Park and the mighty Speed River, having just passed her ninetieth birthday, Dorothy remembers that fateful day:

> Mother thought it was such a neat idea. But those bloomers. They were so voluminous that you wouldn't believe it. You wore them with stockings. They were gathered at the knee and gathered at the waist. I looked like something from the mid-1800s. But I went. I went off by myself, not knowing a soul, down to Union Station, got on a train, in lovely olive drab colouring that wasn't supposed to scare the deer. The idea was to blend in with the landscape.[2]

It didn't take long on the train, however, in a Pullman car chartered just for similarly clad Northway campers and staff, for self-consciousness and homesickness to fade, replaced by a sense of adventure and enthusiasm, massaged and heightened by the rocking and rhythm of the

Temiskaming and Northern Ontario Railway. At Scotia Junction, near Huntsville, the Northway Lodge crew was transferred to an eastbound train on a spur of the Grand Trunk Railway, formerly J.R. Booth's Ottawa, Arnprior, and Parry Sound Railway. With their duffels safely stowed, several dozen girls—a few, like Dorothy, from Toronto but most from places like Rochester, East Aurora, Fredonia, Jamestown, Nashville, New York, Cleveland and St. Louis—looked out the windows at mile after mile of trees, torn between that and returning campers who jabbered on about all the wonderful things they would do on arrival: swimming, canoeing, archery, singing around the campfire and, of course, The Play. Maybe this year it would be *Hansel and Gretel*, or something impromptu entirely made up by the campers about one of their canoe trip adventures.

Eventually the train slowed and stopped at the Madawaska River trestle, where a dam and log chute marked the north end of Cache Lake. Charlie Skuce, an Indian guide from Powassan, met them and helped the girls move their duffels down the embankment and onto a plank platform lashed across two Peterborough sponson canoes. The luggage moved on down the point to the camp's line of canvas wall tents and the girls, led by their matter-of-fact, olive-drab director, marched down a trail into the camp proper to the outdoor hearthstone, the camp fireplace on the south tip of the point, where formal welcomes and introductions were conducted. From that moment on, and in spite of the gruff and enigmatic Miss Case, Dorothy McMichael knew she had found a place that would stay in her heart.

The outdoor life lived by the girls at Northway was to be simple, meaning with the smallest number of necessities possible, living under canvas, and encouraging a full and adventuresome life of service and study in nature ignoring "artificial entertainment" and forms of sport which do not naturally fit into "the open-air life." At root, the idea was to use this spartan venue to develop healthy goals and solid Christian values in young women through close association with nature using canoes as the primary mode of transportation and canoe trips as the principal shaper of experience. Miss Case laid out her aims and ideals in an annual booklet:

Restful, homelike conditions prevail, the tents being placed far apart and composed of four in a family—a counsellor and three girls.

Schedule and **competition** are made light of. Time "to think of and revalue the durable satisfactions of life" seems more important.

Self-help and **democratic ways** are favourite ways, all having a share in the management and contributing to the carrying out of the camp ideals. Camp properties belong to all equally.

Individual, not mass life, and a **full but free environment** for the purpose of satisfying our different tastes and abilities, are goals. Camp is naturally an ideal place for developing social responsibilities and consciousness.

Fun, play and happiness are frankly aims of our summer vacation camp life as well as love for work and service.

A belief in work. The hour or two of real work, mornings before swimming, is connected with building small cabins, clearing out dead trees, cleaning up the forest, blazing new trails, fixing up old trails, painting and mending boats and any other necessary piece of work.[4]

In 1904, at thirty-seven years of age, accepting the invitation of a family friend in Canada, Dr. Howard A. Kelly, Fanny Case took Henderson's ideas and a group of her students from Rochester, to Kelly's cabin on the Magnetawan River in central Ontario. She had such an excellent time over two summers with this arrangement that she felt a permanent campsite for her operation essential. Contacting and subsequently visiting G.W. Bartlett, superintendent of Algonquin Park, she paddled for several days around the Canoe Lake area and settled on a point that caught her fancy across the water from where the new park headquarters was being constructed on Cache Lake. Claiming this land by government lease, Case engaged, through Bartlett, a crew of young men to clear the site, and started with her first group of campers— largely students and offspring of family friends—in the summer of 1906.

Having only a partial idea of what they might do programmatically, Case brought with her some friends from the teaching profession expert in swimming, music, crafts and nature lore and she was able to line up a cook and a medical student to serve as support staff as well. For canoeing and "the camping arts," as she called tent pitching, bed rolling, pack packing and fire lighting, she moved opportunistically and promoted one of the young men who was helping to clear the site to help get a canoe program under way. This was a recent graduate in Forestry from the University of Toronto by the name of Ernest H. Finlayson, who, in turn, was linked with Native guides working in the area, and built for Northway a schedule of routes, plans and logisitics for camp canoe tripping.

Designed to stay clear of Canoe Lake and the mill town of Mowat, which at this time had 500 residents and 18 kilometres of railway sidings, Northway trips with guides like Charlie Skuce, from Powassan, worked their way up the Madawaska from Cache Lake to Tanamakoon and Source lakes and downstream through Lake of Two Rivers, cutting east at Whitefish Lake through Kearney, Pond, Little Rock, Sunday, and Sproule lakes to the Big Water of Opeongo Lake. These trips were never far from regular rail traffic where help could be accessed with nothing more than bloomers on a stick, but this was always a last resort inside Miss Case's rubric of make-do self-reliance. But it was these canoe trips that became the centre of the Northway programming. Writing about these in her memoirs, Fannie Case had this to say:

> Canoe trips are the crowning experience of camping in this country. There is a tang in the deep and lasting memories of camp that undoubtedly is derived largely from this mettle-testing experience ... The trips mean hard work, and every-body works (that is the unwritten law). Arms ache but keep on paddling. Three campers in each canoe, and two canoes. Next day arms are stronger and want to keep going into the unknown, new glimpses always ahead. They are young explorers. Every girl carries her own pack, not too heavy, 12 pounds for beginners, 20 to 25 later in the season for strong campers.

Trippers usually stop well before dark. Making a home in the wilderness is "tops" in clean-tasting joy. All lend a hand in cleaning away brush after finding the right spot for pitching the tent. Some make the fireplace for cooking, others dash off in canoes to catch a fine trout for supper. The guides know these places.

Moral and mental strength and courage, as well as physical, come from these five to nine day trips. The alert posture upon return, shining eyes and new grasp on things are unmistakeable signs. The shorter trips for new campers and younger girls are splendid, too. "Nature and the good earth have their own undefeatable way of working."[6]

Joyce Plumptre Tyrrell who served as assistant director under Miss Case for several years recalled the nature of Fanny Case's unusual brand of leadership:

She was hard to describe and was often baffling, even to those who knew her well, because she never followed a set pattern, but came, fresh and unhampered, to each decision.

On the surface, she was full of inconsistencies, but beneath it, her relations with people were sound and sure, based on the unswerving belief that goodness and fine qualities are in everyone, and need only the encouragement of wise understanding and untramelled surroundings to come to light.

Miss Case's beliefs were expressed at camp in many interesting and challenging ways. There were no set rules at Northway, no boundaries, no whistles, bells or bugles, yet the power of her gentle personality was such that there was camp discipline of the highest sort. Similarly there was no set religious teaching, yet no one who attended her counsellor's meetings or our morning gatherings could have missed the deeply spiritual force that emanated from her.[7]

Dorothy pours another cup of tea with steady hand and looks up with clear blue eyes. She has just told me about a recent, totally frustrating, and humiliating experience of being invited to Georgian Bay and not being able to bend her knees enough to kneel in a canoe. "I had to be paddled," she says indignantly. But, thinking of those Northway days, she is sure about the place that canoeing has had in her life. She can't exactly put it into words, but she says quietly and with conviction of body and face, "Camp certainly made a difference to me. I'm a different person than I ever would have been. I know that. And I value it."[8] As much as anything she says or implies about her canoeing experiences in Algonquin Park, three years as a camper and one year as a staff member, I'm drawn to a carefully folded piece of yellowed paper she hands me. It's a poem, written long ago in prussian blue ink from a fountain pen, she keeps with her Northway mementos. It is evident from our conversation that these images are as vivid now, at ninety years, as they were when she was a teenager:

> The clouds are softly drifting o'er
>   Their lake of spotless blue
> And we are dipping paddles in
>   The same soft water too
> The winds content and do not sigh
> The stately pines are tall and high
> And all are one the lake and sky
>   Where glides our green canoe[9]

For boys, under stately pines to the west of Algonquin, another summer camp was established by A.L. Cochrane, a drill instructor and physical education teacher at Upper Canada College in Toronto. For many of the same reasons as Miss Case—to develop youth in mind, body and spirit in the best traditions of muscular Christianity— Cochrane started with the offspring of friends and UCC students at a site in Muskoka in 1903 and, with the advent of the railway in 1905, moved his operation north to an island in Lake Temagami. Cochrane, founder of the Royal Life Saving Society of Canada, was very much into development and reconstruction of the inner as well as the outer boy through the challenges and discipline of wilderness-skill development, the culmination of which was the canoe trip.

121

The early years of this century were a heady time for innovation in education and training of youth. The manual training school model for education, spawned to meet the needs of the industrial revolution, had grown stale. Progressive educators were fighting back with educational innovations to build experiences into the curriculum that would recognize individual achievement and contextualize learning as a process of total human development (rather than rote learning and the filling of empty vessels with facts of the day). By this time, for her "off season" job, Miss Case was lecturing in the psychology of industrial education at the Rochester Institute of Technology. Robert Baden-Powell and Ernest Thompson Seton were beginning to popularize Boy Scouts and Woodcraft Indians. And the Young Men's Christian Association and Young Women's Christian Association, founded in London, England, in 1844 by George Williams, were taking off in North America. Camping and canoeing became part of this phenomenon.

As it happens, one of Dorothy McMichael's classmates at Brown Public School in Toronto, Adele Statten, had a father who was very active in the YMCA. Taylor Statten would also become a force in the camping world and a significant player in the shifting of canoes and canoe ideology from relative historical obscurity into public consciousness. Statten was National Boys' Work Secretary for the National Council of the YMCA. He had spent some time helping to develop the YMCA camp on Lake Couchiching, north of Toronto, but in the winter of 1911–12 went by train with his wife, Ethel, and several friends for a short vacation at the Highland Inn, a fashionable hotel on Cache Lake in Algonquin Park, not too far from Northway Lodge. For a day outing, they snowshoed back to Canoe Lake, where they eyed for the first time Little Wapemeo Island halfway down Canoe Lake from the railway junction at the north end. Returning the following summer, they paddled from the Canoe Lake train station and camped on this island, eventually requesting a lease from the government to use the property.

In the next couple of years, Statten's tent installation on Little Wap' was replaced by a cabin with the help of various people in the Canoe Lake community. An artist who had been frequenting the area, and who was always interested in odd jobs to raise a little money from time to time, was enlisted to help build a large stone fireplace in the Stattens' new cabin. According to Bernard Shaw's 1996 history of Canoe Lake and area,[10] the artist, Tom Thomson, was enlisted to transport the stone by scow across the lake from a nearby quarry and, when expected assistance didn't arrive, he ended up completing the job on his own.

As part of his work with the YMCA, Statten had become very interested and involved in the TUXIS Movement ("training in service" with the addition of a cross ["X"] and a "U" for pronunciation purposes), which had grown out of work by the American YMCA in Brooklyn, New York. This idea flourished in the National Office of the Canadian YMCA and, in 1917, the same summer that his stone boatman, Tom Thomson, drowned on Canoe Lake, Statten hosted a group of youth leaders at his Little Wap' cabin to discuss putting TUXIS into practice in Canada. The result of this and subsequent meetings was the production by the YMCA Committee on Canadian Standard Efficiency Training of the *Manual for TUXIS Boys*, a guide to creating fine citizens through action, adventure and service, similar to, but distinct from, Seton's Woodcrafter Movement and Baden-Powell's expanding notion of scouting. To put the TUXIS manual into practice, Statten applied for a lease to a sweeping bay on the main shore of Canoe Lake he'd been looking at for years, and in 1921 started Camp Ahmek. Ethel, inspired by her husband and, presumably, by the fine work of Fannie Case 13 kilometres to the east, started a small girls' camp at the Little Wap' cabin, which grew until it had to be moved to a more permanent site on nearby Big Wapemeo Island in 1930. According to Bernard Shaw:

> Early efforts to keep the boy [on the mainland] and girl [on the island] campers apart involved patrols in a motor boat equipped with a large spot light. Boys trying to run the blockade usually had their ardour dampened by having their canoe swamped.[11]

The kind of canoeing done by both Canadian and American camps in Algonquin Park—and there were more camps opening every year throughout the first half of the twentieth century, tended to be less ambitious than the tripping that was going on farther north in Temagami. Unlike other camps, which were more or less stuck on the notion that one should not stand in a canoe and that whitewater was patently unsafe for canoe travel, A.L. Cochrane's leaders were running trips on the Montreal, Lady Evelyn, and other Temagami rivers that involved both poling up (often requiring a standing position in a canoe) and shooting down rapids. More ambitious even than A.L. Cochrane, however, was A.A. Greg Clarke, who founded Camp Keewaydin on Lake Temagami in 1902 and who, by 1911, was running mostly American youths on ground-breaking trips down the old fur-trade rivers like the Mattagami, Abitibi, and Missinaibi from heartland Northern Ontario to tidewater at James Bay.

One of the many aspects that all of these camps had in common, however, was their celebration of the canoe—usually canvas-covered cedar canoes from, for Canadian camps, the Peterborough or Chestnut Canoe companies and, for American camps canvas-covered canoes from the Old Town or E.M. White Canoe companies. (The first Keewaydin trip to reach Moosonee in 1911 arrived with a badly damaged canvas-covered canoe that had to be replaced with the purchase of a birchbark canoe from local Indians.) As a by-product of the leadership and character development that was, arguably, the first aim of the early camps, young men and women participated in tough but significant wilderness experiences that at a most impressionable time in their lives settled their making as people, as citizens. And, as Dorothy McMichael, and thousands of others have testified over the years, the legacy of these canoeing experiences at camps has been signficant and substantial.

In his early years, a young French-Canadian lad from Montreal called Pierre Trudeau turned up at Taylor Statten's Camp Ahmek, where he fell in love with a way of life and an image that would stay with him. A story about a lesser-known Liberal prime minister arises out of the oral history of A.L. Cochrane's camp on Lake Temagami. Like Fanny Case, A.L. Cochrane liked to hire young medical students for his staff because, with these people, who were often former campers, he acquired competent canoe trip leaders, but he also got medical expertise to put on the trail. One such medical student was

Toronto native Alex Bryans. By the time Bryans came to Cochrane's camp in the 1930s, its name had been changed to Camp Temagami, but the thrust was still canoe tripping. It had been a powerful experience for him:

> I think going to camp itself, being away from the family like that, was a very formative thing for me. The first time away, of course, it was. But then I wanted to go away from then on, partly to be away and partly because of the fun we had there. That was all very formative, that time away with kids my own age, and different people calling the shots. Not the teachers, not the family, not the policeman on the street corner and whoever else guides us in the city.
>
> I think what canoe tripping did for me was about that but also about bonding with people and making new friends. Taking responsibility and, above all, getting close to nature—the scenery, the water, the freedom of it that you experience on a canoe trip. It sure got in my blood, and I was keen to go back. And even now, as an adult, I'd rather have a canoe than any other kind of boat.[12]

Like Dorothy McMichael and countless others, Alex Bryans went back to Camp Temagami as staff member while he was at university. In Bryans' case, he was studying to be a doctor. In the summer of 1941, at twenty years old, Bryans was helping to lead a group of ten- and eleven-year-old boys on a canoe trip. The day's paddle had come to an end and they were camped at an ideal campsite, a rocky point protruding into the calm waters of Lake Temagami. When supper and chores were done, the canvas tents set, and the blankets rolled out, it was time to relax. A couple of the boys were out fishing in a canoe off the campsite. Bryans picks up the story there:

> It was just about dusk and all of a sudden about a hundred yards out there was a great scream—a couple of screams. I could see that one of the boys was sort of standing up, and I shouted, "Sit down! Sit down!" And he started yelling at me,

and they were flapping around. And what had happened was, one kid had caught a fish—quite a big fish—and was trying to land the thing into the canoe. He got it up into the canoe. It was on one of those three-pronged hooks and one or two of them had gone into HIM as well as into the fish's mouth. The kid was attached to the fish and it was flapping around like crazy. I took off in another canoe, out to where they were, but by the time I got there they didn't have a chance to take the fish off the hook. The fish had unhooked itself and ended up back in the lake. So I took the kid back to shore and it fell to me to fix the situation. So I got out the sharpest knife—I remember feeling all the knives we had around camp—and I simply cut the thing out. It was my first operation.[13]

What Alex Bryans could not know that day on Lake Temagami was that the recipient of his medical ministrations would become Lester Pearson's minister of consumer and corporate affairs, Pierre Trudeau's minister of justice and later finance and, in his last political incarnation, the twenty-third prime minister of Canada.

Unable to resist getting the other end of Alex Bryans' fish story, I called John Turner, explaining that I'd just had tea with the trip leader who had taken the fish hook from his thigh. "That wasn't my thigh," he spat back, "that was my ASS! And it hurt."

Later in his Toronto office, Turner was more reflective about the camp experience. For him, as an Ottawa boy, it had been difficult fitting into and being accepted by the Toronto boys who, because of Cochrane's work affiliation, came in the main from Upper Canada College. Through the thirties, when he was seven, eight and nine years old, he was an interloper, but with time came more boys from outside Toronto and Turner became fast friends with some of the UCC gang. "Some of my best friends, some of my oldest friends from Toronto, are guys I knew from camp," he said. "You don't see them much, but when you do, you don't need any introductions—you know them well. You pick up right where you left off." The friendship they shared was built as much as anything on learning they had undergone on their Temagami canoe trips:

You learned how to trip. I mean ... you learned how to put an inventory together of what you needed. You learned the food you needed. In those days there was far less of this freeze-dried stuff. I mean, it was all out of cans and you'd have to carry a grub box, and you'd have to pack it. You had to make sure you were warm enough. You learned organization. You learned responsibility. You're talking about leadership. And also you learned discipline. But you also had fun. And you learned to be optimistic. Sometimes the weather closed in for three or four days and it's pretty hard to do that when the guys get wet and cold. You learned about the outdoors. It wasn't as rough as the *coureur de bois*—you learned how to take hardship, you learned how to get along with other men outdoors, you learned friendship, you learned the warmth of a campfire and all the good stories that go with it! You learned the mystery of the campfire. The stars ... the moon![14]

These were grounding experiences for John Turner, who went on to canoe with family and friends, every year if he could, on routes that eventually took him to challenging rivers in the Northwest Territories. Researching these junkets, he became fast friends with Ottawa paddling legend, Eric Morse, who would annotate Turner's maps with river-running details, campsites and other pertinent information gleaned from his pioneering trips that Turner would later take on. He befriended other characters in the elite Ottawa paddling circle, including Blair Fraser, Ottawa editor of *Maclean's* magazine, who lived only a couple of blocks from Turner in Rockcliffe. Turner remembered watching Fraser practise portaging his canoe around the residential street, getting limbered up, the week before he went paddling with Eric Rogers and drowned at Rollway Rapids on the Petawawa River, just as the Liberals formed a government in 1968. Trudeau and Turner were honorary pallbearers because of their canoe connections to the much-missed editor of *Maclean's* magazine.

Like Alex Bryans and Dorothy McMichael, however, Turner's introduction to canoeing at camp lived on in his bones and became a dominant metaphor for him that affected how he saw himself and the country and how he went about his business. For example, in a 1996 speech to the Canadian Club—the club had invited all living former prime ministers, Clark, Campbell, Mulroney, Trudeau and Turner, to deliver addresses that year—Turner's grounding in the Canadian landscape from the vantage point of a canoeist is evident. He opens with an observation that it is Canada's good fortune to "occupy the most beautiful land on earth." And he goes on to celebrate the country from coast to coast through activities, salmon feasts on Haida Gwaii, harvest time in south Saskatchewan, sunsets on Lake of the Woods, hockey in the old Forum, lobster on Passamaquoddy Bay and "canoeing down the Burnside to Bathurst Inlet on the Arctic Ocean."[15]

The only would-be politician who ever actually campaigned in a canoe was Trent University history professor Bruce Hodgins, who ran for the New Democratic Party against Liberal Hugh Faulkner in the Trudeaumania election of 1968. He lost, but not, or so he would like to think, because of the canoe.

Hodgins, who grew up at another venerable summer camp on Lake Temagami, Camp Wanapitei, made a "fetish" of his experience as a canoeist in Peterborough during the 1968 election campaign. "I went up and down the Otonabee and got my picture in the paper nation-wide for canoeing, for canvassing in a canoe." And when his illustrious-but-aging party leader, Tommy Douglas, came to town, Hodgins thought nothing of plopping him into a canoe as well. Speaking about this at his kitchen table along the Otonabee, he smiled and recalled:

> I put him right in the middle of Carol's [his wife] and my canoe, and we paddled him across Little Lake and right over here. We landed at a neighbour's place and walked him right in here for a reception. He was scared, by the way. As a prairie boy, I'm not sure he could swim. He was absolutely positive we were going to tip him. But everything turned out all right and it was a lovely image for the television cameras. People responded to it, especially in Peterborough.[16]

Whether or not there are more people in politics and positions of leadership as a result of character formation in the summer camp crucible called the canoe trip is difficult to say. It is certainly a tempting conclusion. But these camps were founded by privileged people and, with very few exceptions, tended to draw privileged boys and girls, many of whom, by virtue of upbringing and circumstance, would likely have done very well anyway. And, some have argued, the camp experience, with its white Anglo-Saxon middle-class, Christian ethos, was not all sweetness and harmony with nature. Jewish camps, for example, were established because the prevailing Christian ethos was not always welcoming to Jews. The implicit messages in summer camps about who counted, in terms of religion and race, have latterly been roundly damned.

First Nations guides, like Powassan native Charlie Skuce, from whom Dorothy McMichael learned most of her canoeing and to whom she became quite attached over the years, were, in the early years, an integral part of the camping scene. But over the years, especially in the more southerly camps in Algonquin Park and elsewhere throughout Muskoka and Haliburton, the First Nations physical presence in camp programming, if it was ever there in the first place, evaporated, later condensing into aboriginal analogues of the Al Jolson minstrel show, complete with sylized feathers, war paint, breech clouts, braves, and a great chief, usually played by the director.

The messages these Indian Nights sent to campers were decidedly mixed. On the one hand, in the best tradition of Ernest Thompson Seton's Woodcraft Indian teachings, they sensitized these youth of means to a lifestyle integrated into the landscape through which they were canoeing from summer to summer. On the other hand, in the usual absence of real First Nations representatives, these charades of toe–heel campfire dancing, games, stories and ceremony had a pervasive element of parody. For impressionable young people, this was always a little confusing, and could result in unexplored apprehensions that would dog them as emerging leaders, as they moved out into business, industry and government and into decision-making positions across the continent, up to and including the highest offices in the land.

One particularly colourful camp founder, whose legacy registers more than most in today's popular culture, is "Unca" Lou Handler, a prize-fighter from Detroit who came north to Algonquin Park in the mid-1930s looking to start a summer camp. He found a willing partner in a young man who had grown up in the park, Omer Stringer, and the two of them crafted an institution around the romance of the Canadian canoe. A schmaltzy description of how Camp Tamakwa was started is printed in promotional material for the camp posted on the Internet:

> On a cool and misty morning in the year 1936, a red canoe glided silently across the still waters of South Tea Lake. In it were two young men: one with a dream, the other with the skills to make it real. Naturalist Lou Handler and legendary canoeist Omer Stringer had come to this part of Algonquin Park looking for some very special land—a place that would make the perfect campsite. And as the morning sun burned away the early mist, they approached the northern shore of this two-mile lake with their hopes high. The sparkling clear waters revealed a firm and sandy shoreline without any steep drop-offs as it sloped gently up to meet the land. These would be safe swimming waters.
>
> The men left the canoe and scrambled up the embankment. Under the tangle of century-old windfalls they saw that the land was flat, and the sandy soil promised clear drinking wells. The location—just a quick jaunt around the bend from the main park road—was close enough for quick access. But the men thought its distance far enough to assure that this, indeed, would be a wilderness camp.[17]

It would be in this environment, growing up in black and white Camp Tamakwa canoes, that Patrick Watson, former chair of the Canadian Broadcasting Corporation, actor Chevy Chase, U.S. senator Carl Levin and U.S. federal judge Avern Cohen, among many others, would figure out who they were. It would be this place and this camp that would be the subject and the setting for Tamakwa alumnus Mike Binder's Hollywood feature, about a group of friends who return to the camp of their childhood. But most significantly, at least in terms of exposure in the global marketplace, the most pervasive legacy of the Tamakwa canoe camping experience would be established by two young campers from Unca Lou's home town, "The Roots Boys," Michael Budman and Don Green, who packaged their Algonquin Park canoe experience and became millionaires.

Budman and Green burst onto the fashion scene in 1973 with their innovative negative-heel "earth" shoe, which thrived until scientific research demonstrated that the product was detrimental to good orthopedic health and posture. Undaunted, the young entrepreneurs turned to their canoeing mentor, Omer Stringer, and tried to market his particular shape and style of canvas-covered canoe. The "Beaver" canoe, as a boat, flopped, but what took off was the canoe company logo, which was plastered on sweatshirts from coast to coast. Almost magically, when they switched from the Beaver Canoe label on their products to the "Roots" logo with its beaver icon wrapped in wilderness imagery— lakes, rocks, trees, canoes—the ideal lifestyle à la Algonquin that these promoters were selling with their clothing took off, as if an unsuspecting North American public had been waiting for a commercial opportunity to exercise their affection for the canoe way of life. By the late 1990s, Roots itself had become a way of life, the Canadian team at the 1998 Nagano Olympics being the most conspicuous illustration of the Roots Boys marketing savvy and success. By that time there were ninety-five upscale Roots stores around the world, with their log cabin facades and wood-planked floors, where youthful clerks sold footwear, natural-fibre clothing, leather jackets and accessories "inspired by the founders' real-life experiences in Ontario's Algonquin Park."

Without doubt, however, the most substantial material legacy of summer camping on the whole world of canoeing in North America is the collection of canoes that was started by Kirk Wipper, director of Camp Kandalore on Lake Kabakwa, just south of Algonquin Park. After service in the Canadian Naval Reserve during World War II, Wipper, a man of German stock from the Interlake region of Manitoba, came to the University of Toronto, where he studied physical education and subsequently became a professor. But, through his connections with the YMCA in Winnipeg, he became involved with the Y in Toronto, which led him to Pinecrest, their summer camp in Muskoka. Following the pattern of many youth leaders before him, determined to make a difference in the education and training of youth, Wipper eventually found the wherewithal to purchase Kandalore, a fledgling boys' camp, in the late 1950s. And, with a philosophy that embodied the character-development goals of the Algonquin camps and the best wilderness canoe-tripping traditions of the Temagami camps, he built a leadership infrastructure that informed the lives of many Ontario boys. But Wipper had a weakness, a passion for canoes. One of his old professors from the University of Toronto gave him an old basswood canoe, built by the Payne Brothers of Lakefield *circa* 1860, to display in the dining hall at Camp Kandalore and, from there, a collection grew. Quipped Wipper's oldest son, Doug, in later years, "Some people collect stamps or coins, Dad collected canoes."

As Kandalore camper and staff member from 1959 to 1973, I watched this collection grow and grow. It was a matter of course for people at Kandalore to be offered opportunities to paddle bark canoes of all shapes and sizes, historic Peterborough all-wood and canvas-covered craft and to have, as part of summer camp life, experience with all manner of canoes that Wipper was collecting from across Canada and around the world. Some specimens were set aside for conservation, but most of the craft Wipper collected were to be paddled with care and always with impromptu history lessons from their keeper. Whatever their historic value and significance, the message from Kirk was that canoes were important and they were to be cherished and used.

In particular, I have vivid and very happy memories of two 25-foot Couchiching Freighter canoes, built by the Peterborough Canoe Company around 1895. With planks lashed across their gunwales, as with the luggage-toting sponson canoes remembered by Dorothy McMichael at Northway, these beamy craft were used for transportation of heavy loads across Lake Kabakwa, as a multi-person ferry to Chapel Island, as a diving raft, judge's stand and barbeque deck. They were even used for an on-the-water variety night stage one summer, the central event of which was staff member John Fallis, nephew to Alex Bryans of John Turner–fish hook fame, being tied up in chains as "The Great Faldini" and lowered into the lake for an escape act that involved accomplices breathing out of upturned buckets weighted to the bottom of the lake with rocks and lengths of binder twine. And the featured event of every weekly regatta at Kandalore was the war canoe race, in which these big old canoes would be loaded with eighteen or twenty campers and paddled at full speed over the length of a sprint course in Junior Bay. They were even used on one occasion to pull a tiny camper on water skis, an activity now dubbed "resistance training" by dragon-boat racers.

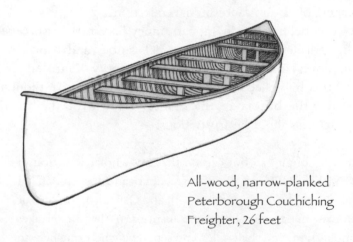

All-wood, narrow-planked
Peterborough Couchiching
Freighter, 26 feet

Staff at Kandalore suspected as much but didn't know for sure the extent to which the stress and strain of keeping this growing national treasure trove was coming to bear on its keeper. In 1976, Wipper managed to negotiate the purchase of the entire Heye Foundation collection of Native craft from the Museum of the American Indian, making the Kandalore—now Kanawa—collection one of the most significant assemblages of canoes and kayaks in the world. But Kirk Wipper was a camp director, a physical education profession, a lover of canoes; he was not a museologist, a fundraiser or a bookkeeper and, in spite of help from a variety of talents, including Richard Nash—New York commercial photographer–cum–bark-canoe-builder, who had worked with legendary canoe builder Henri Vaillancourt on the Quebec canoe—the collection was too much for one man to manage or to look after. Wipper's marriage collapsed. The camp was sold, but even those additional funds were not sufficient to meet the cash demands of Wipper's passion. He was connected to canoe people all over the world. He was travelling, making deals, and finally came to the realization that if the collection was to survive, indeed flourish, it needed to be moved to a better location, one with proper climate control and fire protection, but also a place with operational funding and staff to research the craft and stop their decay. By the mid-1970s, mice, for example, had chewed their way through the taut sealskin cover of a priceless Inuit kayak, and humid conditions in an unheated building had promoted rot in the most heartbreaking of circumstances in the collection.

Forty years before, Edwin Tappan Adney had tried, unsuccessfully, to sell his priceless collection of model canoes and papers to the Canadian government. As detailed by Timothy Kent, Adney was convinced that his collection "ought not to leave Canada, though the [U.S.] shares the history of the canoe."[20] He wrote to his friend Diamond Jenness about his frustrations:

> It is becoming all but certain that my whole collection of Models of Canoes will go to an American Museum, after I vainly sought to place them with the Canadian National at almost any terms. The same institution that undertakes publication, and their field representative who came here to see me over a year ago is coming in the spring to discuss details. The museum is the new Mariner's Museum which has reserved an entire wing for the Canoe.[21]

By return post not a week later, Jenness, the head of the Anthropology Division of the Victoria (National) Museum, wrote back to Adney:

> It is a shame that your model canoes cannot stay in Canada. I would give a good deal to be allowed to purchase them for our museum here, but we operate on a shoe-string and are not able to buy anything at the present time. Some day,

when it is too late perhaps, the Canadian people will wake up and decide they want a real museum in the capital city.[22]

Kirk Wipper ran into more or less the same frustrations, except that his goal was even more ambitious: to have his collection enshrined in a living museum that would see research combined with conservation and a lively program of education and public programming. It was not an easy task. Only after years of frustrating false starts, during which parts of his collection were shipped to various locations around Ontario, and hopes were raised for facilities in Haliburton and on Lake Ontario at Cobourg, Wipper finally gifted his collection to the newly formed Canadian Canoe Museum, a consortium of people from Trent University and the city of Peterborough in 1995 who, in turn, handed over a lump sum of cash to Wipper to help offset the money that had flowed through his hands for close to forty years to build the collection. The canoes would stay in Canada. The Canadian Canoe Museum opened its doors to the public on Canada Day, 1997. Testament to the fortuitous change of circumstances for Wipper's canoe collection is the sentimental opening stanza from George T. Marsh's poem, "The Old Canoe," published occasionally in mailings having to do with the collection, that often includes a hopeful codicil written by Wipper himself:

Tho' they rest inside, in our dreams they'll glide
    On the crests of the streams of yore
In the mid-day sun, they'll make their run
    And light on a distant shore.
The trav'llers are gone with their unmatched brawn
    Who plied the mapless way
But their craft we keep, tho' the paddlers sleep;
    Their stars we seek today.[23]

In the fall and winter of 1997, I walk with Wipper[24] through the damp, cold, hangar-like expanses of the old Outboard Marine Corporation factory on Monaghan Road in Peterborough, where row upon row of plastic-shrouded canoes, complete with paper toe-tags, lie racked like bodies in a temporary morgue, but change is in the works.

135

Stories tumble from Wipper's memory, and today Dawn McQuade, the newly hired collection manager, strolls with us, tape recorder in hand. Lifting the plastic at the end of a 26-foot Haida canoe, Wipper runs thick fingers over the carved cedar prow and tells me of the day in Masset, Queen Charlotte Islands, when he and a crew paddled the boat backwards, not knowing the weapon rest always went first. Sliding his hand down the stem, his fingers find a small hole right on the centre line of the boat. "There used to be a carved eagle that was attached right at this spot. It must have been broken off during shipping," he sighs. After years of moving and storage in less than ideal circumstances, it is a good thing the boats have landed. But it will take time to transform this warehouse into a climate-controlled collections centre.

We rest again at the old Kandalore Couchiching Freighters and reminisce about boys straining every muscle on those worn plank seats for regatta glory on Lake Kabakwa. Wipper smiles and says: "It was essential to get everyone, especially the little guys, involved in canoes at camp. These canoes were perfect for that. Team captains would stand up in the dining hall each week and ask for a show of hands for any paddlers who thought they were strong enough to join the war canoe team. We would fill these canoes with campers, the smaller the better, and they would feel part of a grand event, win or lose. These canoes were about trying your best and having fun. They were about teamwork, finding ways to work together to achieve great things."[26]

In the months since it opened, the Canadian Canoe Museum has evolved substantially. The temporary morgue is scheduled for a new roof to stop dripping water. Some of the craft have been unwrapped and elevated to tiered wooden racks, built by volunteers. There is still much work to be done. The main office building of the Outboard Marine Corporation, located on the same property as the original factory, has also been given to the museum and, with the help of sizeable corporate donations, has been transformed into an education and display centre for the canoe collection, complete with space for working artists and craftspersons. Future plans for the museum include a robust schedule of public programming, craft restoration, and research, as well as a continuing capital campaign to enhance facilities both on Monaghan Road and on a satellite location on the water at Little Lake in downtown Peterborough.

Founding executive director Bill Byrick insists that, in the spirit of the collection's roots in camping and canoe culture, the Canadian Canoe Museum is not solely about canoes as artifacts. His vision is to create a broadly based not-for-profit heritage institution, serving the people of Canada and visitors from around the world, with a dynamic exploration of the canoe in its full historical and cultural context. To support this mission, Byrick and the museum's board of directors have set an ambitious agenda:

- to promote the canoe as legacy and symbol linking the history of aboriginals, French, British and all Canadians to Canada's unique landscape;
- to preserve and augment this unique and valuable collection of watercraft and related artifacts in a suitable setting;
- to exhibit the collection and interpret the skills and stories it represents;
- to develop the world's foremost research institute for the study of canoes and kayaks;
- to develop educational programs both at the museum and across the country based on the canoe in Canadian culture.[27]

In many respects, the entrepreneurial spirit and fierce independence of camping pioneers like Fanny Case, Taylor Statten, A.L. Cochrane and Kirk Wipper are already written into the script of the Canadian Canoe Museum. And, as individual craft are restored and interpreted, as expeditions begin and end in Peterborough, as research gains momentum, and as the body of archival knowledge grows, Wipper's canoes will be part of a living entity. The creation of the Canadian Canoe Museum has been, and continues to be, a collective act, in which the culture of the canoe is developed, explored and interpreted to create historical context for the craft themselves. In many cases the children of nature who benefited from summer camp experiences have become the titans of government and industry, and it is these people who are giving back financially and in kind to develop a home for their favoured craft in Peterborough, Ontario.

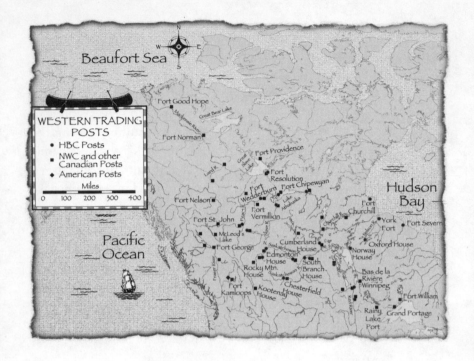

Map legend:

WESTERN TRADING
POSTS
- HBC Posts
- NWC and other
  Canadian Posts
- American Posts
  Miles
0   100   200   300   400

Map labels: Beaufort Sea, Fort Good Hope, Mackenzie River, Great Bear Lake, Fort Norman, Fort Providence, Fort Resolution, Fort Chipewyan, Hudson Bay, Fort Nelson, Fort Wedderburn, Lake Athabasca, Fort Churchill, Fort St. John, Fort Vermillion, York Fort, Fort Severn, McLeod's Lake, Cumberland House, Oxford House, Fort George, Edmonton House, South Branch House, Norway House, Rocky Mtn. House, Chesterfield House, Bas de la Rivière Winnipeg, Fort Kamloops, Kootenay House, Fort William, Rainy Lake Post, Grand Portage, Pacific Ocean

7

WHEN IS A CANOE NOT A CANOE?

Bateaux: a variety of keelless, often flat-bottomed plank boats made with pointed ends and straight flaring sides ... typically propelled by rowing, poling, and water currents, or they were sailed with the wind. York boats were said to be descended from bateaux ... were sometimes called "the white man's version of the canoe."

— "Vessel Types on Minnesota's Inland Waters"[1]

WHEN YOU ARE APPROACHING Manitoba from Hudson Bay, land is an unlikely proposition. Even from the deck of a small sailing vessel riding a tall swell, one must get dangerously close to shallow tidal flats to realize that the thin, green smear between sea and sky is, in fact, that northern doorstep of a massive, fur-rich country with diverse topography. Here an erratic rock or a knoll with stunted spruce can be a scenic event that breaks the monotony of wind-seared sedge and tundra greens. This is Canada still rebounding from the weight of the ice sheets of the last glacial age, a flat, marshly lowland still underlain by continuous permafrost in many places, where occasional hardy conifers eke out an existence on ancient gravelly beach ridges, now distant from the tidal zone, where there is sufficient drainage to put down roots. This is not the imposing rocky coast of Newfoundland, the red rich beaches of Prince Edward Island, the sylvan hills of Nova Scotia or New Brunswick, the welcoming islands and curling green banks of the Rivière du Canada, or anything like the mountain-ringed harbour at English Bay, in the west. This is bog and fen on frozen clay. In summer—coastal lowland home to polar bears and millions of migrant geese. In winter—home to ptarmigan, twisted spruce and frozen stones. Nevertheless, it is in this pitiless environment that the empire of the Hudson's Bay Company (HBC) began, and it is here that another Canadian canoe-like vessel was born.

Having learned on various forays into the interior of North America, via Montreal and the St. Lawrence, that it was possible to exploit the fur riches west of Lake Superior from Hudson Bay (and been fined and frustrated by King Louis XIV for their efforts), Médard Chouart des Groseilliers and his younger brother-in-law, Pierre-Esprit Radisson, took their idea for this trading domain to King Charles II of England. The king, as it happened, was in the process of drafting a plan for an imperial economy in which northern lands would counterbalance tropical territories, and control of trade routes would be all-important.[2] With the help and encouragement of his cousin, Prince Rupert, and statesman Sir George Carteret, King Charles was able to secure enough investment to mount an expedition to confirm the business potential of the plan.

A first voyage to Canada was planned for 1667 but had to be abandoned. The following year, however, the two most entrepreneurial bark canoeists of them all were dispatched from Gravesend, England, on June 3, 1668—Groseilliers, aboard a tiny two-masted, square-rigger, the *Nonsuch*, and Radisson aboard a second vessel, the *Eaglet*, headed for Hudson Bay. The *Eaglet* was forced to turn back, but the *Nonsuch* survived the journey across the North Atlantic, through Hudson Strait, and south to the "bottom of the bay" (James Bay), where they spent the winter trading with the Cree near the estuary of the Rupert River. This foray was so successful—in terms of the number and quality of furs returned to London—that the investors backing the project (who had organized themselves into a public corporation while Groseilliers was away) were able to secure a grant that gave them a monopoly for trade in northern North America. It was modifications of this process of incorporation, energized by the bounty from the voyage of the *Nonsuch*, that gave rise, on May 2, 1670, to a Royal Charter issued to the "Governor and Company of Adventurers of England trading into Hudson Bay," granting exclusive trading jurisdiction to the entire drainage basin of Hudson Bay, lands including 40 per cent of what is now Canada and portions of what is now the northern United States.

Unlike the French, who had made a point of getting into the canoes of the First Nations and learning how to paddle and portage to where the fur-bearing animals were being trapped and skinned, the "Company of Adventurers" decided to build forts or "factories" by the bay, to sit by the fire and wait for the furs to come to them. Two of the earliest of these posts were Fort Albany, built in 1682 at the mouth of the Albany River on James Bay, and York Factory, established by HBC governor George Geyer the following year. The only small boats required by the English to support this trading strategy were craft to ferry cargo to and from ships anchored off shore. HBC personnel saw birchbark canoes of all kinds, in increasing numbers, as the momentum of trade grew but, beyond recreation or curiosity on the part of bored traders, the canoe was a craft of the aboriginals who visited the posts. As a conduit for furs to the point of departure from North America, however, the canoe was as important to the British trading initiative as it was to the French.[3]

Word spread. Post records from York Factory show that in 1715 alone there were 172 bark canoes paddled by Cree and Assiniboine

Indians who came down the Hayes River to exchange furs, beaver predominantly, for European trade goods. According to historians Bruce Hodgins and Gwyneth Hoyle, the Hudson's Bay Company post on the bay drew aboriginal traders from a wide area:

> Many came from what is now southeastern Manitoba and areas between the Saskatchewan and Churchill rivers. There were also Bloods and Blackfoot from the west. Thirty of the 172 canoes were filled with "Mountain Indians"—Hidatsa and probably Mandans from the upper Missouri and as far west as the Rockies: there were even "Sarsi"—Sarcee from farther to the southwest.[4]

Because most of these First Nations people used canoes as their primary mode of transport, many of them travelling round trips of more than a thousand miles, these trading expeditions to the bay had to operate in the slim margin of summer when the rivers were ice-free. Arthur Ray and Donald Freeman contend that this situation represented a significant measure of risk for the aboriginals:

> The remote trading groups who used canoes to traverse part of the distance, such as the Mandan, Blood, and Blackfoot, had to contend with the problem of the short open water season that characterizes the lower reaching of rivers flowing into Hudson Bay. Unless they reached the bay, traded, and departed before the second or third week in August at the latest, Indians from the Missouri, upper Saskatchewan, and Churchill rivers faced the danger of freeze-up before they reached their homeland. Starvation and death were usually the consequences if this occurred.[5]

Competition with Montreal-based French traders intensified. From the point of view of First Nations people, especially those some distance from the bay, given the risks and time involved in this axis of exchange, it made sense to deal with canoe-borne traders at more southerly latitudes inland. And so, reluctantly, the H B C had to leave their posts and the bay and move inland, and with this desire came a need for another type of boat.

The obvious choice, of course, was the canoe that had, since the inception of trading relations, borne people and furs to and from the hinterland to the coast. But the British were reluctant to adopt it immediately. Years of observation, recreational trials and provisional forays upriver had not convinced them that the canoe was their boat of choice. Joseph Isbister, senior HBC employee, at Fort Albany in the 1740s, grumbled in his journal on one occasion that the men in his charge were, "intirly Unhandy in Cannoes," adding, "theres no eand to building cannoes—in one tripp they are spoiled or broake—by the unskillfullness of our men."[6]

A quirk of historical circumstance came into play at this point. During the eighteenth century there was significant demand in London for sailors to man the British, fishing, whaling, and naval fleets, making it difficult for an outfit like the HBC to recruit personnel for work on the forbidding shores of Hudson Bay. But, as it happened, ships headed for North America would sail north from Gravesend and stop at the Orkney Islands, north of Scotland, for a last fill-up of fresh water before heading out on the open ocean. Posting handbills around the port of Stromness, they soon realized there was a pool of Orcadians, undaunted by the prospects of life on the bay, who would work for half the wages expected by Londoners. Happily for the HBC, with these men came a substantial body of knowledge about boats and boat building. This combination of need and know-how gave rise to the so-called white man's version of the canoe.

The development process took place at Fort Albany, spurred on by Orcadian Joseph Isbister's disenchantment with the bark canoe. Winnipeg historian and wooden boat enthusiast Dennis Johnson describes the process of innovation:

> From the beginning, company boatwrights, carpenters, and coopers [built] a variety of "inland boats," including wooden canoes, bateaux, flat-bottomed scows, and European-style boats that were sent out "in frame" from England or constructed locally. From these endeavours, one

particular design emerged that could carry more than twice the cargo of a freight canoe using the same manpower—a significant economic advantage in the competition with the Northwest Company, which had much longer supply lines and relied almost exclusively on canoes ... Eventually, these wooden boats became known as "York boats," after the name of company headquarters at York Factory.[7]

York boats were made in response to these local needs, by arguably "local" people, but they were not—at least not initially—made of local materials, and thereby immediately contravened one of canoe designer John Winters' principal conditions for the emergence of a bona fide canoe. For building materials, Orcadian shipwrights on Hudson Bay used imported hardwoods such as elm, oak and ash, which produced a "vessel without decks" that was pointed at both ends, had a beam to length ratio of about 1:5, but that, at best, could only be declared a first cousin to the original North American canoe. Nevertheless, these inland craft served a critically important function in the fur trade. To the extent that they are somewhat similar to and served the same function as canoes but are not really siblings of the bark craft of the North American First Nations, they help shed light on the essential nature of the truly North American canoe.

York Boat, carvel-built, 40 feet

The boat itself was in the length range of the birchbark freight canoes but was built upwards from a stout, straight keel timber with flared sides and ends raked up about 45 degrees from the waterline.

Stem and stern pieces would be secured to the ends of keel with bolts or rivets and to this central member, temporary rib frames would be attached, over which, through an elaborate bending process involving steaming, brute force and hand-forged nails, the hull of the boat would be built from keel to gunwale. All of the planks—"strakes" in boat-building parlance—would be carvel-jointed (meaning nailed side to side with no overlap) and caulked with pitch and oakum, except the top three, which were usually clinker-built (overlapping) for strength and seaworthiness. When the hull was finished, the temporary internal frame would be removed and replaced by a skeleton of ribs and thwarts. In profile, especially with these last three clinker-built strakes emphasizing the elegantly sweeping sheer, a York boat at anchor could easily have been confused with a canoe with lines like a Gander Bay boat. But in the days of the freight canoe, with its distinctive half-moon ends, or even the classic "C" configuration of the Cree birchbark canoe stems, there could be no mistake.

Similarly, there would be no mistaking a York boat for a canoe when it was under way because these sturdy craft were built to be rowed, not paddled, with boatmen's backs to the direction of travel. Wooden thole-pins on the gunwales alternated positions for six to eight rowers from one side to the other. A steersman in the stern would manipulate a long oar or a rudder straight out the back and, when needed, a man in the bow with long oar or pole would fend off rocks. And, in the spirit of their Orcadian builders, most York boats came with a detachable mast (usually tied below the outer gunwale when not in use) that could be stepped and hung with a 400-square-foot sleeping tarp that would double as a sail. Running before the wind on Lake Winnipeg, York boats had a decidedly Nordic look to them.

On portages, York boats were quite recognizable as well. Most weighing something in the order of a ton, York boats would have to be unloaded to move them around rapids, but with the impossibility of a crew of only eight or ten carrying a craft of this weight, they had to be rolled on timbers on 10-foot-wide paths that had to be cut and smoothed beforehand. But cut they were, the road-like York-boat portages, thirty-four of them between York Factory and Nelson House at the north end of Lake Winnipeg. Some of these were fitted with tracks and small trolleys in time, but moving inland from Hudson Bay still required a certain amount of effort, so much so that at the end of the main climb up the Hayes River from York Factory—a portion of the route the boatmen called "Hill River" for obvious reasons—a place called "Dramstone" was established, where a nip of brandy could toast achievement or soothe the muscles of an aching portageur.[8] Measure of the toughness of this challenge was marked by Sir John Franklin, who ascended Hill River in 1819 in a York boat, making in one full day's labour only $1\frac{1}{2}$ miles upstream. The British explorer remarked in his journal, "It is not easy for any but an eye-witness to form an adequate idea of the exertions of the Orkney boatmen in the navigation of this river."

Beyond their tolerance for devilishly hard work and a certain affinity for alcohol, descriptions of the men of canoes and the men of the "white man's version" were, like their craft, of striking contrast in character and outlook. In a now-classic characterization of voyageurs, Daniel Harmon writes:

> The Canadian Voyageurs possess lively and fickle dispositions, and they are rarely subject to depression of spirits, of long continuance, even when in circumstances the most adverse. Although what they consider good eating and drinking constitutes their chief good, yet, when necessity compels them to it, they submit to great privation and hardship, not only without complaining, but even with cheerfulness and gaity. They are very talkative, and extremely thoughtless, and make many resolutions, which are almost as soon broken as formed ... They are very deceitful, are exceedingly smooth and polite, and are even gross flatterers to the face of a person, whom they will basely slander behind his back ... a secret they cannot keep. They rarely feel gratitude, though often they are generous. They are obedient, but not faithful servants. By flattering their vanity, of which they have not a little, they may be persuaded to undertake the most difficult enterprises.[9]

By contrast, cleric Murdoch Mackenzie characterizes the York boatmen this way:

145

[Orcadians] are healthy, hardy, well-shaped, subject to few
Diseases, and capable of an abstemious and laborious life, at
the same time; but for want of profitable Employment, slow
at work and many of them maligned to Idelness. In sagacity
and natural understanding, they are inferior to few of the
Commons in Britain; sparing of Words, reserved in their
sentiments ... apt to aggravate or magnify their Losses, and
studious to conceal or diminish their Gains ... Honest in
their dealings with one another, but not so scrupulous with
respect to the Master of the Grounds ... Many of these men
bring home with them all the vices without any virtues of the
savages, indolence, dissipation, irreligion and at the same
time a broken constitution.[10]

Still, the "white man's version of the canoe," in the hands of the
British, and its "well-shaped" Orkneymen, outperformed variants of
the real thing, in French hands, on the big lakes and rivers of the
West.[11] The York boat afforded the HBC a competitive advantage
derived from the fact that six to eight employees in a York boat could
transport nearly twice the cargo of that number of voyageurs in a North
canoe. For example, soon after the founding of Oxford House, midway up the Hayes River, William Sinclair accomplished the "all but
impossible feat of transporting a bull and several cows, while they were
yet calves, up the difficult Hayes River route to Oxford House in York
boats,"[12] thereby establishing the first small dairy in Rupert's Land.
Led by the Earl of Selkirk, York boats conveyed dispossessed Irish and
Scottish to the contentious Red River Settlement in 1812. And later,
the same type of vessel transported a 1600-pound carillon made by
Mears of Whitechapel, London (makers of Big Ben's bells), from York
Factory to Saint Boniface Cathedral.

As the birchbark *canot du maître* was to the river route between
Lachine and Fort William, the York boat was to the West. Instead of
heading west on the Nelson River—the most direct but also the most
hazardous riparian route from Lake Winnipeg to York Factory, because
of the high volume of water—traders by-passed the lower Nelson by
heading inland up the Hayes River (which had only a third of the flow

of the Nelson) portages and all, and back across to the navigable portion of the Nelson as it leaves Lake Winnipeg via the Echimamish ("the river that flows both ways"). From there, when the winds were favourable, masts would be stepped, sails would be rigged, and the York boats would sail across the unpredictable northern coast of Lake Winnipeg to the outflow of the Saskatchewan River at Grand Rapids.

A hundred or so miles upstream on the Saskatchewan River through Cedar Lake brought the York boat crews to Cumberland House, the first HBC inland post, established by Samuel Hearne in 1774. From there, continuing west to the forks of the Saskatchewan River and again upstream on the north branch, there were no rapids for which portages were required all the way to Fort Edmonton, even to Rocky Mountain House. This was York boat territory, so much so that in the modern-day interpretation of the fur trade at Fort Edmonton, it is the "white man's version," not the *canot du nord*, that is featured in displays and events for visitors.

On the bicentennial of the founding of Fort Edmonton, in 1995, Tim Marriott, head of the Fort Edmonton Fur Trade Unit, organized a special York boat expedition and re-enactment, travelling with a group of ten in a 44-foot replica York boat[13] from Rocky Mountain House to Edmonton. Amid much hoopla and celebration, six, 16-foot pine oars were settled between thole-pins and secured in place with rope grommets, and the re-enactors set out on their eight-day journey. Historically, on a York boat of this size, there would be room for eight oarsmen, alternating sides, with a steersman in the stern and a bows-man to sound the river and fend off rocks and shoals in the front of the boat, but on this occasion, because of the current on the North Saskatchewan, it was felt they only needed three a side, with sounder and steersman. The crew quickly learned that there was more to running a river in a York boat than they had at first imagined.

The first problem was the rudder, which, in shallow water, kept riding up on the bottom and coming adrift from its iron pin mooring on the stern stem. And, with a ton and a half of gear, in a craft that weighed nearly 2 tons, the boat was of sufficient weight to make manoeuvering with oars a challenge. And, without a rudder, even for a short period, the boat would tend to wallow sideways in the river, exposing its flank to rocks and greatly increasing the likelihood of upset. At one point, during a rudderless moment on the river, the helmsman suggested it might be best to leapfrog the ungainly craft down the bank until such time as they could get into slower current where steering with the oars would once again be possible. Fortunately, though—and very likely in the spirit of the original Orcadian boatmen—the re-enactors worked out a technique with a sweep oar in the stern, instead of the rudder, which, with a few miles of practice, allowed them to maintain control, even in shallow water. On the occasions when the water became too shallow, causing the heavy craft to lumber to a scratchy halt on a North Saskatchewan shoal, the crew would bail out into the icy stream and walk the boat to deeper water.

Rocky Mountain House being the western limit of navigable water on the North Saskatchewan, the re-enactors never had to portage their York boat, but during conversations at the oars and at night when they camped in a riverside tipi, they speculated about what it might be like for even ten strong men to move a craft that weighed an estimated 3,500 pounds bone dry.[14] Apparently soon after these conversations, chief York-boat builder at Fort Edmonton, Joseph Isserlis, started talking about building a smaller boat, perhaps one closer to the 28-foot models that had historically been used in the western range of the York-boat domain. There was a hope, they thought, that such a boat could be moved on a portage by a crew of hearty historical re-enactors. And, a second consideration, discussed after the 44-foot model very nearly broad-sided a cliff in a tricky S-bend on the route, was that a shorter, lighter boat might be more manoeuvrable in the shifting sands and waters of the North Saskatchewan. "The forty-four-footer was so sluggish," remarked Tim Marriott. "Had we the smaller boat, it might have been more responsive."[15]

As a student of history, Tim Marriott never encountered York boats or anything like them. He remembers seeing a reproduction of Paul Kane's painting of a York-boat brigade in a textbook and thinking that it was really not something he should be concerned about, because it was so "exotic." But ending up as an interpreter at Fort Edmonton, one of the places at which the York boat was built, he learned otherwise:

It's amazing. They were in use well into the 1920s. Now they're just gone. They're totally out of the consciousness of the ordinary Canadian. It's not something you read about in history books, which is surprising because the York boat was a vital part of what the fur trade was about out here.[16]

The ultimate irony of the York boat's history takes us back to changes that occurred around the time the North West Company, and its voyageurs, merged with the HBC and its Orkney boatmen. When George Simpson took charge of the Hudson's Bay Company in 1820, and studiously began to celebrate the canoe with his antics, one of his first moves as a businessman was to adopt the York boat, where appropriate, as principal conveyance for the Hudson's Bay Company. While Simpson was roaming the country in his express canoe with piper and his "praetorian guard of Iroquois boatmen,"[17] creating colour and romance wherever he went, it was York boats that were doing the bulk of the freighting. For all its faults and failings, the York boat did yeoman's service for the fur trade, for which it has yet to receive proper recognition. D.F. Johnson offers this explanation of why that might be the case:

> Throughout most of their history, York boats operated beyond the accepted boundaries of civilization in North America, beyond the sight of journalists and writers of the Eastern establishment whose imaginations were instead captured by the "voyageurs" and the birchbark canoes of the Eastern fur trade. As a consequence, the exploits of the York boats went largely unheralded.[18]

To that, Tim Marriott adds:

> The York boat is not a canoe, but it would have to be considered a cousin of the canoe. The canoe is this wonderful, versatile, beautiful craft but there's more to the story than just the canoe. The York boat met a real need, because it gave the Hudson's Bay Company a boat that "even an

Englishman could paddle" and a cargo vessel that became
the mainstay of fur-trade transportation on the
Saskatchewan. The York boat broadens the story of water
transportation in the west ...

The York boat deserves a better knowledge, to gain some
kind of reputation. It's a beautiful thing to see in the water.
The lines are quite spectacular. And when we were fully
laden with everybody in it, rowing from Rocky Mountain
House to Edmonton, it was a beautiful sight. People
followed us from bridge to bridge, just to get another look
at this unsung piece of our history.[19]

The York boat was a product of European need in the Canadian
landscape, and although not canoe-like, at first glance it had much in
common with other craft of the fur trade. In fact, Montreal canoes and
north canoes also appeared only in response to the transportation
demands of a growing fur industry in Canada. The First Nations had
large canoes of one kind or another but nothing like the size and sheer
number of craft that ran the Voyageur Highway at the height of the fur
trade. These large canoes could only be considered "white man's
versions" as well, to the extent that they were longer, wider, deeper and
heavier than the traditional aboriginal craft made of bark and cedar. The
York boat was made to ply the exact same geography and to serve the
same commercial purpose as these freight canoes, but it was of different origins, its roots tracing back through Orkney to Scandinavia,
perhaps even to the lines and sensibilities of Viking craft.

As demonstrated by the way in which the Hudson's Bay Company
went about "waiting at the bay" and subsequently going inland in a boat
of European design, there was a certain reluctance on the part of the
English to adopt the canoe or anything else about North America in its
aboriginal form. And this sensibility only grew through the nineteenth
century as the notion of recreational boating in North America took hold
in the colonies. A late nineteenth-century reply by the editors of the
American magazine *Forest and Stream* to a request for information about
birchbark canoes for recreational purposes, illustrates this aversion of
some people of European stock to adopt the aboriginal craft:

> We are reluctant to inform our anxious inquirer that the
> birchbark canoe is not named or known in the category of
> civilized craft which our modern canoemen paddle and sail
> ... It is the peculiar toy and vehicle of the aboriginal redskin
> and although it is light and buoyant and full of poetry and
> well adapted to his requirements the palefaces are conceited
> enought to believe that they can manufacture something
> better in all respects.[20]

What the "something better" might have been in the 1870s could have been just about anything *but* a classic birchbark canoe. A *New York Times* article published at this time, entitled "The Canoe Pastime," notes that members of the New York Canoe Club had in their possession "many curious models of canoes" that were paddled or propelled by other means on the Hudson or around Long Island. There were canoes made of rivetted and soldered tin, canoes made of India rubber and even canoes made of paper, in addition to small wooden craft of various shapes and sizes. According to the newspaper, none of these non-wood canoes had really amounted to much in the eyes of the canoe-club members except the paper canoe—no relation to the paper birchbark canoe—which had impressed the gentlemen with its lightness, its rigidity, and its imperviousness to water.[21]

The paper canoe appears to be a North American invention that came onto the canoeing scene from a paper and box manufacturer 125 miles up the Hudson, in Troy, New York. The invention on which this technological development hinged was the Fourdrinier machine, which allowed paper to be made in continuous sheets. Experimenting with the possibililities for this new rolled product, George, son of Elisha Waters, the business owner, found a way to fix a leaky cedar rowing shell by gluing and varnishing portions of thick paper stock to the hull. He was so impressed with the maleability of the wet paper and the toughness of the varnished, finished product that, with the help of his father, George Waters covered his rowboat with whole layers of paper pulled from newly made rolls that were still damp, moulded them to the form of the wood and finished up with a paper mirror of the original craft with no joints, laps or seams on its surface. Moving quickly to other shapes, refining their technique as they went, by the following year the Waterses' family business was listed no longer as a box manufacturer but as a boat-making firm. By 1875, the *New York Daily Graphic* credits E. Waterses' and Sons, Paper Boat Builders, Troy, N.Y., as the "largest boat factory in the United States."[22]

What is interesting about the paper canoe is that it appeared to be lighter and stronger than any other non-Native canoe on the market at the time. This advantage was demonstrated by Nathaniel Holmes Bishop, an inveterate rambler, who had been captivated by Scotsman John MacGregor and his peregrinations through Europe in the Rob Roy canoe.[23] Bishop set out on a canoe adventure in 1874 from the Gulf of St. Lawrence, heading south along the east coast of North America in an 18-foot wooden Rob Roy–style canoe, with a pile of gear and an assistant to help him on the portages. The two men made it as far as Troy, New York, and the Waterses' boat factory, where the intrepid adventurer tried one of George Waters' impressive new canoes, summarily dismissed his assistant, abandoned his 90-pound wooden canoe, and continued on down the Hudson River to the coast and south to Florida in a brand-new 58-pound paper canoe he called "Maria Theresa." Explaining to his readers in an account of this epic journey, why paper might be just the thing from which to make a long-distance touring canoe, Bishop credits a Cornell University student who helped him understand the virtues of his new craft:

> Let us take a piece of wood and a piece of paper of the same thickness, and experiment with, use, and abuse them both to the same extent. Let the wood be of one-eighth of an inch in thickness ... Hold them up by one side, strike them with a hammer and observe the result. The wood will be cracked, to say the least: the pasteboard, whirled out of your hand, will only be dented ... Wood, being stiff and liable to split, can only be moulded into comparative form. Paper, since it can be rendered perfectly pliable, can be pressed into any shape desirable ... after which it can be water-proofed, hardened and polished.[24]

In profile, the lines of the "Maria Theresa" look like no bark canoe of the eastern woodland region of North America[25] but with stems raked at 45 degrees, a relatively straight keel and a sheer that sweeps up quite dramatically at the ends, there is a marked resemblance between Nathaniel Bishop's paper canoe and the York boat. And, as it happens, there is reason to think that these two North American craft, constructed by builders of European descent, are of common ancestry that stretches back across the Atlantic.

It turns out that another adventuresome soul who was impressed with the exploits of John MacGregor and his Rob Roy canoe was one Warrington Baden-Powell, an officer in the British Merchant Navy and brother to Robert, of scouting fame. As a sailor, Baden-Powell the elder was interested in boat design, having in his library a 1793 book of naval architecture which allowed him to place the Rob Roy in a category of vessels called "yawls," an old-time term for boats of light construction, long in form without fixed ballast, that could be sailed, rowed or paddled. This old text, referred to in an article by Baden-Powell in *Forest and Stream* magazine,[26] gave the French equivalent of yawl as "canot." Baden-Powell made connections between what he was reading and what he knew from his naval training of Viking yawls, sharp, raked ends, bold sheer and canoe-like form. Having procured a Rob Roy–style canoe and gone on some grand adventures of his own, Baden-Powell knew that to correct the one significant failing of the Rob Roy—its unseaworthiness in waves—he should take a leaf out of the Viking-yawl design handbook, and add a higher bow and stern to MacGregor's design. The result was a highly symmetrical, barely rockered canoe with high bow and stern that imparted a dramatic sheer, a design he called the "Nautilus." Records show that in 1871 members of the New York Canoe Club wrote to Warrington Baden-Powell, having heard about his new canoe design, requesting that he send along plans for "Nautilus No. 3." It may well be that, as part of the New York Canoe Club fleet, subsequent renditions of Baden-Powell's Viking/MacGregor "yawl canoe" became part of the design inspiration for George Waters and his dad up in Troy.

While the members of the New York Canoe Club were playing with canoe designs originating across the Atlantic, a classically trained shipwright in Canton, New York, J. Henry Rushton, began building small craft for use on the St. Lawrence River, specializing in so-called pulling boats, like the Adirondack guideboat and the St. Lawrence skiff. Using conventional lapstrake or clinker construction, in which longitudinal planks are overlapped from keel to gunwale, both of these boats were rowed or sailed. The guideboat was built for stability and for carrying ease on the hilly portages of upstate New York, while the skiff was built more for speed and manoeuvrability in the waters of Lake Ontario and the shifting currents of the Thousand Islands region of the St. Lawrence River. Both of these beautifully constructed wooden boats had decidedly canoe-like lines, but in appearance they were definitely much more closely related to the classic European yawl than they were to any North American aboriginal canoe design.

It was because of his growing reputation as a superb builder of these light craft that another MacGregor fan, George Washington Sears, approached Henry Rushton about building him a canoe for adventures that he had planned. Sounding like a historical version of the diminutive canoeist Bill Mason, at 5 feet, 110 pounds, Sears was too small to lug hefty Adirondack guideboats over portages. So his challenge to Rushton was to build him a wooden canoe that would weigh less than 20 pounds. It took him a few years, but Rushton fashioned an ultralight canoe he called the "Wee Lassie" that just met Sears' challenge for weight. This canoe was carvel built (planks flush, in contrast to overlapping clinker construction) with 3/16-inch planking, light ribs, no seats, and only one thwart, but it suited Sears' needs to a tee. Sears began a series of journeys around North America, writing about them under the *nom de plume* "Nessmuk," meaning "wood drake," after the name of a Narragansett Indian boy he had befriended in his youth. Sears did so much to promote Rushton's prowess as a builder of light canoes, that Rushton Boat Shop catalogues in the final decade of the nineteenth century included items Nos. 161 and 162, the Nessmuk Canoes, with a testimonial from Nessmuk himself to help a buyer decide:

> You ask what of the little canoe? and you say you think she is too small? I don't know: she was large enough to carry me (110) and forty pounds of duffle on all the Fulton lakes, on

the Moose, on Blue Mountain lake, on Raquette, Eagle—
anywhere I wanted to go. Too small for handling a *very* large
salmon, or an open contest with a deer on the lakes perhaps,
and not as comfortable as a larger, broader boat. But for a
cedar boat of 15 pounds or less, she was, and is, a marvel of
steadiness; and she is tight yet, after being paddled over 550
miles on lakes, rivers, outlets, inlets, creeks etc., and jumping her over rocks in the rapids that might have wrecked a
heavier boat.[27]

There have been many other "white man's versions of the canoe"
created since J. Henry Rushton. In 1891, for example, aluminum
became available and this material was added to the list of sheet metals
that were hot-rolled, cold-moulded, hot-rivetted, soldered, screwed,
hammered and cajoled into canoe-like shapes. Each time a new canoe
came onto the market, the imagination of the advertising copywriters
would be plumbed to come up with a reason why this craft was the
greatest thing. In 1902, the yearbook of the American Canoe
Association (founded in 1880 by George Washington Sears) contains
an advertisement for a "Galvanized Sheet Steel Indian Canoe" made by
the W.H. Mullins Company of Salem, Ohio, with two models, "14 and
16 feet long, with air tight compartments, indestructible, and durable,
also made sectional, saving half the freight, and convenient for handling
or carrying."[28]

If there was a positive spin-off from World War II, it was the refine-
ment of construction techniques for the aircraft and armament industry that translated into Plycraft canoes of laminated wood from the
Mosquito bomber plant in Montreal, Grumman canoes from the
Grumman Aircraft Company in the United States, and eventually into
a whole family of epoxy and polyester resins that could be worked into
fabric to make vehicles of any and every description, including canoes.

But what is interesting about all of this is that there are some lines that
canoeists, especially Canadians, have a very difficult time getting used to.
The York boat, in spite of its history, is not considered a canoe, although
it looks and behaves very much *like* a canoe—pointed ends, open top, no
decks, seats, thwarts, portageable (in a manner of speaking), used in the

North American fur trade. The Adirondack guideboat and the St. Lawrence skiff, with their Vikingesque lines, to many are not really canoes. And yet the decked Rob Roy canoe, which was paddled with a doubled-bladed paddle, like that used in a kayak, and the Nautilus, which was rowed, have yawl lines and are called "canoes" by people in the know.

Many traditionalists would say that anything made of sheet metal could never be called a canoe, that many of the canoes people of European descent have produced historically and are producing up to this moment are not really canoes. Bill Mason's son Paul is part of a phenomenon called "creekin" and "canoe rodeo" which involves paddling doubled-ended boats less than 10 feet long,[29] filled with airbags, through souse holes and over waterfalls that his traditionalist father would most certainly have portaged, probably painted. Are these revolutionary high-tech boats canoes?

To appreciate today's "white man's version," we must turn to an advertisement which boasts "The Canoe Redefined." The text of the ad reads as follows:

> A canoe is so much more than just a canoe. It is a part of the heritage of everyone in North America. Everyone knows how to canoe. It is a right of childhood passage. A quick paddle will bring it all back, even if you think you've never done it before.
>
> The Escape Canoe line was born out of a deeply held belief that a canoe should be more user-friendly, and more safe. And at the same time, become an object, that once seen, would touch your soul. Canoes should create passion, and grace the waters that they slice.
>
> Until now, the recreational canoe has not been improved in decades. The shape of the master canoe builders succumbed to tin cans. The tin cans gave way to bulbous sheets of plastic. The entry level canoe lost its beauty, passion and innovation. The enthusiasts say this traditional activity cannot be improved. Why can't entry level canoes become more attractive, easier to use, and safer?[30]

What the Escape Canoe Company offers, ironically, is a craft shaped just like the beautifully proportioned, gently sheered and rockered, symmetrically rounded bow and stern of the classic aboriginal canoe. The difference with this craft is that it is made of some kind of high-tech plastic that is moulded into "lightweight monocoque hull construction." The moulded plastic seats in this strange vehicle are above the waterline, so that if water splashes in around the seat, it simply returns to the lake via the drain holes in the side. Like a glori-fied surfboard with double sidewalls, this craft has many fine qualities but, as many among us would argue, it is not a canoe.

If we were to ask the question "When is a canoe not a canoe?" the answer would be quite clear. As long as the shape of a craft conforms to the curves set by the bending limits of natural birch bark and cedar, and as long as it is paddled with a single-bladed paddle, then it is a canoe in the eye of most North American beholders. In the face of more than 150 years of European attempts to better the design of the original aboriginal canoe, in spite of the fact that many of these innovations represent improvements in one dimension or other of canoe perfor-mance, and notwithstanding the fact that some canoe companies have done quite nicely with canoe-craft of European design, it is the classic lines that draw the most attention. This is unfortunate because our history—the white man's version—is not quite as uniformly uninter-esting as it may first appear. For to mount the Hayes River from Hudson Bay, as it was done when the HBC was young, it is the York boat that one must row and drag—heaven forbid!—up the knarled fingers of the sea to mountain heights.

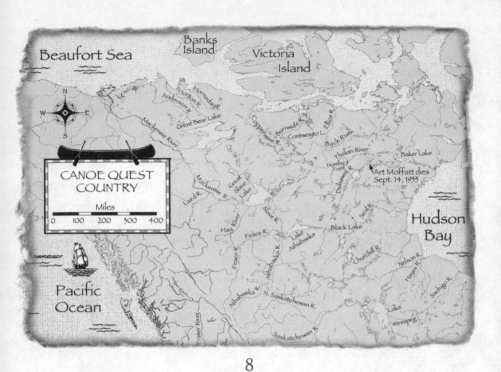

8

THE CANOE QUEST

The bugs have been terrible.
The company has been tremendous.
My husband has been tolerant.
My tan has ... what tan?
My partner is tired and techy.
I love this CANOEING!

—Sarah, Duchess of York, August 1987[1]

IN A FINISHING ROOM at the Peterborough Canoe Company plant on the site of the old Adam Scott Mill at Water and King streets in Peterborough, Ontario, an epic adventure begins. It is early 1893, and in the incandescence of bare lightbulbs accented by harsher white light reflected from frozen Otonabee River outside, a strong hand plaits thick spar varnish on the satinate hull of a sturdy 18-foot all-wood cedar canoe. Applied with the exact balance of frugality and generosity required for varnish to set but not to dribble, braided brush lines smooth to a thick, perfect coat that reflects the proud face of the finisher. Left to dry on spattered trestles beside a second sturdy and identical specimen, the canoe has a tag tied to the dry inner surface: "H.B.C. Edmonton via C.P.R.: Hold for J.B. Tyrrell, Geological Survey of Canada."

Once the finish is completely dry and hardened, the two 120-pound canoes are wrapped in burlap and crated for shipment. With other orders headed northwest, they are carriage-drawn to the Peterborough train station and loaded aboard a freight car destined for Toronto, then on to the prairies. Even wrapped, the lines of these brass-accented all-wood canoes are simple, strong, elegant—distinctive sheer with curving decks, clean entry lines, broad in the beam, ample curving chine, straight and strong along the keel. When loaded with people and gear for a northern journey, they will each carry more than a ton. And in this case, the people and gear these two Peterborough canoes will carry (along with a third made of basswood shipped west the previous year) will be Joseph Burr Tyrrell, of the Geological Survey of Canada (GSC), his younger brother James William, a civil engineer, along with brothers Pierre, Louis and Michel French, expert Iroquois canoemen from Caughnawaga, Quebec (following in the spirit of George Simpson's express paddlers), a Métis, John Flett, thought to be an excellent portager and Eskimo linguist, and, finally, two men, James Corrigal and François Maurice, of European stock engaged through the employment network of the Hudson's Bay Company.

In what became a model and precursor of many epic northern canoe journeys to follow, beginning at Edmonton on May 22, 1893, the Tyrrell party made their way north on wagons, scows and steamers past Athabasca Landing, Fort McMurray, Fort Chipewyan, and across Lake Athabasca to Fond du Lac and Black Lake, Saskatchewan, before setting their canoes in the water and heading north, without guide or map, over the divide, across the treeline, and into the unknown Barren Lands. With those hardy Peterborough canoes they paddled down the lakes and rapids of the Dubawnt River to the Thelon River, west to Baker Lake, out to the unpredictable tidal waters of Hudson Bay, and south to Fort Churchill, where the lateness of the season forced them to trade their venerable canoes for toboggans and snowshoes that took them to York Factory and eventually Winnipeg on New Year's Day of 1894.

Ostensibly, the motivations for this epic journey were scientific and exploratory in nature. Of course Samuel Hearne and his Chipewyan confrères had reported on much of this territory a century before and various other people, including the infamous John Franklin, had made exploratory journeys into the barrens, but in the middle to latter portions of the nineteenth century there appears to have been a bit of a lull in northern activity,[2] especially in what is now Nunavut, west of Hudson Bay. This is what allowed an adventuresome, Canadian-born character like J.B. Tyrrell to report to his superiors at the GSC with enthusiasm sufficient to have them underwrite a journey to document and map this region that was not well known to, at least, Canadian government brass. Although J.B., the serious brother, reported on the journey, a popular account written by younger brother J.W.[3] left readers "spellbound,"[4] not so much by the science but by the Odyssean sense of adventure that rang in the prose. Describing what they set out to do, in the opening of his book J.W. wrote:

> [J.B.] had been authorized by the Director of that most important department of the Canadian Government to conduct, in company with myself, an exploration survey through the great mysterious region of *terra incognita* common known as the Barren Lands, more than two hundred thousand square miles in extent, lying north of the 59th parallel of latitude, between Great Slave Lake and Hudson Bay. Of almost this entire territory less was known than of the remotest districts of "Darkest Africa," and, with

but few exceptions, its vast and dreary plains had never been trodden by the foot of man, save that of the dusky savage.[5]

That the Tyrrell brothers lived to tell the tale of their northern adventure is likely due in large measure more to daring, chutzpah, good luck, and to the land skills of their First Nations canoemen than it was to any kind of unusual skill or competence on their part. Nevertheless, they purposely planned an expedition, crossed the threshold from the known to the unknown in a canoe, and returned with a great story to relate. Bitten by the adventuring bug, J.W. mounted a parallel journey on the neighbouring Kazan River immediately following his return from the Dubawnt trip and, six years later, led a Dominion Lands Survey through the Keewatin, adding the entire Thelon River and lands east of Great Slave Lake to the 1900 official map of Canada. J.B. confined his further explorations with the GSC to more southerly climes, discovering, among other finds, the rich dinosaur beds of southern Alberta. What is most intriguing about their original 1893–94 canoe adventure, and J.B.'s later northern river trips, however, is the way in which these journeys captured the imaginations of others, and became the basis and inspiration of a surprising number of adventures to follow.

Just as John MacGregor's European "grand tour" in his Rob Roy canoe inspired Warrington Baden-Powell, Nathaniel Bishop and George Washington Sears ("Nessmuk"), the Tyrrell brothers became model adventurers/explorers, thanks largely to the publication of J.W.'s accounts. Their deeds, when coloured by the frosty romance of the Klondike gold rush that occurred the same year *Across the Sub-Arctics of Canada* was published, helped establish the canoe as a vehicle of quest in the Canadian context. Among those to take up this challenge were David Hanbury, who ascended the Thelon River between the months of May and October 1899, and returned to descend the same route and engage in various winter travels a couple of years later, producing a classic article and popular book about his adventures.[6] Another was George Mellis Douglas, who led a remarkable trip to the Coppermine River in 1911, to investigate the possible mineral potential of that region. Like the Toronto-born Tyrrells,

Douglas was from Lakefield, Ontario, and, instead of relying exclusively on watercraft he might find in the Northwest, he took care to secure and ship west two classic 18-foot all-wood canoes from craftsmen in his home town. According to historian Shelagh Grant:

> He took great pride in his selection of boats—here the more romantic side of the competent organizer emerges. The two 18-foot canoes were handbuilt in Lakefield from specially selected wood "by men who took a keen personal interest in their work." One was christened *Polaris* after the North Star, the other *Procyon*, a star of the first magnitude in the constellation Canis Minor. [A] freight canoe purchased in Edmonton was built by the Peterborough Canoe Company of longitudinal basswood strips with close ribs and rigged with a lug sail [this may well have been a craft identical to the Tyrrells' third canoe, which was also purchased in Edmonton]. This craft was named *Aldebaran*, also a star of the first magnitude, the eye of Taurus. [A] York boat acquired to transport the heavy load of supplies up the Great Bear River was called *Jupiter* after the largest planet in the solar system.[7]

Douglas's notion of naming his craft imparts decidedly mythic overtones to later accounts of his quest—*Aldebaran*, *Procyon*, and *Polaris* evoking the best of the ancient sojourner, Jason, and the famous ship *Argo*. His book *Lands Forlorn*[8] has become a classic in the literature of canoeing.

Most notorious of all descendants of the Tyrrell questing spirit was an English friend of George Douglas's, John Hornby, who amply demonstrated that an epic quest can become tragic without notice in a land of short summers and slim margins. As it happened, John Hornby and his associate, James Cosmo Dobrée Melville, son of a wealthy English cotton merchant, were camped below the village of Fort Norman, on the Mackenzie River, on the morning of July 5, 1911, when Douglas and his celestial livery of canoes arrived on a big smelly steamer named after the river. Melville made quite a good impression on Douglas as they breakfasted together on the Mackenzie

River, taking time to draw the newcomer a map of canoe routes linking Great Bear Lake with the Coppermine River. Hornby, by contrast,
made Douglas suspicious. Historian George Whalley describes the
meeting this way:

> Hornby made on Douglas no very prepossessing impression.
> Small, fidgety, voluble, 'just like a monkey,' he chattered,
> pouring out incoherent conversation. He gave facetious or
> misleading answers to Douglas's perfectly grave questions,
> and seemed to know nothing accurate or certain about the
> country he had spent nearly three years in. Worst of all he
> kept dipping filthy fingers into the sugar bowl to the grow-
> ing annoyance of Captain Mills.[9]

In contrast to the meticulously organized and prepared Douglas,
Hornby and his associates over the years were anything but, always
suffering privation and usually existing in squalid camps, ill-clothed and
usually hungry. Always the wanderer, Hornby used copies of J.W.
Tyrrell's maps to move from Great Bear Lake to lands east of Great
Slave Lake in the years following his encounter with Douglas at Fort
Norman. By the autumn of 1924, having nearly starved to death innu-
merable times, Hornby was resolved to continue and to make a living
by trapping the valuable white fox in lands north and east of Artillery
Lake, on the edge of the Barren Lands. Hornby had also managed to
secure a modest arrangement with the Northwest Territories and
Yukon Branch of the Canadian government to make observations of
caribou migration and musk oxen of the upper Thelon and in the
McKay Lake area, which included provisions and a small stipend to
finance his continuing adventure. He teamed up with Captain James
Charles Critchell-Bullock, a naturalist of sorts, and his two canoes,
Yvonne and *Matonnabee* (which appear in photographs to be canvas-
covered craft). Hornby and his new companion carried canoes and gear
up Pike's Portage, linking Great Slave Lake and Artillery Lake, and
paddled north, settling eventually in a grotty little cave dug into the
side of an esker in the vicinity of the Lockhart River at the north end of
Artillery Lake. In no time at all, the two of them were living among a

delicate amalgam of green hides, fox innards, caribou blood, mixed into the dark, damp and cold recesses of a windowless enclosure heated with a small, smoky tin stove for which, because of their location, there was precious little fuel wood.

By late December, their canoes now buried in drifts of snow outside their esker home, Hornby headed south to Fort Reliance for supplies and left his beleaguered companion "in a state of abject misery and self-pity," his only companion a dog with a frostbitten paw that was becoming gangrenous. In a gem from the annals of the Canadian adventuring literature, Critchell-Bullock mused about his Yuletide situation in his journal:

> Alone this Christmas Eve on the Barren Lands of the Sub-Arctic of America, when those outside are contemplating the morrow with hearts full of happiness and pleasurable excitement. Alone in a dug-out beneath the sand and snow when but one thousand miles away home are alight with fairy lights and decorated with those little frills pertinent to Christmastide. Alone in this awful shack of continual discomfort with its subsiding walls and crazy roof likely at any moment to fall and entomb me in a living grave. Alone with sufficient wood to make only one more fire. Alone with a dying dog whose foot is stinking with decay consequent on frost bite ... Can a man without empirical knowledge of such unhappiness possibly grasp the full meaning of what all this means to me and teaches. I cannot believe it. Such is the penalty of attempting the so-called impossible ...[10]

Drawn further into the Barren Lands by Tyrrell's map, having miraculously survived another winter and wanting to make good on their promise to the Government of Canada to investigate the caribou and muskox populations east of Great Slave Lake, in May 1925, Hornby and Critchell-Bullock headed east, across country to Campbell Lake and into the headwaters of the Hanbury River. The good ship *Yvonne* did not survive the winter, so it was their other canoes, *Matonnabee* and the basswood freight canoe, they dragged across rotting ice and spring eskers, with the help of four dogs and travelling mostly at night, until reaching open, moving water on the lower Hanbury River after about a month's heavy hauling.

As seems to happen on all epic quest journeys, talk on this two-canoe, two-man expedition turned eventually to fantasies about food. Writing about this, George Whalley compares the food fantasies of these two adventures with "the meals desired with a poignant and hallucinatory intensity by Scott and his party when they were dying on their way home from the South Pole only a few years earlier."[11] Detailed in Critchell-Bullock's journal, in the middle of their Thelon River canoe trip, inspired by a steady diet of fish, caribou and simple bannock, the two men thought that these menus would break the monotony and tedium of the trail:

HORNBY
One magnum best Heidseick
Salmon mayonnaise
Egg soufflé
Roast pheasant and chips

Mince pies
Preserved assorted fruits
Ice cream
Cheese
Coffee
Crackers
Hot Rolls

BULLOCK
Roast dressed pheasant
Mashed potatoes
Best brandy trifle
Assorted crystallised fruits
Ice cream and sponge fingers
Stilton

Turkish coffee
Nuts
Marsala[12]

Apparently, at some point during this discussion about high-life food, which occurred while the two men were storm-stayed on the banks of the Thelon River, Hornby told his companion that the meanest eating he had ever done was eating bannock made from flour on which a skunk had squirted. Food was of such consequence to Hornby, as a result of his northern experience, that he decided somewhere along the way that one day he would write a book about his adventures entitled *The Land of Feast and Famine*. The irony of this, as history would show, is that the book was never written. One sidebar to the Thelon canoe trip with Critchell-Bullock, however, was the report that Hornby eventually submitted to the Canadian government which initiated the establishment of the Thelon Game Sanctuary. In an uncharacteristically pre-emptive frame of mind, Hornby wrote in a now-famous piece of text in the Canadian conservation canon:

> The results of this trip show that there is a large uninhabited area where musk ox are plentiful, swans and geese nest, and caribou have their young[13] undisturbed by man. This wooded area possesses no minerals, containing only sandstone and sand, consequently can afford no inducement or excuse for men to go on a prospecting trip. If it is desired to protect the game in this part of the country it is essential to take measures to prevent traders form encouraging natives to hunt in this district. A few years, perhaps, it will be too late.[14]

But it was not conservation that really motivated John Hornby, it was adventure—canoe adventure in particular—in which he could exercise ultimate brinkmanship with the forces of nature. Returning to England after his first Thelon River trip, with his tales and his offhand, iconoclastic manner, he entered the world of his seventeen-year-old cousin, Edgar Christian, as a larger-than-life hero. And Hornby's stories of survival and unspeakable hardship at Great Bear Lake, in the esker with Critchell-Bullock and, later, on the Thelon caught not only young Edgar's attention but the notice of Edgar's parents as well. When the possibility of Edgar accompanying Hornby on another grand Thelon canoe adventure emerged, the teen was understandably over-the-moon and his parents were convinced that such a quest would "give the boy something to build his life on."[15] What Marguerite and Colonel Christian did not know, because Hornby never cast his own adventures in anything but the rosy glow of ultimate success, was that he was a dangerous person to travel with. He didn't like to plan and thought if he had survived his various scrapes and near-misses then he and anyone accompanying him would do the same. And so it was that John Hornby, now in his mid-forties with more than twenty years' experience in the North, returned to Canada with young Edgar Christian in tow, sailing from Liverpool on the SS *Montrose* in April 1926.

Crossing Canada by train, they picked up a third member for their party, an old friend of Hornby's and an ex–Royal Air Force pilot named Harold Adlard, twenty-seven, ostensibly as a companion for Edgar. The three of them made their way north from Edmonton by train, and then by various motorized means to Fort Reliance before heading up Pike's Portage toward the Thelon River under their own steam. All along the way, in the tradition of a British prep school boy, Edgar wrote copious letters to his family that detailed his continuing excitement and occasional disbelief at his good fortune to be heading into the unknown hinterland with "Uncle Jack." And, once they had followed J.W. Tyrrell's map, now modified by Hornby's previous experience in the area, into the headwaters of the Hanbury River and down the Thelon to a place Hornby knew there was enough wood to build a cabin, Edgar started keeping a journal that came to contain one of the most macabre tales imaginable.

The short version of the story is that Hornby had once again gone into the Barren Lands ill-prepared, blithely assuming that they would be overrun by caribou and musk oxen and that they would live out the winter, hunting, gorging, and telling stories around a hot stove. The musk oxen were, as it turned out, somewhere else. And, by the time the three men arrived sometime in late summer at the double-bend in the river where they built their tiny cabin, the caribou migration had come and gone as well. Meagre rations quickly dwindled. They spent the winter trying to trap animals and fish but with little success. For a time, they were able to dig discarded fish and animals' entrails out of the snow and eat those, but these thin soups eventually gave way to ground-up bones and animal hair that bunged up their insides. Hornby died first, of starvation, on April 17, 1927—just about the time the federal government was getting ready to pass the order-in-council that established the Thelon Game Sanctuary. Adlard was next, on May 4, leaving eighteen-year-old Christian to contemplate an uncertain future. On what may have been June 2, he wrote:

> 9 a.m. Weaker than Ever. have Eaten all I Can have food on hand but heart peatering? Sunshine is bright now see if that does any good to me if I get out & bring in wood to make fire to night.
> Make *preparations* now.
> Got out too weak & all in now. Left Things Late.[16]

Whatever else Edgar Christian did in his last living hours, his preparations included writing to his father on a sheet of stationery he had saved from the Windsor Hotel in Montreal a year earlier. He wrote:

> Dear Father,
> My address is not the above but I hope that this find you one day.
> Jack Hornby always wished to see this country sometime before he gave up his life in Arctic Regions & wanted someone with him & I was the one this time I realize why he wanted a boy of my age with him and I realize why one other should come in order to make sure I got out safe, but alas the Thelon is not what it is cracked up to be I dont think. I have now been trying to struggle by myself for over a month & help my other poor pal but spring is late here and I cannot get fresh meat although have always had food to eat at times some jolly good meals only a few days ago which did

not put me in condition to hunt fresh food but the weather
blew cold & to-day June 1st has seen me with fine weather
food but not fresh and unable to get fresh being too weak &
played out.

Adamson Corona Hotel Edmonton finds two trunks of
mine. In one that 'Bible & Prayer Book' which Jack refused
to let me bring. Do not be annoyed but I know why now and
Jack alone was one man in this world who can let a young
boy know what this world and the next are. I loved him and
he loves me. Very seld is there true love between 2 men!

> Bye Bye now. Love
> & Thanks for all
> you have Ever done for
> me Edgar.[17]

In a final heroic act, before he, too, died of starvation, perhaps antic-
ipating the future significance of their story, Edgar Christian took his
diary and his letters and placed them inside the cold metal stove,
thereby protecting them from the elements. On another slip of paper,
placed on top of the stove he wrote the words "WHO LOOK IN
STOVE." With that, he lay down on his bunk in khaki shirt, grey flannel trousers with a silk handkerchief for a belt, a scarf around his neck,
winter moccasins and puttees, pulled up two red Hudson's Bay
Company blankets over his head and died.

The following summer, 1928, a party of prospectors saw a canoe by
the river and stopped to investigate.[18] They found the shrouded skele-
tons of Hornby and Adlard outside the run-down log cabin, and
inside, when someone touched the ten-point blankets on the lower
berth, as the story goes, a skull rolled out one end and foot bones skit-
tered like dice across the cold earthen floor. A year after that, alerted
by the prospecting party, a detail from the Royal Canadian Mounted
Police canoed in to bury the remains and conduct a formal investigation. It was the police who found Christian's faded note on the stove
that led them inside to his diary and its shocking contents. The diary
was published nine years later by John Murray Limited in London,
England, entitled *Unflinching: A Diary of Tragic Adventure*, a

cautionary tale that captivated armchair and other adventurers throughout the English-speaking world.[19]

Not surprisingly, interest in recreational canoe adventuring on the Barren Lands waned in the thirty years following the Hornby disaster.[20] And, when another trip was organized in the early 1950s, this time entering the Thelon River valley from the south via the Dubawnt River, in strange and portentous ways it was informed by the experiences of the Tyrrell brothers and by the demise of John Hornby, Harold Adlard and Edgar Christian. This next trip was organized by Arthur Moffatt, an adventurer and writer who was about the same age as Hornby when he died. In addition, a fact that may shed light on just what it was that Art Moffatt might have been searching for on his northern quest: he had been hardened during World War II as an American attached to the British Eighth Army in Africa, carrying dead and wounded back from the front, for the duration of the conflict. Hornby had also done military service, and the connection between military service and high-test canoe adventure is not as unlikely as it might at first seem—both in their own way building character in circumstances of limited control, adventure being what philosopher William James called "the moral equivalent of war." Whatever his motivation, whether it be to replicate something of the awe he held for the Tyrrell exemplar or to recapture something of the positive essence of his war experience, sometime in 1953–54 Art Moffatt decided that he needed to retrace the Tyrrell route across the Barren Lands and began recruiting volunteers. It was to be an ultimate adventure, described by Moffatt in the trip prospectus this way:

> The canoe route from Lake Athabasca over the Great Barren Grounds to Chesterfield Inlet on Hudson Bay was first explored by Dr. J.B. Tyrrell of the Canadian Geological Survey in 1893. With his brother and six Indian canoemen, Dr. Tyrrell left on July 2. Almost two and a half months

later, after running scores of dangerous rapids, the party reached the coast.

Since Dr. Tyrrell's exploration of the route, no other party has made the trip. We will be the first all-white party ever to make the trip. In our journey north we will pass into the hunting and trapping grounds of the Chipewyan Indians and out onto the Barren Ground, beyond the northern limit of trees. This is the summer range of the vast herds of caribou. The lakes and streams are reported to be full of trout up to 25 pounds in weight ...

Two of the major problems we shall face are food and fire. The greater part of the route is through the treeless tundra, and what fuel there is is often too green or wet to burn. We will not be able to pack enough gas to cook two meals a day.

Food may be even more acute. I have a letter from Dr. Tyrrell ... He writes: "You will need to have a couple of high-powered rifles so that you can shoot game at long range, otherwise starvation is likely to threaten the trip ...

To conclude, the hardships we face, besides those already mentioned, are bad weather, unbelievable swarms of mosquitoes and black flies and the lack of fire. Always we face the possibility of illness, accident or starvation 500 miles from help.[21]

With this prospectus and some old-fashioned charisma, Moffatt (thirty-six) was able to assemble an expedition of six, including Skip Pessl (twenty-two) and Peter Franck (nineteen) who had canoed the Albany River with Moffatt after the war, Bruce LeFavour (twenty-one) and Joe Lanouette (twenty) recruited from Dartmouth College in New Hampshire, and a friend of a friend, George Grinnell (twenty-two) who was coming out of a two-year stint in the American Army and looking for a new adventure.

In the spring of 1955, each of the participants was asked to contribute $200 for a half-share in an 18-foot Chestnut Prospector canoe, and an equivalent sum to grubstake food for the three-month expedition. On June 25 of that year, the crew assembled with their gear on the dusty airstrip at Stony Rapids, Saskatchewan, on the Fond-du-Lac River at the east end of Lake Athabasca. Like the Tyrrells, sixty-two years earlier, they reached this northern departure point via "public transport," only in this case instead of trains, scows and York boats, the Moffatt crew had lumbered north in scheduled DC-3 aircraft, proven in World War II, and in the process of becoming the transportation workhorses of the Canadian North.

Following the Tyrrells' route, they made their way from Stony Rapids to Black Lake, and up the Chipman River toward the height of land at Selwyn Lake. The scope and intensity of the challenge they had taken on tightened around the Moffatt party almost as they came closer and closer to the divide that would commit them to running downstream on the Dubawnt River into the unknown Barren Lands. Participant George Grinnell describes how his perception of the adventure changed as they approached this turning point in the trip:

> Up to this point, I had thought of the trip as a kind of interlude between two cocktail parties; one before the trip and the other at the end of the trip in which I would have, at last, something to talk about. I had imagined myself making sacrifices on the trip, like not eating for two or three weeks and other such heroics, but all of a sudden I was terrified, and I did not think cocktail party conversation was all that important any more.[22]

Suddenly for Grinnell, and presumably the others, reality dawned. There were ways a person could die in the wilderness. A person could break a bone, succumb to a latent disease, get appendicitis, pass kidney stones, suffer hypothermia, run out of food, or upset and drown in a rapid. They could starve. They could die. And, as Grinnell tells the story, this frightening realization manifested itself in a certain brooding reticence the night before the trip crossed the height of land. The six of them sat quietly around the fire, slurping down their steaming bowls of Spam-and-macaroni stew—thinking. Maybe thinking about the Tyrrells and how, in earlier days, before airplanes or topographic maps, they had completed the trip safely. It was Bruce LeFavour who finally broke the silence by asking Moffatt to tell the crew a story. The story he told? What else but the tale of John Hornby. Knowing the resonance between what they were doing and where they were relative to the setting of the story, and eyeing a chance to draw some lessons for his young expedition mates, Moffatt likely unravelled an unabridged version, complete with details of slow starvation, homemade devices to administer warm-water enemas to relieve lower bowels impacted with skin, bone and animal hair—a good story, dressed, and seasonally adjusted for a band of young adventurers about to cross the threshold of the Barrens.

What the members of this pioneering recreational canoe trip of the modern era could not have known as they heard the grisly details of the deaths of Hornby and company was that in two months less two days one of their number—their leader, Arthur Moffatt—would be dead on the tundra as well, from exposure and cold following an upset in the rapids of the lower Dubawnt River. On September 14, 1955, the party inadvertently floundered onto a series of ledges. In a series of events that went from bad to worse in less time than it takes for cold water to knock the wind out of a startled paddler on immersion, Moffatt and his partner Joe Lanouette swamped and upset. Grinnell and his partner Peter Franck also swamped but were able to get to shore, empty their canoe and quickly paddle back to rescue Moffatt and Lanouette. But as soon as Grinnell reached from his bow position in the empty canoe to pull a pack from the river, he lost his balance and their canoe was swamped for a second time. The third canoe containing Skip Pessl and Bruce LeFavour also swamped but these two were able to put together the rudiments of a rescue and restoration plan. The events that ensued involved a desperate attempt by six wet and freezing paddlers to draw each other one by one back from the brink of death. Numbed by cold, fingers like mitts, limbs like unresponsive logs, precious core heat ebbing away with every movement, they eventually got to shore, struggled to change and to set up camp and to warm each other skin to skin. For Moffatt, who had been in the water the longest, it was too late.

In the years following Moffatt's death, having very nearly died himself, George Grinnell tried to come to terms with what had happened that fateful summer. Work as he might to write about the summer of 1955, and put it behind him once and for all, the beleaguered Grinnell could not. Eventually, he was beset by another canoe disaster. In 1984, Grinnell's two grown sons perished in a storm as they tried to paddle along the coast of James Bay from Fort Albany to Moosonee at the end of their Albany River canoe trip. But in the years following these events, Grinnell persisted with his search to find meaning in these hard lessons. In 1988, he published an article in a popular canoeing magazine entitled "Art Moffatt's Wilderness Way to Enlightenment."[23] In 1995, he spoke publicly about his Dubawnt experience at the Wilderness Canoeing Symposium in Toronto, and again for CBC Radio's "Ideas" program. And, in an act of continuing courage, Grinnell finally published a full account of the deaths of Art Moffatt and his sons in a 1996 book called *Death on the Barrens*. This remarkable volume, unlike anything else in the non-fictional literature of canoeing, includes the details of his own near death on the tundra beside his leader. In a particularly poignant description of the Dubawnt scene, Grinnell recounts an encounter between himself and Skip Pessl that demonstrates the power of the place—the North—to transcend even death on a canoe trip:

> When Skip came near, I smiled up at him; but instead of smiling back, he looked down at the ground as if at a loss for words. I thought he was preparing another lecture on "group consideration and altruistic behavior," but he was looking for other phrases.
>
> Finally, he said: "You were right all along, George" [referring to a disagreement about whether the rapid was shootable in canoe].
>
> "I have never been right about anything in my entire life," I replied.
>
> "At 'the moment of truth' I had always thought I would have done the courageous thing."
>
> I looked at him with a puzzled expression on my face.
>
> "If I had not called out, you would have rescued Art first."
>
> "We picked you and Bruce because your canoe was in current."

"I should not have called out," he repeated.

"I should not have crawled into Bruce's sleeping bag."

He paused, then looked down: "I just came over to thank you for saving my life."

"You are welcome. Thank you for saving mine," I replied. Art lay dead on the tundra next to us.

"It is because of me, not you, that Art is dead," he said and turned away. Then he paused and turned toward the sun. "I can understand why 'primitive' people worshipped the sun."

The wilderness around us filled us both with awe. On the one hand, we were terrified of it: on the other hand, its beauty elevated us to a plateau of sublime peace.

Skip spent the remainder of the day knocking the ice off the other people's clothing, drying everything on his own body.[24]

What is fascinating about Grinnell's three accounts of his Dubawnt River trip is that they all focus on different aspects of the learning. In the book he describes the immediate response to his own near death, and Moffatt's passing in the vignette with Skip Pessl. But he also chooses to relate a story of the first meal the five survivors shared as Moffatt lay dead on the tundra. Peter Franck had cooked a can of corn-meal mush. Earlier in the trip there had been much bickering and jockeying at mealtimes about who scooped how much from the dinner pots, but on this occasion there was new magnanimity of spirit and cooperation amid communion overtones with Moffatt's passing. Grinnell writes:

What we had all learned was that there are things more frightening than death. What we passed around that night was more than just a can of lumpy mush. "Take, eat; this is my body which is given for you: do this in remembrance of me ..."

When the corn meal was gone, Peter passed in a package of Velveeta cheese. I handed it to Skip. He took out Art's hunting knife and sliced the cheese into six equal pieces and then passed them around for us to choose, as was his

custom. When the cheese came back to him, he picked up
the fifth piece, and we all stared at the sixth remaining piece.
Art lay outside. We all wondered if we should bring him into
the tent with us and give him his piece of cheese, even
though he was now dead.[25]

By contrast, in the magazine account he dwells more on the legacy
of his own near demise, writing: "during one of my periods of uncon-
sciousness, I thought about the meaning of life and death, and I asked
myself if I believed in God, and I decided I probably did not."[26] And
that other-worldly sense of spirituality is extended when he speaks
about the same circumstances on the radio:

We all came close to freezing to death. I can remember passing out from the cold several times, and having pleasant
dreams. The pleasant dreams would revive my will to live. I
had time to reflect, in these sober moments, on what it
meant to die. I thought, would I like not to have been on
the trip, but to have stayed in civilization and live? Or to
have been on the trip and die right then and there? I was
hoping to die, because freezing to death is, after all, a very
painful process. I'd hoped to pass out, but that's the easy
way out. I'd hoped to go crazy, and that hadn't worked. It
wasn't until I really wanted to die that I was able to pass out
and have these pleasant dreams.

But the point was that I had gotten to the point where I
really wanted to die ... I can't explain why I was so happy.
But to me it was that we had killed a lot of caribou, and the
caribou had become one of us; and we had gotten into a
relationship with the natural world, and death was not the
separation. The separation was the separation from civilization, and it was a separation that I was very happy [about].

But what I would mourn was the separation from nature,
from this relationship we had gotten into: with the caribou
and the fish and the mushrooms, with the weather, with the
beautiful lakes and rivers, with the sky. This was a relationship

that it would have been death to be separated from. But it wasn't separation to die, if you can see what I mean.[27]

Queen's University Professor of Religion William C. James has argued that it is the heroic quest[28] that links people like Art Moffatt and George Grinnell to those who have gone before—from Odysseus to J.B. Tyrrell—in the classic pattern of preparation, separation, tribulation and return. For those who survive, there are lessons learned through the trials of afar that are brought back home for the betterment of all. Art Moffatt's death, in the end, empowers the narrative of the Dubawnt River adventure in a literary dimension. We listen to George Grinnell not only because he has a good tale to tell, but because in his canoe he crossed to another world in which one of his party carried on over the ultimate threshold

Besides Art Moffatt, John Hornby, Harold Adlard and Edgar Christian, in the literature of canoeing is a host of other unfortunate characters who have died questing for adventure of one kind or another. Most notorious of all was Sir John Franklin's ill-fated expedition by canoe down the Coppermine River, along the coast and back south via river and land to Fort Enterprise, on which a record ten men died in the final six weeks of the trip. Junius, Eskimo translator, canoeman: vanished September 27, 1821, without crossing the Coppermine River; Mathew Pelonquin, voyageur: unable to keep up, left behind after Obstruction Rapids on October 6; Registe Vaillant, voyageur: collapsed, left behind October 7; Ignace Perrault, voyageur: collapsed, left behind October 8; Antonio Fontano, Italian voyageur: collapsed, left behind October 8; Gabriel Beauparlant, voyageur: collapsed at Round Rock Lake while looking for Indians with Back's party, left behind October 16; Michel Terohaute, Iroquois voyageur: shot by Richardson on October 23 (thought to have shot and eaten flesh from Belanger or Perrault); Joseph Peltier, voyageur: died of malnutrition after the Franklin party reached Fort Enterprise, November 1; François Samandre, voyageur: died of malnutrition at Fort Enterprise, November 2.[29] And there are others: adventurer Leonidas Hubbard (1903);[30] artist Tom Thomson (1917); the eleven youths who died after falling from a canoe into Balsam Lake (1926); journalist Blair

Fraser (1963); the dozen schoolboys and a teacher who died in the frigid waters of Lake Temiskaming (1978); Sandy Host and Betty Eamer, who died in 1984 on James Bay with George Grinnell's sons—and the list goes on. But as Margaret Atwood points out, these deaths may be a necessary feature of the experience of the Canadian landscape and to acknowledge them in one's quest is to embrace a condition of participation in a country where wilderness can reign supreme. However tragic, canoe deaths gird the continuing significance of the canoe trip in Canadian experience. To leave home and travel by canoe on a northern river—the more barren the better—is to return a hero because, as Atwood writes:

> Every culture has its exemplary dead people, its hagiography of landscape martyrs, those unfortunates who, by their bad ends, seem to sum up in one grisly episode what may be lurking behind the next rock for all of us, all of us who enter the territory they once claimed as theirs.[31]

And so, when one reads the accounts of northern canoe trips, there is invariably acknowledgement of the heroic tradition via citation and reference to those who have gone before. The Tyrrells acknowledge Hearne and Franklin. Hornby uses the Tyrrells' map. The Hornby story is told at a pivotal point in the Moffatt journey. And, when Eric Morse, the acknowledged "father" of modern-day canoe tripping, decides to head to the Barrens in 1962, he continues the tradition. In his memoirs of planning this excursion, Morse writes:

> In the Arctic Institute in Montreal, and also in my own library, I read all the accounts I could find of canoe and overland travel in the area of the Hanbury and Thelon—J.W. Tyrrell, Critchell-Bullock, Hanbury, and others—but only Tyrrell gave enough detail to be useful to us in navigation. The Tyrrell brothers, J.B. and J.W., were the last of our Canadian explorers and their epic journeys in 1893 and the early 1900s had included the route we took, down the Hanbury and Thelon to Hudson Bay.

Another indication of the novelty of our plan was the concern of the RCMP. Superintendent Bill Fraser, then in charge of the northern division and himself a legendary dog-team traveller, seemed worried for our safety. He was adamant that we should take firearms for protection and insisted on alerting the relevant police detachments along our route.

With all of these portents, we took extra care over our preparations. Pam [Morse's wife], a born worrier, spent sleepless nights reviewing her food lists after reviewing Edgar Christian's *Unflinching*, the poignant story of the slow death by starvation of himself and his two companions in 1927, on the very river we were to travel.[32]

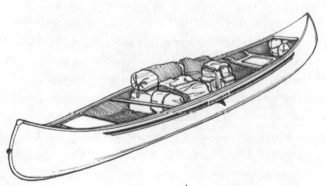

Grumman Aluminum tripping canoe, 17 feet

Although death seems necessarily a part of the canoe-tripping quest, more recent canoe-trip narratives do not seem to be limited exclusively to the monomythic notion of quest as tragedy.[33] In 1977, a group of adventurers entered the Thelon River valley by canoe, hoping to mark the fiftieth anniversary of Hornby's death by overwintering near Lookout Point and paddling out the following year. Having chosen this remote wilderness context for their canoe quest, these intrepid canoeists hoped to live in harmony with nature and without undue interference from the so-called civilized world. Unfortunately, it was at this exact location, fifty years after John Hornby's untimely death, that the errant Soviet satellite *Cosmos 954* crash-landed, bringing the full force of the Canadian and American military into the Thelon area. Having found bits of the satellite, the adventurers found themselves secured in their cabin by armed commandos before being whisked out to Edmonton for radiation tests, and returned, bewildered if not amused, by these rapid transitions.

Christopher Norment, one of the members of this unfortunate Hornby fiftieth-anniversary trip, writes that their trip was informed by the travels of David Hanbury and the Tyrrells and that (putting a bright spin on the *Cosmos* debacle) the satellite "forced us to confront much of what we had sought to escape." But in his book about the trip, *In the North of Our Lives,* Norment hangs onto the notion of wilderness seeking:

> So where is the all-out struggle against fierce river, bitter cold, and voracious insects? Mostly in other books. What's worth the telling lies elsewhere—in part, along the route of an interior journey that paralleled our travels through the vast northern wilderness. There were many aspects to this quest, but three seem most prominent. First, the duration of the expedition gave us the opportunity to become intimately familiar with the land ... and strip away some of the barriers that Industrial Man ... erects between himself and the earth. Second, a group of novices inexperienced in the North envisioned a goal, traveled out into the Barrens, and survived in reasonably good style. Third, six people mostly unknown to each other before the journey began spent more than a year in isolation and emerged still on speaking terms. The lessons that we learned (or failed to learn) about cooperation and communication should have a range of applicability that extends beyond the confines of the journey.[34]

Christopher Norment spoke at the Wilderness Canoeing Symposium in Toronto soon after completing his book and told a slightly different, and even funnier, story. He reported that, in proper military fashion, joint commanders of the satellite clean-up effort—called "Operation Morning Light"— dropped bulldozers from cargo aircraft to clear ice runways and created an instant camp for hundreds of military searchers. Into "Camp Garland" were flown all manner of experts to see to it that the situation was put right. Some of these personnel were put in charge of Norment's crew, while others tended to a variety of tasks on the land and in the camp. Reports about his experience from the military person's perspective were of an operation conducted in a hostile and unforgiving wilderness—impenetrable darkness, unspeakable cold, isolation like nowhere on earth. Norment, by contrast, recalled settling back into their log cabin, after the trip to Edmonton to be checked for radiation poisoning, and watching the proceedings. They even visited Camp Garland and, in a neighbourly sort of way, appreciated just how ferocious were the dragons the solders had to confront on their clean-up quest. "As far as I was concerned," quipped Norment, "the worst thing those people had to cope with was an outbreak of crabs in the portable showers."

Fictional accounts of the Hornby story have a similarly wry and ironic twists to them. Novelist Thomas York secured a government grant in the early 1970s to investigate the economic potential of gathering the valuable *qiviut* (underfur) of the musk ox from the bushes in the Thelon River valley. At the end of this $10,000 canoe adventure, he produced 2 pounds of the cashmere-like fibre, which were duly filed in a Yellowknife bureaucrat's desk drawer, but in labour of more lasting substance he went on to write *Snowman* (1976) and *The Musk Ox Passion* (1978), both of which draw substantially on the legend of John Hornby in anything but tragic terms. The latter of these two novels explores the whole nature of the Barrens as a venue for the playing out of dreams, real and imagined. Although not as dramatic as Conrad's classic, *Heart of Darkness*, there is much in York's work to reinforce the "otherness" of the Canadian North, as foreign and forbidding in some respects as any jungle or hidden mountain range. Theatrical plays,[35] radio dramas[36] and other novels[37] have been written about the Hornby story, and each, in its own way, amplifies and enriches the mystique of the Thelon River valley.

The "ultimate adventure" is not a phenomenon that occurs during the physical passage from the known to the unknown and back, but in the journey of the imagination that occurs before, during and after the tangible encounter with bugs, wind, rapids and weather. But one must point out that there is the journey in the imagination of the adventurer, and then there is the journey in the imagination of the followers of the adventurer, the readers of the adventure-quest literature. It is this inner journey on which the potency of the canoeing quest is founded and it is the ethos arising from these imagined journeys, as they make their way into public consciousness and add layer upon layer to the foundation of history. The adventurer becomes a participant in history, not a bystander, as he or she embraces Tyrrell, Hornby, Hanbury, Moffatt or Grinnell and heads into the Thelon River valley (or wherever) by canoe. But so, too, does the consumer of these stories make a tangible link to history by reading these accounts and, more importantly, by linking to these accounts by canoeing in less forbidding places.

In a country where the same routes paddled by the explorers are in many cases, especially in the North, in the identical wild condition as they were one, two or three centuries ago, the imagined journey happens without provocation. In a land where the most appropriate vehicle today is exactly the same as the most appropriate vehicle historically, this lends potency to the quest. The myth underlying the canoe quest is one of seeking.

In his classic essay about canoe-tripping, written after an extended trip on the Harricanaw River in 1941, Pierre Trudeau probes into the notion of personality development as legacy of the canoe quest. He writes:

> I would say that you return not so much a man who reasons more, but a more reasonable man. For, throughout this time, your mind has learned to exercise itself in the working conditions which nature intended. Its primordial role has been to sustain the body in the struggle against a powerful universe. A good camper knows that it is more important to be ingenious than to be a genius. And conversely, the body, by demonstrating the true meaning of

182

sensual pleasure, has been of service to the mind ... Purely physical is the joy which the fire spreads through the palm of your hands and the soles of your feet while your chattering mouth belches the poisonous cold. The pleasurable torpor of such a moment is perhaps not too different from what the mystics of the East are seeking. At least it has allowed me to taste what one respected gentleman used to call the joys of hard living.[38]

Trudeau is actually an instructive example of a variety of ways in which the legacy of the canoeing quest can inform subsequent endeavours. Canoeing was central to not only his image of himself but also to the image he projected publicly.[39] On the sad occasion of Trudeau's son Michel's accidental avalanche death in November of 1998, for example, veteran journalist, Roy MacGregor wrote:

> Michel had chosen, as his own father once had, to "test his strength against the strength of the country." A lifetime earlier, Pierre Trudeau took on the mighty rapids of the Peace River and even a paddle to Cuba—and lived to brag about it ... They shared an attraction for wilderness, a need both to test oneself and to come to understand oneself. It is a peculiarity, a rite of passage even, more for those born to privilege than for those born to the bush itself, but this makes it no less valid an experience—certainly not for the vast, vast majority, anyway, who survive their self-imposed tests.[40]

Where did Trudeau go when he and the Liberals lost the election of 1979? In the wake of Hornby and the Tyrrells, on a canoe trip down the Hanbury/Thelon River. What motif did he choose to open his television memoirs? Paddling a red canoe. What metaphor did he choose to title his collected writings? *Against the Current.* Building on the groundwork done by a young Jean Chrétien, minister responsible for the National Parks Branch in Ottawa, following a trip down the Nahanni River in 1970, Trudeau put in place the Canadian Wild Rivers Survey, precursor to what became the Canadian Heritage Rivers

System. Trent University historian Bruce Hodgins sees both of these initiatives as a direct legacy of convictions confirmed by Trudeau through his love of canoe-tripping. Says Hodgins:

> I happen to think that the Wild River Survey was positively *his* initiative, despite what minister happened to be doing it ... his commitment to canoeing and to wilderness is something that transcends everything else, and there's an element of tremendous genuineness in this idea.[41]

One could argue, along similar lines, that John Hornby's move to establish the Thelon Game Sanctuary and, in more southerly reaches of the country, the great imposter Archie (Grey Owl) Belaney's conservation efforts on behalf of the beleaguered Canadian beaver were similarly secured and authenticated by the canoe-tripping experience. What it might be, exactly, that the canoeing quest *does* to the questor, in the end, to make him or her care deeply about the land and the country is probably in the realm of the unknown, described in 1915 by journalist W.R. Bocking as follows:

> There is a secret influence at work in the wild places of the North that seems to cast a spell over the men who have once been in them. Once can never forget the lakes of such wonderful beauty, the river, peaceful or turbulent, the quiet portage paths, or the mighty forests of real trees. It is really getting to know Canada, to go where these things are. After having made camp along the water routes, one feels a proud sense of ownership of that part of the country, which must develop into a deeper feeling of patriotism in regard to the whole land.[42]

The legacy of George Grinnell's canoe quest—courage to carry on and tell his story. His persistence to carry on, having reached the point of death on the shores of the Kazan River in 1955, is outshone only by his persistence in finding the will to live following Moffatt's death and later the death of his two sons. Time after time, he tried to find a publisher to allow him to tell his story to the world, so that others might learn from the tragedies; finally his book found a home at Northern Books in Toronto. At the end, he writes:

> Art's journey ended in death, and so did, unfortunately, the journey of my sons; all journeys end in death; it is the nature of the human pilgrimage; but there is another point: part of Art's journey and the journey of my sons lives on. It lives on in me, and it lives on in others.[43]

Secret or not, the influence of the canoeing quest is tangible to anyone who has crossed the threshold of adventure. Even now, I sit inside looking at a tired green hull upturned in the shadow of a rough canoe shed at the edge of the wood outside my window. A 17-foot Old Town Canoe Company "Tripper" model canoe. The points in its yoke match the dents in my shoulders and bring back memories of wind-swept tundra portages where I cursed the sheer size of the boat as it weather-vaned at the whimsy of the breeze. The crimps in its vinyl-clad aluminum gunwales remind me of the day we came a cropper at McCoy Rapid on the Ottawa. And inside, although I can't see the details from here, there are the forgotten footprints of little feet that stood as we paddled with our two daughters, even as they were learning to walk. I think of a two-year-old studying the bottom of the canoe as its bottom oil-canned with the rhythm of a regular tripping stroke, thirty-three beats per minute. And I remember with great fondness that exclamation of sheer delight when she said, "Hey look, the canoe is breathing!"

9

FROM SEA TO SUDS

So you have a French guy and an English guy in the same canoe, paddling around Canada and getting along. People saw this as a sort of symbol of Canadian unity. In fact, it's not. It was not our intention to make a political statement with the William and Jacques ads. All we wanted to do was sell beer.

—Mark Solby, Labatt's Brewery[1]

THINKING ABOUT CANADA is a lateral process for most of its residents, from east to west, an exercise that inevitably involves furtive glances over one's left shoulder to the south. The phone lines follow the railway; the roads move west with the rivers; the sea's fingers set the essential pattern and character of a nation. Aboriginals in dugouts become voyageurs in trade canoes, then surveyors in canvas-covered craft, who in turn become truckers and tourists, making their way across the country, and stopping at trading posts along the way for ersatz pemmican, beaded leather belts, paddling postcards, *coureurs de bois* on playing cards, Mounties on quick-shellac paddles, and miniature bark canoes made in China or Cincinnati. At Richelieu on the St. Lawrence, the water and souvenirs lead southeast, to New England through Mohawk lands to Indian territory on the coast. Through the boundary waters between the Lakehead and Winnipeg, the canoe line points south, as it did for La Salle and, latterly, country rocker Jerry Lee Lewis, who sang about travelling down the Mississippi to the Gulf of Mexico.

Whether you are a paddler or not, canoes and canoe imagery are part of life across Canada and through at least the northern United States. Somewhere along the way, from Lachine to the Rocky Mountains, from the Great Divide to the Pacific, from the Mackenzie Delta to New Orleans, the canoe has, over time, changed from a simple conveyance to a symbol, an evocative and saleable image laden with overlapping and conflicting or confusing meanings.

The American dry-goods retailer Currier and Ives has, over the years, rendered all kinds of historic canoe paintings of voyageurs and gentlemen adventurers on all manner of household items from playing cards to painted porcelain tiles, featuring the work of artists, including Adirondack outdoorsman and painter Arthur Fitzwilliam Tait. In Canada, long-standing connections between the railway and the canoe endure in the ephemera of the CPR and in the art that plaques the plastic walls of LRT trains racing between Windsor and Quebec City. Today, besides the clichéd trinketry of roadside stops, there are canoes on calendars, greeting cards, calling cards, wrapping paper, and fancy cheques; T-shirts, sweat shirts, nighties and nappies. There are canoes on public pavilions, like that on the waterfront in Sault Ste. Marie,

Ontario, and on billboards throughout New Brunswick, Quebec and Ontario; and there are canoes in ads for just about everything under the sun: from milk to malt whiskey; relaxation tapes to RRSPs; books and beer to boots and cigarettes; airlines to Internet service providers.

If one were to track back to the place or point at which this symbolic transition began in earnest, one would need to move west from Lake Winnipeg, through Cedar Lake to the Saskatchewan River; upstream, past The Pas, over the border into Saskatchewan, past Cumberland House and the road to Love; veering left into the South Saskatchewan before Prince Albert, then through Saskatoon and again west into Alberta. Over the border, not far from Medicine Hat, where the Old Man River enters from the south, take the right fork, the Bow River, and persist all the way upstream through Calgary, and eventually to the railway town of Banff, home of the Banff Springs Hotel.

There, on a hot day in July 1953, after breakfast and before the lunchtime rush, kitchen helper Glenn Lewis, on summer holidays from high school from Kelowna, BC, acting on a tip, was hopping about on the dock on the banks of the Bow River near the Banff Museum, snapping photographs of a remarkable scene—Hollywood movie siren Marilyn Monroe in a canoe. Lewis recalled that day in a recent conversation:

> She was making a movie called *River of No Return*. Actually, there were several movies being made at the time. Shelley Winters was there making a film too, *Saskatchewan*, I think it was called. Anyway, they used to hang out together at the Banff Springs. I was working at the Cascade Hotel and my roommate was the photographer at the Banff Springs, and he told me that she would be at this particular place at this particular time. I went down and there she was, posing with the Mountie, taking publicity shots for the hotel. I had a little Brownie my mother had given me, a used camera. They're just snapshots, but they turned out okay. I've exhibited these shots as art prints, a series of six, along with a poster that goes with them and kind of conceptualizes the package.[2]

They are complex and confusing, if not memorable, images. Helped by a member of the Royal Canadian Mounted Police in red serge with all the trimmings, Ms. Monroe has removed her flip-flops and striped socks, and left them on the dock, and she sits in the stern seat of a canvas-covered pleasure canoe, looking back over her left shoulder, smiling for the young fan with the camera. The mountains and forest as backdrop, iconic in themselves, set off in high-sun relief the Mountie, the curvaceous canoe, and the platinum blonde. If there ever was a photograph of love in a canoe, this is it. Monroe is there following the success of her 1952 film, *Niagara*, and before her next hit, *The Seven-Year Itch*. Uncle Sam's siren daughter meets the eligible and ever-so-helpful Canuck bachelor, but no nonsense: he's on duty. Noticeable about the canoe is the fact that it lacks a centre thwart.[3]

The *River of No Return* would be a forgettable film, but the picture taken by the young kitchen helper would go on to be published and republished in books and magazines up to and including the cover of a 1997 volume by Citizen X entitled *Who Are the People of Canada Anyway?*[4] A person might ask, "Who are the people of Canada?" with three such incongruous elements in one picture. A strikingly similar image, which may well also have been taken along the Bow, involving another Hollywood leading lady, a big white dog, and another Mountie who is paddling his two best friends in a ghastly re-creation of a birch bark canoe (a still from the film *Yukon Manhunt*) bedecks the cover of another book, the gently titled *Why I Hate Canadians*.[5] Although it is often impossible to say where or in what circumstances a notion for a photograph has its genesis, in this case there are clues—the big railway hotel, the location, the mountain scenery, the canoe, the Mountie— that point in the direction of one person.

If there is one historical figure we might thank or damn (besides HBC governor George Simpson, who was one of the very first people to recognize the symbolic possibilities of canoes) for the proliferation of canoe imagery in North American culture in general, and for the creation of the Alberta Mountie/canoe/damsel motif in particular, it would have to be Canadian Pacific Railway publicist John Murray Gibbon.

The Canadian Pacific Railway, in contrast to the railways in the western United States, was, in essence, a private undertaking, generously supported by government grants of cash and land, but nevertheless an undertaking that took with it across the country its own form of discipline and order, its own rules and assumptions, just as the corporate policies of the Hudson's Bay Company and the North West Company had done for the previous two centuries. It was a fine railway, but, unfortunately, when it was built people did not rush to ride it. And so, from the last ping of the last swing of a 9-pound sledge on the last spike at Craigellachie in British Columbia (a photo that some credit as being *the* most famous in Canadian history), it was corporate policy to actively encourage ridership. And this initiative, of course, involved creating or manufacturing reasons to travel west by train and finding ways to insert these in the plans of immigrants and travellers, wherever they might be. In an early book about the building of the railway, CPR general manager William Van Horne is quoted as saying, "Since we can't export the scenery we shall have to import the tourists."[6] Filling the trains required serious public relations.

Early CPR publicists, like George Ham, working with photographers, writers, film-makers, and artists of various sorts, set to work creating all manner of ephemera—maps, posters, pamphlets, postcards, prints, view books—to promote the railway in England and central Europe. Agents of the CPR travelled around with lantern slides and with some of the earliest ciné footage and projectors, telling people about the virtues of Canada, the CPR and the West. And, of course, these romantic images, especially those depicting the land between central Alberta and the Kicking Horse Pass, included canoes, sometimes in an aboriginal context, but more often as a transportation device for a Mountie or a recreational floater for a courting couple on a train holiday to the West. The results of this PR program are described by Daniel Francis in *National Dreams: Myth, Memory and Canadian History:*

> The CPR publicity machine succeeded in turning the country into a story. With the help of the company's promotional material, the rail journey unfolded like a book, leaving thoughtful travellers to contemplate the rise of civilization

and the majesty of wild nature. The transcontinental trip became a narrative by which visitors interpreted the country as they passed through it, beginning in the settled East, where cultivated farms and growing industrial cities gave evidence of a long history of occupation, and progressing onto the plains, which were being transformed into a world granary. Everywhere the signs of industry and growth indicated a prosperous future, while here and there a picturesque Indian village exposed vestiges of the "primitive" peoples who first occupied the region. Finally, visitors arrived at the wilderness of mountains, the ultimate scenic experience.[7]

By far the most ambitious and energetic publicity agent for the CPR was John Murray Gibbon, who, as a scholar trained at the universities of Aberdeen, Oxford and Göttingen, combined intellect and curiosity with a certain fearlessness when it came to staging public events to promote the railway. Imagine a hybrid of Pierre Berton and P.T. Barnum, with the most finely tuned sense of cross-cultural pageantry of any man on Canadian soil since George Simpson. Aided and abetted by dime novelists, Hollywood film-makers, and the writers of children's adventure publications like *Chums* magazine and *The Canadian Boy's Annual*, Gibbon was a significant force in the elevation to iconic status of the mountain, the Mountie, the pretty woman, the Indian and the canoe. His genius was to make these images move and dance, wrapping them in the sights and sounds of cultural festivals cooked up by the CPR to fill the railway hotels and bring Canada alive: at the Château Frontenac in Quebec City, it was the Folksong and Handicraft Festival, an event that was restaged at various other railway installations through the twenties and thirties, including the Hotel Saskatchewan in Regina in the spring just prior to the stock market crash of 1929; at the Royal Alexandra Hotel in Winnipeg, it was the New Canadian Festival, involving a colourful whirl of performers exhibiting the arts and dance of the Middle European countries from which the immigrants had come; in Vancouver, Gibbon organized the Sea Music Festival; and in Banff, in honour of the Scottish place of the same name, he introduced a Highland Gathering at the Banff Springs Hotel to complement the annual spree called Banff Indian Days, in which canoes paddled by actors dressed up as Indians performed scenes from Longfellow's poem "Hiawatha." Publicity posters from the 1920s advertising Banff Indian Days, the Highland Gathering, and other railway-sponsored events, etched images in public consciousness that substantially shaped future imaginings, to the point that when a winsome figure like Shelley Winters or Marilyn Monroe turned up at the Banff Springs Hotel to shoot a movie, it was a reflex to drop her in a canoe, aided by a Mountie, with forest and rock in the background, for a few publicity shots.

Gibbon engineered these cultural celebrations for the CPR into a regular radio program and eventually into a book called *Canadian Mosaic*, for which he earned a Governor General's Award just prior to the outbreak of World War II. He was alive and prolific, in ten places at the same time, always moving, always doing something. Gibbon is recognized as the person who attached faces, sounds and public experiences to the notion of "mosaic" Canada as a new-colonial multilingual blend of people from disparate cultures living together, happily along the ribbon of steel. Gibbon was also a prolific writer and was founder and first president of the Canadian Authors Association. But one of his most enduring interests, and the feature that brought him to Canada in the first place, was the canoe.

Benefiting from the exploits of John MacGregor in his famous Rob Roy canoe and members of the Royal Canoe Club, Gibbon first encountered an all-wood Canadian canoe, made in Peterborough, at Oxford University. This was not only his introduction to canoeing but also to Canada. When not rowing, or studying of a Saturday, Gibbon would borrow a canoe and make his way up the Cher River to the village of Islip and return, for a pleasant afternoon of sunshine and activity. These outings kindled Gibbon's interest and imagination and led to several transatlantic trips for him, as an undergraduate and, as a graduate in the early years of the twentieth century. Drawn by his reading of the fur-trade literature, on one of these first trips, Gibbon and a friend somehow orchestrated a fishing canoe trip on the French River. With his training as a journalist, his own study of Canada, and now with this experience and interest in things Canadian—notably the canoe—Gibbon was appointed director of European publicity for the CPR in 1907. Because of his Canadian experience, unlike his colleagues in the London office, who continued with lecture tours throughout Britain to promote the railway, Gibbon's first assignment was to take a group of British newspaper editors to Canada where the railway laid on a sumptuous first-class journey from Montreal to Vancouver, pulling out all the stops, bringing to life all the poster images. Gibbon's growing knowledge of the country, his enthusiasm for its people, and his technical prowess in a canoe must have impressed these editors, and his bosses at the CPR, because in six years, Gibbon was back in Canada to stay, moving to Montreal to take up his post as the railway's publicity director.

Based in Quebec at Ste-Anne-de-Bellevue, Gibbon travelled the country as a tireless ambassador for the railway, but always found ways to engage his passion for canoes and canoeing, and for fishing. Along the way, he met Harry Allen, head of the New Brunswick Guides Association, who took him to the salmon-rich rivers of the east that so reminded him of his school days in Aberdeen, fly-fishing on the banks of the Don and the Dee rivers. Writing about his passion for canoes in later years he recounted his entry to Canada via its boats and rivers:

> I made canoeing and fishing trips to Lake St. John, the Bostonnais and the St. Maurice Rivers, Lac Archambault in the Laurentians, and Rivière du Lièvre and Lac des Ecorces; and right at home at St. Annes on the Ottawa River and Hudson on the Lake of Two Mountains, not to mention one trip on the Gatineau.
>
> In Ontario I naturally tried out the Muskokas, but returned to my original stamping ground on the French River. Then I sampled the Michipicoten, the Nipigon River and its neighbour, the Steel River, and so on to Kenora, the old Rat Portage.
>
> From there I skipped over the prairies to the Canadian Rockies, the Bow River at Banff and the lakes in the higher altitudes—Lake Louise, Lake O'Hara, Rock Isle Lake and Sunburst Lake near Mount Assiniboine—then over the

Great Divide to Emerald Lake and the Upper Columbia Lakes ... There were canoes at Lake Windermere and on Kootenay Lake as well as at Skookumchuck, and canoes also on the Arrow Lakes and Lake Okanagan.[8]

Gibbon's teaming with Charles Marius Barbeau, fellow Oxford graduate and founder of professional folklore study in Canada, put the CPR publicist in contact with not only the substance and context of a rich array of Canadian folk tales but also with the process of lore and lore-building. When Gibbon couldn't find an appropriate song to infuse into his festival mix to advance a particular view of life or people, he did what folklorists had been doing for years—he made one up, and matched it with a catchy tune already in existence. A shining example of this practice is a song called "The Ghost Canoe," the lyrics of which Gibbon wrote upon hearing the story of "La chasse-galerie" from his friend Barbeau. To an ancient German tune "Der Erlkönig" by Carl Loewe, Gibbon wrote the following words:

Come shantymen, come fly with me
Above the topmost branch of the tree.
Be jolly fellows and have no fear,
And you'll spend at home a happy New Year.

He ran to join them, and swiftly on high,
No water beneath them, they paddled the sky—
Their souls at stake in ghost canoe
On dread adventure far off they flew![9]

Not surprisingly, when this song was published, it was accompanied by two illustrations: one, the classic black and white drawing of the flying canoe by George Pepper "courtesy of Marius Barbeau"[10] that accompanied the music; and two, on a page facing the lyrics, on the exact same Bow River setting as Glenn Lewis's Marilyn Monroe photo, only a little wider view, another CPR publicity shot showing a happy couple paddling a canoe on the Bow against a background of conifers and snow-capped Banff peaks.

In fact, John Murray Gibbon wrote a number of ballads of the canoe, but his interests went beyond this aspect of Canadian history into ballads of Jacques Cartier, the *coureurs de bois*, David Thompson, the fur brigades, Sir Isaac Brock, Laura Secord, Henry Hudson, George Vancouver, mountains, Mounties, the Yukon rose, the Elfin People and, my favourite, a group of ballads about "Jenny, a Canadian girl."

Gibbon was savvy enough to realize that there was a gender imbalance in the historical accounts of Canada's early days. His interest in folklore had shown him that women had played as substantial a role as men—a reality of the pioneering experience that was reflected in his folklore festivals. But when it came time to put a face and an image to the female equivalent of "The Canadian Summer Boy,"[11] Gibbon conjured from his imagination a canoeing cousin for the celebrated (but not very tanned or bush smart) Anne of Green Gables. Introducing this character, Gibbon writes: "With Anne in mind, I venture to present one or two ballads about her cousin Jenny, of whom not so many have ever heard. She is an outdoor girl who likes to go camping, she is a lover of wild flowers, she is at home in a canoe, she is an expert at canning, and she has enough imagination to believe in fairies."[12] And, in an effort to use Jenny to promote the notion of Canada as a benevolent playground for women as well as men, for girls as well as young boys, Gibbon wrote songs like "Jenny, Jenny, Brown as a Penny," sung to the English country dance tune "Grimstock":

Jenny, Jenny, brown as a penny,
Eyes of sky-blue, lip as of clover;
Jenny, Jenny, jolly as any,
Linnet, the rover,
Lingers for you.
Jenny, Jenny, days are a-winging;
Out on the lake the loon is hallooing.
Jenny, Jenny, sure he is singing,
"What are you doing?
Bring your canoe."
Down on the water the wild duck advancing
Swim out from the lilies that silver a pool.

Paddle along while sunlight is dancing
Until under willow you find it more cool.[13]

A goodly number of ballads about Gibbon's imagined Canada were published in books called *Northland Songs No. 1* (arrangements by Harold Eustace Key) and *Northland Songs No. 2* (arrangements by Sir Ernest MacMillan) and several were interpreted by the Westhill High School Singers from Montreal and recorded by the R.C.A. Victor Company of Montreal.[14] Three of his canoe songs were rendered by singer Frances James on a Victor record as well.[15] Although none of Gibbon's songs became classics, they did add substantially to earlier music celebrating the Canadian experience, such as Laura Stevenson's "Paddle Your Own Canoe" (recently reinterpreted by Toronto-born concert performer Mary Lou Fallis in her 1997 CD, *Primadonna on a Moose* [Open Day Recordings]), and became a solid foundation in the canon of Canadian canoe songs which now includes contributions from contemporary selections like Ian Tamblyn's "Woodsmoke and Oranges" and Connie Kaldor's classic "Canoe Song."[16]

The last of John Murray Gibbon's publications, published fifteen months before his death in 1952, and without question the best example of his role in celebrating the canoe in Canadian culture and elevating it from a functional device to an enduring symbol, was *The Romance of the Canadian Canoe*. In the introduction, he writes simply this about where the idea for this groundbreaking book came from:

> When recently I turned to see what books had been written about the Canadian canoe, I was amazed to find how few there were, considering how much of the social history of Canada was linked up with the canoe before the building of roads and canals and railways.
>
> It seemed that something was lacking—hence this new book.[17]

For the first time, between the covers of one book were words from explorers' journals, folklore, folk songs, Indian legends, poems and prose, all about the canoe and all liberally interlaced with canoe artwork

by W.H. Bartlett, Paul Kane, Frances Hopkins, Guy Laviolette, etch-
ings and sketches by various people, including the venerable "chief
illustrator of Canadian history" and once art director of the Toronto
Star Weekly, Charles William Jefferys, and photographs by many
people, including several specimens by CPR photographer Nicholas
Morant, one of which—an early Kodachrome—shows a man and a
woman and a canoe against snow-capped rock and green trees on azure
waters of Lake Louise ... Gibbon couldn't resist.

What Gibbon had done, with his books, songs, festivals, posters,
songs and pageants for the CPR, was to add an iconic dimension to the
Canadian landscape. He was not the only person to take a part in this
process, but he was a significant player, especially with respect to the
canoe. Throughout the century, as the canoe took on values and meaning, and increasingly was used in graphic art and advertising to convey
certain types of messages, its portrayal often echoed the clichés of CPR
publicity.

In his incarnation as cartoonist for the *Toronto Star* and freelance
illustrator in the early 1900s, C.W. Jefferys frequently used the canoe to
stand for Canada in general, Canadian industry in particular. For example, in a cartoon that shows "Hard Times Rapids" flowing into
"Prosperity Bay," Jeffreys' character Jack Canuck has hauled his canoe,
Canadian Industry, onto shore and is inspecting its bottom. The
caption reads, "Well! We're past the bad spot and there's not damage to
the canoe."[18] Interestingly, the cartoon is set up with canoe and character in the foreground, placed against a backdrop of water, rock and
trees, the quintessential Canadian scene, but a scene that evokes as much
as anything a railway poster, a link immeasurably aided by the fact that
Jack Canuck is wearing a Mountie's starch-brimmed Stetson. A walk
through North American print advertising reveals similar echoes and
also depicts the gradual permutation of canoe from craft to icon.

The only canoes that turn up in early consumer publications—newspapers, magazines, catalogs—are those in advertisements for the boats
themselves. The 1902 catalogue for the "Cheapest Supply House on
Earth, Chicago"—Sears, Roebuck and Company—has lovely line
drawings of 16-foot canvas-covered Peterborough canoes ($62.50,
single-bladed paddles extra for $1.75) and a veritable sideshow of

other canoe-like craft for the budget-conscious fisherman or hunter. The "Get There" sheet-metal hunting boat ($17.50), which looks like a bad copy of a John MacGregor Rob Roy; the "Bustle" sheet-metal hunting boat ($24.50), which is exactly like the "Get There" except for the addition of 5-inch wide air chambers, or sponsons, on either side of the canoe to stop it from sinking to the bottom too quickly in the event of upset; and a "Special Folding Canvas Boat," which looks for all the world like a knock-off of the folding canoe design Dr. Mellis Douglas of Lakefield pioneered thirty years before. It had heavy canvas duck skin held to shape with "bent wood ribs instead of common iron ribs, which rust easily."

By the 1920s there were magazine ads from a large variety of other canoe companies besides those in Peterborough, New Brunswick and Maine. For example the Gagnon and Jobidon canoe company in Loretteville, Quebec, is flogging their "famous Huron Canoe, built by genuine Huron Indians." And, in 1928, the Thompson Brothers Boat Manufacturing Company in Peshtigo, Wisconsin, is selling canoes, "$48 and up, some all wood, others canvas covered. Light, swift, safe, strong, and durable. Choice of many distinctive colour combinations." But also in the twenties makers of outdoor gear are starting to attach the fine qualities of their products to canoe imagery. In a 1928 issue of *Rod and Gun and Canadian Silver Fox News*, the Canadian Milk Products Company of Toronto is targeting canoeists to buy "KLIM" their powdered whole-milk product. And regularly in issues of *Maclean's* magazine and the Hudson's Bay publication, *The Beaver*, the Canadian National Carbon Company of Montreal, Toronto and Winnipeg is selling their Eveready flashlights and batteries with exclusive use of canoe imagery and slogans like "Play safely this summer," "See and Be Safe." On the back cover of the December 1924 issue of *The Beaver* the ad reads, "Splits the Night Wide Open—An Eveready searchlight makes canoeing at night possible."

Also in the 1920s, Canadian National Railways and Canada Steamship Lines are running ads in *Maclean's*, promoting their travel services. With canoe imagery, CN tells the reader that they can "open for you the door to the Playgrounds of Canada, in the Maritimes, Quebec, Ontario, British Columbia and the North Pacific Coast." Also with canoe imagery, but used in a more symbolic way, Canada Steamship Lines is promoting a 1,200-mile boat trip from "Niagara to the Sea," using one of William Henry Drummond's pidgin French poems, "The Song of the Saguenay," to invoke the spirit of the voyageur for would-be passengers on their steamers:

> The French-Canadian "voyageur" whose home is Quebec and whose fame as riverman and philosopher has reached the furthermost corners of civilization, is justified in his feeling of pride for this, his land of green rivers and blue skies. His enthusiasm is matched by that of every traveller who visits this beauty-spot of the North ... Our steamers, luxuriously equipped and specially designed for every type of voyage, touch at Toronto and thence wind their way through the 1,000 Islands. Transferring to a smaller boat, we make the descent of the far-famed rapids of the St. Lawrence. Montreal is visited, then the rock-girt city of Quebec, and the beautiful summer resorts of Murray Bay and Tadoussac; the trip terminating in the wonder voyage up the Saguenay—and the awe-inspiring beauty of Capes Trinity and Eternity.[19]

Swift's Premium Ham and Ingersoll Watch Company as well are using canoes in their ads, extolling the virtues of their products. And an ad by the L.E. Waterman Company of Montreal uses the qualities of a paddle motif to illustrate the super light weight and even balance of their "Ideal Fountain Pen."

The 1930s opened with the publication by Canadian National of "Canoe Trips and Nature Photography," a promotional pamphlet that institutionalized the notion of canoe trip as a formal and somewhat exclusive alternative to workaday life and other types of holidays. Detailing trips across the country, from Nova Scotia to British Columbia, the prose here started to define the type of person whose life and image would be enriched by a canoe experience, not with rod, reel, or gun, but with camera, a non-consumptive alternative to hunting and fishing. These were exclusive trips for "all who know the pulse of youth," for those who could muster train fare:

Adventure, to most of us, is a summons to the unknown, the uncharted and it may be, the hazardous. It is the very antithesis of the "organized" and personally conducted outing, for it demands above everything the unorganized, the untrammelled, where the independent judgment, the power of a nimble body, the sense of caution, the readiness to take a dare, are the only buffers against discomfort, the only assurance of times worth remembering. But thousands of young men today are looking for just the self-reliant adventurous type holiday. They demand action. They insist on novelty. They are not afraid of distance or solitude. Portages and camp fires, beds of balsam boughs, the straining muscle, the dip, dip of rhythmic paddles, the nervous approach to the river bank above "white water," the twice-told tales as the moon sails upward from the pine tops. To all who know the pulse of youth, these things are instinctive and laudable.

Yesterday such experiences were the privilege of the occasional argonaut who "knew the ropes" in northern Canada. To-day they are available to any individual or party through Canadian National Railways, the most extensive railway system on the continent.[20]

During the Depression, though such pamphlets were designed to fill trains on the steel rails of Canada, they would more likely have reached the imaginations of those purchasing magazines or newspapers, because CN edited similar copy into print ads of all kinds with all manner of evocative canoe images in them. A would-be, wannabe lifestyle was represented in ads from other firms as well, depicting men and women relaxing as if without a care in the world, the woman reclining in centre-thwartless pleasure canoes, the attentive man sitting up, paddle in hand. The June 15, 1939, issue of *Maclean's* magazine, for example, contains a full-page advertisement by Agfa Ansco Limited of Toronto showing a woman, who looks like Marilyn Monroe's twin, stretched out in a tailored skirt and jacket with blouse and tie, ensheafed bulrushes in hand, with her handsome man in collar and pressed flannels. "A hard picture to get—but Agfa Film got it!" The RCA Victor Company indicates that a couple's company in a canoe is not sufficient, suggesting instead that people purchase a new suitcase-sized RCA Victor Portette to take with them. "Just pick it up and take the world of radio with you. Nothing to connect, no aerial to put up, no electric current needed, complete ... ready to turn it on and tune in anywhere," perhaps pulling in John Murray Gibbon's landmark "Canadian Mosaic" program.

"Girling" with an RCA Victor radio—
from a 1939 advertisement in *Maclean's*

In 1940, announced by the heading "Then came the rain and the first thing they sought was shelter," was an ad for Barrett Roofs, "Canada's largest manufacturer producing coal-tar products." Here, the canoe image is not picturesque and sublime, but dark and wet, associating the canoe with all that is exposed and uncomfortable in the great outdoors. The Beech-Nut Candy Company persists with lifestyle ads, drafting an ad, under the slogan "Refresh Yourself," that shows a pretty woman in a natty bathing costume lying over the stern deck of a Peterborough canvas-covered canoe, one hand holding a paddle, one hand idling in the water, sucking, all the while, on a Beech-Nut Lemon Drop. "You'll love the keen, juicy flavour," it says. But with that, canoes all but disappear from advertising during World War II. When they appear again, in the postwar period, they signal an explosion in the popularity of canoeing, of camping, and the beginning of the long connection between brewers and distillers with canoe iconography.

In 1947, Carling Breweries Limited, Waterloo and Walkerville, Ontario, mount a conservation-oriented campaign that attaches a quasi-moral dimension to the straight-ahead escapism of the previous decade. In one of the ads of this era, the main element is a painting of two Canada geese by artist T.M. Shortt, accompanied by a drawing of a man with a shotgun on his lap being paddled down a river. "The Guide—a conservationist," it says, "helps the cause of conservation by setting an example in obeying the game and forest laws—the laws of Nature and Man." Though the emphasis is on nature, there is a subliminal connection between canoes and the good life, the lifestyle that now, necessarily, involves Carling beer.

In 1949, Calvert Distiller (Canada) Limited of Amherstburg, Ontario, advertising in *Maclean's* magazine, take a more historical tack and begins the use in advertising of the canoe as symbol of Canadian tradition. "Great Families Create Great Nations" is the message and, with a text and a painting of a voyageur canoe being portaged up to a trade house on the St. Lawrence, it tells the story of Pierre LeGardeur, a contemporary of René-Robert Cavelier, Sieur de La Salle, who was granted the seigneuries of Cournoyer and Repentigny. Calvert the distiller, by contrast, came from English stock who founded pioneer colonies in Newfoundland and Maryland. The ad reads, "The family is the corner-stone upon which great nations are built. Let each of us promote within the great Canadian family the same concepts of freedom and tolerance pioneered by the Calvert family over three hundred years ago." The implicit message of the ad, and the one that links it to the Calvert spirits, is "toss back a few shots of our whisky and you too will think you and one friend can toss a 35-foot Montreal canoe on your shoulders and carry it to the party, just like the hardy voyageurs in the picture." Or maybe, remembering the legendary drinking prowess of the fabled Nor'Westers, to some viewers the ad might be written to read: "Buy our product and you too can carry on into the wee hours like William McGillivray and the rest of the members of the Beaver Club, drinking until you, too, slide from the table, unable to 'recover your seat.'"

During the 1950s and 1960s, as canvas-covered canoes were replaced by aluminum canoes and canoes made of other manufactured materials—notably fibreglass—the canoe as an icon fell out of favour. Out was tradition and in was modernity, that is until the Centennial Canoe Pageant, which, along with other factors, led to a renaissance of interest in the canoe and a return to the pages of newspapers and magazines of the image of a canoe. The link between conservation and canoes, raised by Carling years before, was particularly popular. And, as the notion of getting back to nature in a non-consumptive way took hold, there was even a renewal of interest in the building, selling and owning of wooden canoes. With the passage of time, however, the canoe, as symbol, became more complex and convoluted. The virtues it came to represent were no longer just tradition and link to wilderness rest and recreation. There was a class-consciousness and pretension that perhaps always underlay the whole idea of having the time and money to "escape." In latter-day ads, this was much more visible, more obviously included in the messages. The idea of the "good life" attached to the canoe image that was expressed in early railway ads was transmuted in the seventies, eighties and nineties to the canoe as an evocation of good health, youthful vigour, durability, tradition and clean living—and these messages have become attached to a bewildering array of products and services.

In the 1980s, the Dairy Farmers of Ontario mounted the "Irreplaceable Milk" campaign on billboards across the province, showing a robust, healthy, youthful, powered-by-milk couple paddling their shiny canoe across a foaming, squeaky white clean sea of nature's wonderfood. And more or less the same images that evoked risk in the ads of years gone by were being used, in a curious way, by R.J.R. Macdonald Inc. to sell Export "A" cigarettes. In the early 1980s, huge billboards along big city expressways in Canada showed Madawaska Kanu Camp instructor Dirk van Wijk, a non-smoker, crashing through white water in a fiery red canoe—a youthful, vigorous, competent, healthy Canadian at play on the voyageur highway. I always looked at those ads and, after smiling about Dirk's embarrassment over doing the shoot (he used the money to finance a paddling trip to the Grand Canyon), thought that the main message, to one viewer at least, was "Smoke Export 'A' and risk your life."

Conscious use of the canoe as a symbol of risk was employed in a 1990s ad campaign to promote Guardian Mutual Funds. In these print ads, over the slogan "Ah yes, the risk," a man in a lone canoe is just about to be swamped by the prow of a passing freighter. What is intriguing about the ad is that, at first blush, the canoe appears to represent intolerable fragility and unacceptable risk, but as one reads through the text of the ad, including a secondary heading, "Discipline, through proven performance," it seems that, in a most ingenious way, the copywriters have invoked the best of the tradition of competence and expertise, and the inevitability of risk, that also attend the canoe.

Beer-makers, however, remain the kings of canoe imagery in 1990s advertising. It is a historical connection too. When the highwine (a fortified alcoholic beverage carried by canoe brigades) was gone, in a pinch the voyageurs made *biere la pinette*, a turpy blend of water and spruce needles that, with a bit of sugar, sunshine and miscellaneous "natural" fermentation agents (perhaps from under the fingernails of the cooks), turned into a mildly uplifting, if warm, intoxicant for use on the trail. That tradition has today become big business. Four Canadian beers and at least one American brew have canoe imagery on their labels. There is Maudite, made by Unibroue of Chambly, Quebec, that shows a rendering of the classic "La chasse-galerie" image; Niagara Falls Brewing Company, of Niagara Falls, Ontario, has a thick, bearded chap—a young Bill Mason on steroids—complete with plaid shirt and toque, paddling his way into pubs throughout Upper Canada. There is a canoe, almost identical to the one on the old Canadian silver dollar, on Canadian Light beer made by the Northern Algonquin Brewing Company in Ontario; the Upper Canada Brewing Company's house lager is also adorned with a canoe image that appears to be inspired by

Arthur Heming's improbable depiction of voyageurs shooting rapids which was painted around the turn of this century.

Perhaps no beer-marketing plan was better conceived or better executed than a 1996 television campaign organized by Labatt's Brewing Company to sell their Blue lager, a beer that has not a canoe on its label, never did, never will. In the "William and Jacques" promotion, the first of a seventeen-part series of thirty-second commercials was shot—where else?—near the iconographic home of canoeing in Canada, on the Bow River, at Banff. The camera pans down the side of an austere, snow-shrouded mountainside, past a grazing moose, to the crystalline, glacial waters. White text comes up on the screen that says, "Somewhere in Canada, 1734." A voice with noticeable French accent asks, "How far to go, William?" The scene cuts to two youngish men in what looks like an extremely rockered Cree-style birchbark canoe. William, who is a seer of the future, is in the stern. As he speaks from a shot close-in on his head, the canoe recedes into the frame, setting the two of them in a magnificent, late-fall snow-dusted wilderness landscape. William answers Jacques philosophically, a question with a question, as Socrates might have done, had he been a paddler: "How far is far, Jacques?"

The surprising extent to which this particular ad caught the imagination of the nation was exemplified for me at a First Nations youth leadership conference convened for communities of Manitoulin Island and the North Shore of Georgian Bay at the Anishnabe Spiritual Centre, south of Espanola, Ontario. A large group of people from all walks of life—education, social services, police, clergy, youth workers, and dozens of young aboriginals—had come together to talk about issues of mutual concern, many of them contentious and difficult to deal with. As a way of processing what had gone on each day, just before supper, with the guidance of an improvisational theatre group from a nearby community, the youth improvised and performed skits based on the discussions of the day. Early on in the proceedings, two youth stood centre-stage in the small, timber frame Jesuit chapel. They spaced themselves about 10 feet apart, faced in the same direction, put their hands up as if carrying a canoe, and before one of them could finish an opening sentence that began, "You know, William ..." in a contrived French accent, all-knowing laughter from the crowd drowned out the rest of the sketch.

Curious about this ad, and its apparent popularity, I contacted Mark Solby, marketing manager for the Labatt's Blue family of products. He explained that, traditionally, Labatt's Blue has been the best-selling beer in Canada but that to maintain these sales Labatt's is obliged to mount continuous, multi-pronged advertising campaigns. The marketing "mix" for Blue in the warm months of 1996 was called "True Blue Summer," and involved a host of "Escape" events, including a "Blue Escape Bus" and rivers of free beer, as well as canoe events such as the "Blue Urban Portage," which raised money in Toronto and Ottawa for a charity called "Tree Canada." Solby also put blue fibreglass canoes in every liquor store in New Brunswick and Nova Scotia that were awarded to lucky winners (no purchase necessary) throughout the beer-drinking season. About William and Jacques, he said:

> It was really just an idea to portray Blue as something of a shared Canadian experience. Beer brings us together as people. It's part of the fabric of our community and Blue is one of those common Canadian experiences. Once you come up with the voyageur concept, if that's what you call them, you're in a canoe.
>
> The core concept is simple. You have the classic "buddies." You have an English guy and a French guy because it makes for good copy. It's colourful. And it's a historical bridge.
>
> They worked great! Jacques and William gained us a lot of attention and notoriety. The ads are different from what a lot of people think of as traditional beer advertising. They're extremely entertaining and, at the end of the day, they actually SELL BEER.[21]

In Solby's words, the campaign "dialed him in" to the canoeing community in Canada. "I'd never heard the name Kirk Wipper before this," he said. But taking a close look at the demographics and appeal of canoe imagery, as a product marketer must, he learned that canoeists in Canada come from all walks of life. "Everyone aspires to be a canoeist," he said. He also noted that what he learned about canoeing and Canadians was similar to what he had learned about driving and Canadians. In a parallel manner to market-research findings that indicate most Canadians consider themselves above-average drivers, similar polls suggest that most Canadian rate themselves as part-time canoeists. Solby thinks that making this assertion, whether or not a person actually does have a canoe or know how to use it, makes a person feel "part of the family."

What took Mark Solby by surprise, however, was the extent to which the viewers of the "Jacques and William" campaign thought that Labatt's was making a political statement with William extolling virtues of goodness and cooperation and Jacques turning to him in one sequence and saying, "I could build a country like that!" Calls to the marketing manager asking for money to assist with federalist rallies and other causes indicated unequivocally that there was a healthy dose of political patriotism in the ads.

Whether or not Canadians bought beer, and whether or not they knew why they responded so soundly to this concept, its symbolic place in the national consciousness has been established to such an extent, in so many ways, with fixed-element images, conveyed through a multiplicity of media and in a cacophony of voices, that the connection is now, for many, reflexive. Pondering that, we might raise a glass to the man and the woman, to the mountain and the trees, to Lake Louise and the Bow River, to the Mountie and Marilyn Monroe, to George Simpson and John Murray Gibbon, to William and Jacques—wherever they are—and, of course, to the canoe in its myriad forms.

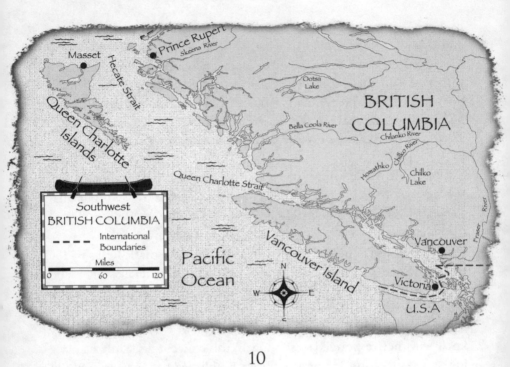

10

THE PATHS OF PEOPLE

When I hear a canoe referred to as a boat, I get insulted. With a boat there is no spiritual connection. With the canoe, at one time the whole thing was living, and you can see, you can touch the canoe, you touch the paths of people. You touch a boat and there is no feeling there, just nails, fiberglass, screws, paint. It doesn't have any real meaning. You know that your history is written in the canoe somewhere, not just you, but your people.

—Peggy Ahvakana, *Our Chiefs and Elders*[1]

RISING IN THE WESTERN SLOPES of the Rocky Mountains near Jasper National Park, the Fraser River drains only about one quarter of the land area that the St. Lawrence does, but the role that its valley played in the evolution of life in the Pacific Northwest is of equal significance. Anthropologists believe that many thousands of years ago, as the ice sheets retreated from the lower altitudes of British Columbia, the first migrants from the interior would have made their way down the Fraser valley on foot, making crude rafts when passage on one bank was impossible, to cross the river on their way to the sea. Along the way, canoes of cedar or spruce bark may have been constructed by people who chose to stay on the plateau, but those who worked their way through the expansive delta of the mighty Fraser needed larger and more sophisticated craft for access to rich food and fur resources of the ocean. It was here, at the western nexus of salt water and fresh, amid the towering redwood trees, that the great dugouts of the Pacific may have had their genesis; majestic sea-going canoes that anchored the most advanced and complex maritime aboriginal culture on the continent.

Speculating on how this technological innovation might have occurred, Roberts and Shackleton observe:

> The earliest canoe, of course, might have been a naturally formed dugout, half of a hollow log found among the masses of beach driftwood. As did primitive boat builders elsewhere in the world, they may have plugged the ends of such natural troughs with clay before the predictable step of burning out a simple dugout. As they developed confidence in their seamanship they made larger, improved dugouts that carried them out of the tranquil waters of the deltas into the Strait of Georgia and along the coast and out to the sea-girt islands. The development of a satisfactory marine canoe evidently came early; the Namu archeological site, in Kwakiutl country, dates back eight thousand years, and yet this camp is virtually inaccessible except by salt water.[2]

Whatever their origins, the great dugouts of the Northwest coast were developed in a north–south cultural continuity that was distinct from the people and canoes of the east. The massive dugouts evolved from available materials to meet the needs of the Haida to the north, the Nootka on Vancouver Island and the Coast Salish people along the Straits of Georgia and Juan de Fuca, and Puget Sound. And what impressive boats they were, carved from trees 600, 700, 800 years old that were 8, 10, 12 feet across at the butt. Canoe builders of the west coast learned to carve their craft with concave keels and straight, initially hogged (upwardly curved, like the Beothuk and Micmac lines) gunwales, so that when the inner cavity of a new canoe was heated with water and red-hot rocks and spread laterally with cross-members of increasing length, the keels of these massive canoes, often 40 feet or more in length, would curve back die-straight, or even become slightly rockered, as the sides curved outward and the gunwales achieved a sweep and two-plane curvature that gave the boats strength, power, seaworthiness and majesty in line, look and capacity.

These were the boats that fired the imaginations of early artists such as John Webber, who travelled with Captain James Cook in 1778, Paul Kane in the 1840s, and other lesser-known painters like Rudolph Cronau and Belmore Brown in the 1890s. They continue in modern times to inform and inspire a nation about the ways of the Pacific Northwest through the work of twentieth-century creators, including Emily Carr, Bill Holm, and Haida artist Bill Reid. Carr, in particular, left a body of work that celebrates the canoes of the northwest coast and illustrates unequivocally the centrality of these craft to aboriginal life. Sometimes in her paintings, such as *Alert Bay*, the canoe with its arresting curves and exterior artwork is the dominant element in a painting, but in other works, such as *Cumshewa* and *Memaliaga*, the canoe falls to secondary significance as a compositional element beside something else, often a totem pole. Alberta-based scholar and artist Donald Burry was especially intrigued by a work entitled *Kispiox* in the McMichael collection in Kleinburg, Ontario:

> In this painting a totem pole is pictured in front of a large wooden house. There is not an actual canoe shown in the work, rather, there is a canoe which has been carved into the totem pole and in this way becomes an integral part of the

representation of the pole on the canvas. The canoe is located across the arms of the lower figure of the pole but it does not appear that this figure is supporting the canoe in any way.[3]

But, like the big canoes of the fur trade that were replaced by more efficient, more modern conveyances, the great canoes of the Pacific Northwest were eventually overtaken by mechanized travel. With the march of progress of church and state that took with it the desire for aboriginal people to hold onto their time-tested traditions, the great canoes were left to rot. By World War I, the last of the great canoes had all but disappeared, leaving only memories of the sleek, strong lines, paddles and "pullers" that built sea-going nations along the coast. The only west coast dugouts that survived in any number were a few racing craft of the Salish canoe tradition.

Why then would the great canoes be resurrected in the mid 1980s? As David Neel reminds us, the reappearance of the high-prowed dugouts of the early days was both symbolic and political. Leading this renaissance was the magnificent 50-foot *LooTaas*, or "Wave Eater," built by Bill Reid, who would go on, in future years to create the *Spirit of Haida Gwaii*, a giant bronze statue of a west-coast canoe and cast of mythical paddlers who now ply the public concourses of the Canadian Embassy in Washington, DC, the Canadian Museum of Civilization in Ottawa and the Vancouver Airport.[4] Using lines adapted from museum models and word-of-mouth, Reid and his helpers fashioned first a half-size canoe to reacquaint themselves and their people with the techniques and innovations of big canoe building. This preliminary step complete, the team set to work and by 1986 had crafted the full-size renaissance canoe that became for the Haida and, by example, for the other First Nations of the Northwest, a symbol for a way of life worth restoring, a potent political icon rediscovered.

Bill Reid's challenge to come up with a workable and authentic canoe after all these fallow years in the all-wood maritime tradition was great. He spoke about the absence of documentation with David Neel:

There wasn't anyone really doing it when I got started. There was a lot of published material, though you did have

to sort through it. A lot of it is wrong. One anthropologist
I read suggested steaming a canoe for two days! There are
canoes in museum collections also. The Haida canoe in the
American Museum of Natural History is actually built backwards. The bow of the canoe is carved from the butt of the
log, where it is supposed to be the reverse. That very large
canoe would be for ceremonial use. On those big canoes, the
stern should be higher than the prow by about six inches,
because the trouble with navigating those big vessels is in a
following sea. With those war canoes in the old days most of
the fighting was done with paddles; that's why the paddles
are pointed. The reason is, when they were navigating the
boat, they wouldn't have had time to change weapons.[5]

With the help of Al Dewar, personnel manager at the forest products
multinational firm MacMillan Bloedel, Reid found the ideal tree, near
Skidegate on Haida Gwaii, remarking to reporters at the time that
however much cooperation there was between the Haida and Mac Blo'
people should remember that the land from which the tree came was
only under temporary lease and that, in fact, the logging company was
a tough squatter to get rid of. With considerable difficulty and delay, the
canoe log was cut and moved to a carving shed, where it was blessed and
the canoe construction began, enveloped in the reflected red-gold light
and aroma of fresh-hewn red cedar. People reported that it was inspiring to watch Reid, who at the time was shaking uncontrollably from
Parkinson's disease, pick up his carving tools with a steady hand, as if the
artist's force or the canoe transcended the disease during the periods
when creative work had to be done.

Through three months of building, with all manner of glitch and
delay, Reid managed to keep his sense of humour. After a few nicks and
cuts with sharp tools on the limbs of his helpers, he posted a sign in the
carving shed that said: "In case of serious accident, don't bleed on the
finished part." And, by the time the canoe, *LooTaas*, was ready for its
debut at Expo 86 in Vancouver, the *Globe and Mail* was reporting that
"the first large Haida canoe to be carved in living memory"[6] had been
nicknamed "Murphy" after the well-known law of catastrophe—

anything that can go wrong, will go wrong. Nevertheless, the canoe was finished and was proudly paddled before an appreciative international audience on the Vancouver waterfront in the summer of 1986. Among the on-lookers was a substantial contingent of Kwakwaka'wakw, Haida, Coast Salish, Tsimshian, Nuu-chah-nulth, Tlingit and other northwest coast First Nations people, who were deeply moved by this symbolic reclaiming of old ways. For them, the canoe was a metaphor for community and commitment to First Nations capability, dignity and shared experience.[7]

Driven by this enthusiasm, a mould was made of the *LooTaas* after its initial voyages in Vancouver. This allowed west-coast canoe builders to fashion lighter, more portable, but nevertheless resonant fibreglass replicas of Reid's original design. These craft, along with the original, became the inspiration for other would-be canoe builders in other west-coast First Nations to try their hands at joining the canoe revival. Communities began to coalesce around these canoes and a new tradition of "paddles" was established, in which whole communities gathered at landing places along the coast. Dozens of great canoes from many nations would converge after, in some cases, long sea journeys, and paddle in fun and solemn ceremony, re-enacting past traditions and reasserting aboriginal pride.

This connection between the canoe and modern northwest First Nations sensibilities is highly significant to the extent that the canoe has been honed as an effective political tool. It is visible and, when paddled in large numbers, quietly asserts in the midst of colour and circumstance a way of life that has in recent years been largely invisible. "What greater way to assert our presence, and the indomitability of our traditional culture, than by bringing fifteen or twenty great canoes into a coastal harbour?" asks David Neel. One of the most visible instances of the *LooTaas* being pressed into political action was when a band of paddlers from the Haida Nation paddled this imposing craft, 50 feet long, its prow rising higher than a man out of the water, to protest unregulated sport fishing in traditional waters.[8]

David Neel, in *The Great Canoes*, suggests that this canoe-building renaissance, often attributed directly to Bill Reid and the *LooTaas*, started in the mid 1980s. However, this is not entirely correct. Nearly two decades earlier, another Haida canoe builder, Victor Adams from Masset, on the north end of Graham Island in the Queen Charlottes, began the revival of the great canoe-building tradition, a process catalyzed, ironically, by a canoe enthusiast from the east, the ubiquitous Kirk Wipper.

Through his contact and correspondent on the west coast, anthropologist Alika Webber, Wipper learned sometime around Centennial year that this man in Masset, Victor Adams, might be a person to approach to build a Haida canoe for Wipper's growing canoe collection. Strapped for money, the perennial problem, Wipper took advantage of a holiday taken by the elderly office managers from Camp Kandalore to begin negotiations. Harold and Marion Penny were heading for British Columbia after the close of camp in the summer of 1968, and so Wipper, always thinking, offered to pay their way from Prince Rupert by ferry across to the Queen Charlotte Islands to visit with Mr. Adams. That they did. Victor Adams agreed to take on the project and was subsequently sent an advance of funds from Wipper to begin construction.

Going through the halting steps of refinding the canoe-building tradition that Bill Reid and his team would encounter fifteen years later—the shaping, the wood-working techniques, the sheer labour of manipulating a massive redwood log, the heating, the bending of the sides, the artwork—Adams laboured for at least three years to complete this very first new canoe. During the building, Adams would write to Wipper to explain delays saying: "We haven't done this for so long that it's hard to know whether we're doing it right." But in the late winter of 1971, Wipper got word from Masset that the canoe was ready. And with that, never one to miss an opportunity for ceremony and adventure, Wipper cobbled together a crew of hardy voyageurs and headed west with the intention of accepting the canoe from its Haida builder and then, in the fine tradition of great canoes, paddling this 26-foot craft 90 miles across the waves and currents of Hecate Strait to the mainland at Prince Rupert.

When they met Adams and members of the Haida community in Masset—where they performed a ceremonial transfer of ownership in which Wipper traded an inscribed hardwood paddle from the east for a hand-engraved eagle pendant made of silver—the crew from the East noticed a certain standoffishness on the part of the Haida. During their trip, Wipper's crew had talked about what it might be like to see a canoe built that has not been seen on local waters in living memory. They thought the Haida would be quite excited about the prospect of floating this new canoe. To their dismay, the people of Masset were quite the opposite. They appeared quiet and cool, even pensive.

Still, the canoe was duly trucked from town down the road to Masset Sound, where it was set in the water for the first time. Wipper and his eastern crew piled in, knowing canoes as they did, and took the canoe for a short spin in front of the assembled company. They thought they were doing quite well, but the crowd on the shore remained silent. Finally, the chief beckoned them in, whispering in Wipper's ear, "You know, our canoe goes better the other way around." Wipper was mortified. He had interpreted the rounded end of the boat to be the bow, but in the manner of a Russian warship (or so he thought at the time) the sea-going end of the Haida canoe was in fact that with the sharp, angular lines, overflown by a beautiful carved eagle that hung just above the water.

By this time the Haida men, who were slated to join the eastern crew for a maiden paddle, backed out, leaving Wipper and company to put the craft through its sea trials. Right way around, the canoe moved with speed and grace in Masset Sound, as smooth and as fast as everyone had hoped. And as this performance registered on the crowd of onlookers, there was a marked change in demeanour, from seeming desolation to celebration. Describing this moment to me, Wipper becomes animated:

> All of a sudden I realized what was happening. They didn't know that the canoe they'd built would even float, let alone perform on the water. They were nervous. They were fearful that they would be totally embarrassed, you see, but it worked out so well. So then they took all the children out

because, you know, these Haida children had NOT had the experience of being out in one of their own dugout canoes. That's how long it had been, see? So we took the kids out, and we had just a great time.[9]

University of Ottawa Recreology professor Claude Cousineau, one of Wipper's crew that day, remembers what he had learned on his own while walking around Masset before the maiden voyage. He knew why the Haida people were so quiet. They were worried that their canoe was not seaworthy because they had tried it the night before and everybody had dumped with it. And that in itself was a scene. So when the eastern crew got in, the whole village was there, waiting for the white men to dump. And, when it was clear that the canoe moved through the water with grace, there was relief all the way around.

In truth, there must have been an element of confusion, if not resentment, about the fact that the first great Haida canoe to be constructed in living memory was commissioned by a non-Native from the East, and slated for immediate removal, on completion, out of Haida territory. But Victor Adams was true to his word and the boat was duly commissioned, built, tested, and readied for its journey east.

Following the maiden voyage in Masset Sound, there was much else to do, to execute the plan to transport this magnificent black and white dugout back east to Ontario and up to the canoe museum at Camp Kandalore. The first step was to paddle across Hecate Strait. Easier said than done. With much celebration, laughter and congratulations, presumably tinged perhaps with regret and sadness, the eastern canoeists settled onto the hand-carved cedar-plank seats, with Wipper at the helm, and began the long journey to Prince Rupert. What Wipper had not anticipated was an 18-knot rip-tide in Masset Sound that swept them north to the sea and ultimately away from where they were headed. Heading out, it was all they could do to steer the canoe away from rocks in Masset Sound. Paddling against this current was out of the question. Learning to watch 50- and 60-foot long filaments of seaweed on the water's surface to find out which way the tide and currents were heading, the crew flailed away through the afternoon into darkness, exhausting themselves, making almost no headway, and heading back for shore on Graham Island.

By midnight on this moonlit night, the crew was spent and looking for a place to land among the palisade of errant logs from broken booms that the tide had piled along the beach. At the only opening in sight, they noticed two figures on the shore, walking and watching, apparently through binoculars. One of the silhouetted figures on the beach called out and said, "Kirk, is that you? We were worried about you." Adams and some of the Haida from Masset had been following their progress, or lack of progress, throughout the afternoon and evening and had come to the place where they knew the canoe and its eager but ocean-new crew would surely end up.

Accounts about how the Haida canoe got to the mainland from there vary. In some versions, the intrepid crew paddled all the way across to a triumphant finish in Prince George. In other versions, the scare of that first outing in the surf of the Queen Charlotte was of sufficient gravity to ship the whole contingent, boat and all, to the mainland via the Big Canoe (ferry). In still other versions, the crew set out the following day for Prince Rupert with favourable wind and tide but were beset by fog and lost their way, only to be rescued by trawlermen who hoisted them aboard for a slightly less triumphant but safer entrance to the mainland harbour.[10] In any case, they eventually made it to the mainland at Prince Rupert, Wipper and the crew flew home to Ontario, leaving the prodigal Haida canoe in the hands of another colourful character, Jim Munster—a.k.a Chief Kitpou— who, over the next twelve months would transport the canoe east, eventually to Toronto.

Kitpou, whose full story is yet to be told, is an enigma. In the early 1970s he was in the employ of the Canadian Imperial Tobacco Company as some sort of public relations or sales officer, but it was his alleged First Nations heritage and his connection to various Indian arti- facts, including canoes, that made a friendship with Kirk Wipper possi- ble, if not inevitable. They met through Hugh MacMillan, revitalizer of the North West Company, at the Mermaid Restaurant on Bay Street in Toronto.[11] In 1970, Munster accompanied MacMillan and a crew of voyageurs, including a group from Camp Kandalore, on a trip in North canoes from Grand Portage to Winnipeg. On the contract for that expedition, he signs himself Chief Kitpou Shaman, Lytton Reserve, British Columbia. Earlier, Kitpou, perhaps in the tradition of Grey Owl, had parlayed himself into a variety of theatrical roles, including that of Screaming Chicken in the Hollywood series "F-Troop." But by the summer of 1971, all that was behind him and he had committed himself, from his home near Winfield, BC, to assist Wipper by transporting this priceless canoe across the country. This he did, giving talks to various groups along the way, raising money, until Thunder Bay.

Winter set in, or Kitpou's old Ford Falcon wagon gave up the ghost, or both. In the winter of 1971–72, Kitpou ended up leaving the first dugout of its kind in many, many years, right side up in Thunder Bay, just in time for it to fill with snow and ice. Wipper didn't get wind of this predicament until nearly spring of 1972, and he rushed north to Thunder Bay to rescue the priceless artifact, which, by this time, had suffered cracking and other damage from the freeze–thaw cycle it had undergone in its first woodland winter. The damage, he discovered, was serious, but fixable with a modicum of fibreglass cloth and resin and various other materials, and so Wipper was able to transport the Haida canoe to Toronto. There, he stored it in the lobby of the Ontario Institute for Studies in Education on Bloor Street, where he occasionally taught, a dry venue that proved to be an even more hostile environment for a canoe made of rainforest wood than the wilds of Thunder Bay. In the OISE building, the Haida canoe suffered another very serious horizontal crack, through the bow section, but this, too, was fixed and the canoe was again made more-or-less seaworthy for the next leg of its voyage.

It was a grand plan, to be sure. Determined to get the canoe to Kandalore as cheaply as possible, with as much public exposure as possible, and involving as many people as possible, including staff and campers from Kandalore, Wipper decided that the Haida canoe should be paddled from Toronto to Minden via Lake Ontario and the Trent Canal. And, as a former Navy man, he couldn't resist the temptation to begin this odyssey by putting the Haida canoe in Toronto Harbour, at Ontario Place, beside the Canadian Navy destroyer HMCS *Haida*.

The Kandalore counsellor to whom it fell to orchestrate this was John Fallis, who was dispatched in July 1972, with a group of fifteen-year-old boys and a number of other staff, to put the canoe in the waters of Lake Ontario and to create a pageant set against the backdrop of the huge destroyer of the same name. Surprisingly, he learned from his Kandalore boss, Kirk Wipper, that while he and his campers were paddling around the harbour, they would be accompanied by another member of the contingent, Chief Kitpou, whom Wipper had forgiven for the storage oversight at Thunder Bay. The "Chief" would stand in the canoe with staff, fur headdress and breech clout. Fallis recalls the day with a wry grin:

> We had to make ourselves look like Natives, despite the fact that a good number of the paddlers had blue eyes, braces and blond hair. So we covered ourselves with coconut butter and put on some loincloths that I guess were fairly typical of Plains Indians, who had never seen that amount of fresh water in their lives.
>
> Kitpou was standing in the front while we paddled around. He had his full regalia on, complete with the ... I always thought it was a cross between eastern Mohawk/Iroquois motif with sort of a Viking thing thrown in for good measure, that wolf headdress with the antlers on it. I think he claimed that he was Shaman Chief of the Haida, but it was all very sketchy. Very sketchy.
>
> It was a nice day. We paddled around. We waved at people who were paddling around in paddle boats. It wasn't anything too official, but there was something on a PA that said, "Now there are these people here from this camp and they're going to get on this boat, the *Haida*."[12]

The paddle-by was a big public-relations success for the canoe, if not for the Indian cause. A photo of Fallis and crew, with Kitpou standing in the eye-catching black and white dugout canoe, eagle on the prow, set against HMCS *Haida*, was published the following day in the *Toronto Star*. From Toronto, the canoe was trucked to the Trent Canal, Wipper, presumably, with memories of Masset Sound and Hecate Strait, a little shy of open water on Lake Ontario. From there, up through Peterborough and the Gull River system, with two Chestnut canvas-

covered 25-foot North canoes as tender vessels, the Haida canoe made
the last leg of its trip to the Kanawa Canoe Museum in Haliburton.

Haida canoe, west coast dugout, 26 feet

As a senior counsellor at Kandalore that summer, it fell to my group
of fourteen-year-olds to paddle these canoes from Buckhorn to
Minden. Until that point in my paddling career, I had never been on
lakes with a water horizon. Paddling across the top end of Pigeon Lake
under the Highway 36 bridge, south of Nogies Creek, and being
confronted with head winds, high waves and water as far as the eye
could see, was a scene and circumstance that still flutters the heart. The
Haida canoe took some getting used to. It was much more buoyant
and sat higher in the water than either of the North canoes and, being
round-bottomed and much heavier than the voyageur canoes, it
handled much differently from the craft we were used to. The Haida
canoe, it seemed, asked for a completely different set of reflexes, which
we did our best to learn. Nevertheless in the surf of Sturgeon Lake that
day, it was all we could do to keep the boat from rolling right over in
the waves and, with all of the publicity that seemed to accompany the
arrival of this boat in the East, what an embarrassment (to say nothing
of the safety of the campers and staff) it would have been to have to be
rescued. Mercifully, by this point in the trip, Kitpou had gone elsewhere, promising to meet up with us again for our ceremonial arrival
in Minden, so, with no one standing in the canoe, at least we were able

to keep our centre of gravity low enough to get the boat and its nervous crew into the lee of a point.

Seated on the shore in the sunshine, we watched the wind continue to blow and the waves continue to roll by us. Time ticked by. The campers got restless, and it became quite apparent that, unless we did something to make headway, we were going to be the crew responsible for knocking the whole escapade off schedule. Hence, driven by that pressure, and the need to do something creative to break the monotony, we procured three long poles which we used to lash the three canoes together: the Haida in the middle with a North canoe outrigger on both sides. And off we struck, into the evening sun.

By the time we turned north around Sturgeon Point, heading to the head of Sturgeon Lake at Fenelon Falls, it was pitch dark. By then the water was calm, but we had done so well in the trimaran configuration that we continued on, buoyed by the adventure of the whole day. But the boys were getting decidedly fatigued, and hungry, cranky even. So, in the best of summer camping spirit, we sang a few songs— voyageur songs from the camp song book that everyone knew by heart. Paddling through the darkness, singing in rhythm, eighteen paddlers in three canoes, lashed together on the water, someone yelled, "Shhhhhhhhhh. Somebody is calling." For a second, it occurred to me that the calling could not possibly be directed our way because here were we, in the dark, well behind schedule, approaching a place where none of us had been before in a dugout canoe from the Queen Charlotte Islands. But we dipped along in silence anyway, and the voice rang out again, this time to everyone's comprehension. Wafting across the star-sprinkled water came the memorable question "Do you know Kirk Wipper?"

Well, as a matter of fact, we did know Kirk Wipper, and to tell the caller so, turned our unusual rig shoreward and headed in where friends of Wipper's, who knew we were coming by ... sometime ... produced a feast of buns and hot soup, gallons of milk and hot chocolate, and a lawn on which to camp for what was left of the night.

The big push to make time in the wind and waves was driven largely by an event in Minden that would celebrate the arrival of this unique canoe in Haliburton County and its new home at the Kanawa Canoe

Museum. With surprising good humour, the crew was up early the following morning and back on the water, making its way over the next couple of days, the canoes now separated, up Balsam Lake to the locks at Norland, and hence up the Gull River to Gull Lake, past Camp Kilcoo to Minden. By the time we arrived in Minden, having paddled a hundred or so kilometres in the Haida canoe, I was still not sure about its stability. On arrival, we met Kirk and Kitpou, who let us know that the local reeve and the Chief himself would be riding with us for the river pageant. Imagining Kitpou standing up as we tried to negotiate the big canoe up the current of the Gull River made me fret all the more. However, when the time came to load the Haida canoe for its final, triumphant entry into Minden, Kitpou, reeve and all, the strangest and most satisfying lesson occurred.

While paddling up the Trent, we had decided to place all of the food and camping gear in the North canoes, thinking that the smaller the load in the Haida canoe, the quicker it would travel with its allotted six paddlers. With the reeve, though, a stout chap, there was no choice, we had to take the load. And so while we were nervously feathering our paddles in the water to steady the canoe at a dock just downstream from Minden, the reeve, chain of office and all, with the help of Wipper, Kitpou, and a number of aides, was lowered amidships. From the stern, I took one look at the bow in the middle seat and suggested that his lordship kneel for the trip. "Perhaps you'd be more comfortable," I lied. "Perhaps you will keep the centre of your bulk a little closer to the earth," I thought to myself. But then Kitpou jumped in, not a big man or tall in stature, but a thick little customer, complete with fur headdress and staff, who sank the canoe even farther into the surface of the river. With this load, it was as if the canoe became a rock-solid platform. With the extra weight of the reeve and Kitpou, even with the Chief standing, the Haida canoe was finally being paddled with something close to the load for which it was designed. The last hundred strokes in the big dugout were the best. The Minden pageant was a great success. The following day, the Haida canoe was trucked up Highway 35 to the museum, its home away from home, its fair-haired "pushers" or its original makers on Haida Gwaii having no real idea of its significance to the museum, or to the revival of canoe culture on the west coast, until much, much later.

In time, Alika Webber's insight, Kirk Wipper's forethought and Victor Adams' courage in making this Haida canoe idea real must become part of the overall historical account of the revival of the great dugout canoe in the Pacific Northwest. Like any worthwhile human enterprise, the great canoe renaissance is not the result of any one person or persons, or even of any one group of interested and committed people. The legacy now of many people of aboriginal and non-aboriginal extraction, in Canada and in the United States, in Oregon, Washington and Alaska, the Northwest-coast canoes have become symbols for a way of life, for a relationship among nations and between people and place.

The First Nations of the Northwest are taking the canoe idea forward as a central motif in teachings for young people. At an educational conference sponsored by the Association for Experiential Education, held near Seattle in 1990, a group of paddlers from Quileute Hoh Nation on the south shore of the Strait of Juan de Fuca came up with a set of universal teachings to be drawn from the canoe experience. They called them "The Ten Rules of the Canoe":

1. Every stroke we take is one less we have to make.
2. There is to be no abuse of self or others.
3. Be flexible.
4. The gift of each enriches all.
5. We all pull and support each other.
6. A hungry person has no charity.
7. Experiences are not enhanced through criticism.
8. The journey is what we enjoy.
9. A good teacher allows the student to learn.
10. When given any choice at all, be a worker bee—make honey![13]

Always eager to embrace traditions that will broaden the organization's diversity, the Association for Experiential Education, who formulated these rules, is but one example of how canoe teachings and traditions are breaking into the mainstream of educational and leadership training. There seems to be a natural resonance, a comfortable fit, between these teachings and the needs of a civil society. As canoe builders of the Northwest coast have asserted their independence and won back land, dignity and sovereignty, their canoe and canoe teachings, as emblems of a way of life regained, have crossed cultural barriers and found their way into decidedly non-aboriginal settings.

It is instructive to examine another canoe tradition, dragon-boat racing, that is moving east from British Columbia and finding a less-warm welcome than Northwest coast canoe teachings along the way. Dragon-boating is a canoe-racing phenomenon with Chinese roots. The original flurry of paddles, people, and long, narrow canoes with dragon heads happened on the fifth day of the fifth moon, in the fourth century B.C. on the Mi Luo River in central China. Chu' Yuan, a popular political dissident, tried to commit suicide by tying a rock to his waist and jumping from a boat into the river. Seeing this catastrophe, people paddled in vain to his rescue. It was out of this valiant effort and Chu' Yuan's sacrifice that the dragon-boat tradition began.

The Chinese have had a long history on the West Coast. The first to settle in Canada arrived in 1788, only five years after the formation of the North West Company, to assist Captain John Meares with the development of a trading post to support sea-otter commerce between Canton and Nootka Sound on Vancouver Island. Over the next century, in spite of systemic racism, head taxes and other confounding factors, Chinese took their place in history, labouring under appalling conditions to build the CPR up the Fraser valley, and persisted, settling on Vancouver Island and in Vancouver itself, especially at the mouth of the Fraser River.

With two long-standing cultural traditions in the Fraser delta, it was only natural that, sooner or later, the Chinese tradition of dragon-boat racing would find a home. But, as with the revival of the great canoes of the Northwest Coast Indians, the introduction of dragon-boating was symbolic, as much as anything, and highly political.

The creation of the Vancouver International Dragon Boat Festival was started to ease racial tension that had risen through the 1980s with high numbers of immigrants from the countries of the Pacific Rim, such as Hong Kong. David Lam, a local philanthropist, and British Columbia's first lieutenant-governor of Asian extraction, promoted the idea of dragon-boat racing and a festival that could be used to unite Vancouver's various factious cultural constituencies into one harmonious whole. Business people in the greater Vancouver area were so enthused by this idea that funds were raised almost immediately and a contagious tradition began. In a decade, the Vancouver International Dragon Boat Festival had grown to the point that the city was hosting the prestigious 1996 world championship of dragon-boat racing. That year 109 local crews with a total of 3,000 paddlers were joined by 19 international teams from seven different countries. As significant as the racing, however, were the goodwill and cross-cultural fellowship engendered in the audience for this grand occasion.[14]

Dragon-boat racing is the most unlikely sport to catch on, but catch on it did. Like canoe racing throughout North America, this form of canoe sport very much counters the notion of elitism and canoeing. Contrary to the days of fancy canoe clubs which, as a prerequisite to membership, had the condition of owning a canoe, racing in big canoes was something that anyone could do, whether you owned a boat or not. Racing made canoeing accessible to working-class people, but there was, at least until the advent of dragon boats in Canada, the requirement of physical prowess on which participation hinged. To join a canoe-racing club, as participant, a person needed to be fit, more of the athlete type than not. But dragon-boating, although it has its highly competitive side, has been as much about participation as it has been about competition and, with lots of space on the side of the boats for corporate logos, and lots of razzle-dazzle hoopla in the cultural events that tend to envelop the races, it has attracted an unprecedented following in Canada, the United States and around the world.

Two aspects of this canoeing innovation are instructive: the response dragon-boat racing had received in the "traditional" canoeing community; and the way in which, as with the great dugout canoes of the Northwest, the dragon-boat spirit of team play, endurance, fitness and good old outdoor fun on the water has been picked up by the community as a metaphor for a positive, healthy life.

Not surprisingly, there is an anti–dragon-boat constituency within the canoeing community, including particularly those for whom the fur trade and the North canoe loom large, and those who resonate with the blue lake/rocky shore/red canoe paddling experience *à la* Tom Thomson, Bill Mason and Pierre Trudeau. For these people, the canoe as a symbol of Canada, includes, in theory, at least, west coast dugouts, but in practice the imagery is largely that of woodland canoes, *coureurs de bois*, voyageurs, portages, and long, hot days on inland, freshwater lakes. For people of this tradition, the notion of dragon boats just doesn't fit: it's perhaps too plebeian, too accessible to anybody with a life vest, a paddle and a few free Saturday afternoons; but, more significantly, dragon boats are not of the land, they are un-Canadian, not even, some would claim, of the North American continent.

In fact, there is a significant portion of Canadian history that has, in a sense, been eclipsed by the domination of central Canadian canoe motifs in the overall story of canoes in Canada and North America. As important as the beaver was as cargo and *raison d'être* to the Nor'Westers and the traders of the Hudson's Bay Company, adjusted to monetary scale, the sea otter was of equal import and significance to the west-coast dugout tradition and traders in China, Russia and the Pacific Rim. And while the *canot du nord* and *canot du maître* were fundamentally European enlargements and adaptations of smaller aboriginal craft, the west-coast dugouts, were, throughout their period of use in the Pacific fur trade, in purely aboriginal form, unaffected and unaltered by Asian or European sensibilities. Who is to say that in time the dragon boat will not add to the rich and varied tradition of canoeing in Canada?

With events now in many Canadian cities and North American dragon-boaters competing in events around the world, this is a paddling sensation that commands notice, whether traditional canoeists, of whatever stripe, like it or not. In my home town of Guelph, Ontario—in the heart of traditional canoe country—the local Rotary Club organized a dragon-boat race on the local reservoir. In 1997, there were twenty-eight teams in attendance, and in 1998, in spite of gale-force winds and rain, there were sixty-seven teams in attendance. Next year they are expecting even more growth.

There is an ecumenical, international flavour that has developed as the idea of dragon-boat racing has spread around the world. Unique in its promotion of fellowship and fun, unlike the Olympics or any other kind of bilateral or multilateral professional sporting event, dragon-boat racing is as much about the people who paddle the canoes as it is about the craft themselves or the act of racing. And out of this rapidly spreading international phenomenon is growing a canoe ethic that is not only healthy, but inspiring in its own way.

Take, for example Dr. Donald McKenzie, one-time Canadian Olympic paddler and now physician who decided to challenge the notion that women with breast cancer should never involve themselves in physical activity requiring strenuous upper-body exercise, a dispiriting prescription that often accompanies the even more shocking news and treatment of breast cancer. After trying out a paddling exercise regime on a small scale with a few patients in kayaks, Dr. McKenzie approached a breast cancer support group to see if there were women who would join him in creating a dragon-boat team, for fun, for companionship and team play, for therapy. Out of this notion came first one group—a twenty-two-member team that called itself "Abreast in a Boat"—followed by two others called "Breasting the Waves" and "Breast Strokes" (there is a tradition in dragon-boat racing for building bad puns into team nomenclature, such as "Sho No Mercy" and "Oarsome Intellect"). The exercise has had no ill effects and in fact has given the women, in many cases, new hope. Says one team member, "What tremendous power we all have ... it's the power to overcome the lingering spectre of breast cancer and the power to inspire others to do the same."[15]

The 1998 World Dragon Boat Championships were held in Wellington, New Zealand. Reports about this sporting event have precious little in them about times and results of who won and who lost, although these parameters did figure in the competition somewhere. Instead, the face of dragon-boat racing that emerged was one of canoe as crucible for international cooperation in which full-out human striving is mixed with the unimpeachable virtues of sportsmanship, friendship and fun. "Abreast in a Boat" from Vancouver managed to pull together the funds to attend and, although they did race and did place somewhere in the standings, they're noted in one report for their rendition at the Thursday Team Talent Contest of an original song about breast cancer written by Tim King. As with the Ten Lessons of the Canoe that have been drawn in recent times from the Great Canoe Experience by First Nations paddlers from the Northwest coast, canoe-learning from the dragon-boat experience is becoming part of something quite marvellous that is crossing Canada and making its way around the world. And, depending on who is doing the reporting, the accounts of what happens in the wee hours at the boat races sounds more than a little like the absolute best of what went on around the voyageur campfire or in the bawdy days of the Beaver Club dinners at Lachine.

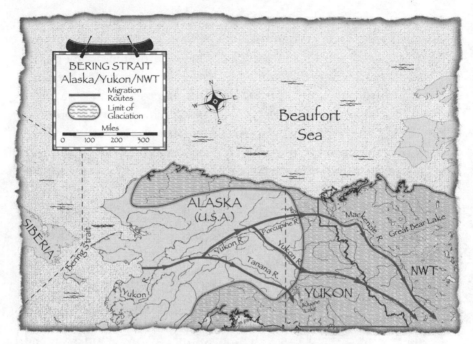

11

THE DOMESTICATED TREE

The primary fact of the Canadian experience is a geographical
one, whose major ingredient is the presence of the Canadian
Shield, which dominates our country, comprises most of its
wilderness and ... is still best explored by canoe.

—William C. James, in *Nastawgan*[1]

HIKING ALONE UP THE STEEP SIDE of Sheep Mountain in Kluane National Park, I rise beyond the limit of trees and look out across the Slims River Delta to Kluane Lake. Born in Ontario, summering on the Canadian Shield, I'm not a mountain person. Today, catching breath in the Yukon sunshine, my eyes are drawn to impossibly blue water far below, and a picture of Robert Service in a birchbark canoe pops into my head. The photo may even have been taken in England or on the Seine, I can't remember for sure. It's just a man in a canoe on the water with nothing identifiable in the background, no rocks, no trees, no Marilyn Monroe. He's wearing a broad-brimmed hat, looking like a Mountie or Robert Baden-Powell. What I do remember are snippets of his poem "The Call of the Wild":

> There's a whisper on the night wind,
> There's a star agleam to guide us,
> And the Wild is calling, calling ... let us go.

Moving on, a snippet of "The Law of the Yukon" wanders in and out of memory, like the braided channels in golden mud and silver strand just beyond my feet:

> Searching my uttermost valleys, fighting each step as they go,
> Shooting the wrath of my rapids, scaling my ramparts of snow.

Grace Reid, an old family friend, gave me *Songs of a Sourdough* when I was far too young to appreciate the fact that the leather-bound book was the 1909 William Briggs edition of the Yukon poet's first published work. It was the pictures I remember and the poems—Grace's favourite was "The Cremation of Sam McGee," mine "The Shooting of Dan McGrew"—full of words and images that made me think of summer camp:

> A bunch of the boys were whooping it up in the
> Malamute saloon;
> The kid that handles the music-box was hitting a
> jag-time tune;

Back of the bar, in a solo game, sat Dangerous Dan McGrew,
And watching his luck was his light-o'-love, the lady
    that's known as Lou.[2]

We acted out the poem one summer, after a long canoe trip in
Temagami. For a time, I was cast as the lady that's known as Lou, until
one of the kitchen girls relieved me of yet another drag part—camps
had lots of these—and I was promoted to the role of piano player.
Walking, thinking, breathing the cool air, looking for sheep on Sheep
Mountain, listening to the beat of my own heart, I'm thinking about
camp, thinking about paddling, and how if God had really wanted us
to climb mountains, he would never have given us the canoe.

At the summit of Sheep Mountain, if you can call a grassy knoll such
a thing, the view extends nearly 20 kilometres up the Slims River's
"uttermost valley." Tracing west with binoculars I can just make out the
tip of the famous Kaskawulsh Glacier, where this water begins. From
there, at the limit of ancient ice, this gnarled finger of the ocean carves
a mountain valley through Kluane Lake, then down north to meet the
Yukon River, upstream from Service's cabin at Dawson, before sweeping northwest across Alaska to another bigger delta at Norton Sound
on the Bering Sea. One day, I think, this would be an excellent place to
start a canoe trip, to paddle from ice to ocean. But that conflicts with
another dream of building a raft on the Yukon and playing cards in vest
and Trilby hat from the "marge of Lake Lebarge" to Dawson. Not to
worry: two trips, two separate outings, chasing Service, seeking adventure but from now on, by boat. This hiking thing is for people who
don't know canoes.

Today, twenty years later, having never returned—yet—to paddle in
the Yukon, I think back on that place, of the mountains and ice, and
rivers to the sea, and wonder how it was and in what form, if at all, that
the canoe found its way to this part of the world. From the stiff-keeled,
hog-sheered Beothuk canoe and the heavily rockered crooked canoes
of the Cree and Montagnais, to the fine lines of William and Mary
Commanda's classic Algonquin craft, west and north to the decked and
dimpled bows of the Dogrib and Chipewyan bark canoes, to the sturgeon-nosed Kootenay canoes of the BC interior and the massive

dugouts of the coast, there are differences in line and detail in the canoes of North America and striking similarities in construction methods and materials. The first people, the anthropologists tell us, came from Asia, but what about canoes?

During the height of the last ice age, the only part of North America to be ice-free was a corridor of land in what is now Alaska and the Yukon. And because an inordinate amount of the earth's water was bound up in ice hundreds of metres thick that covered much of North America, ocean levels went down, creating Beringia, a broad isthmus of land connecting Asia with Alaska. Based on a prodigious body of research and evidence, prevailing wisdom suggests that the first people to enter North America did so on foot via this bridge, nomadic peoples with coppery skin, dark eyes, straight black hair, wide cheekbones and shovel-shaped incisors. These people followed large game animals like the woolly mammoth, American mastodon, short-faced bear, Alaskan camel, muskox and giant beaver (estimated to be 2.5 metres long and 200 kilograms! with a pelt the size of a black bear) across the hardy grasses and through the dwarf willow and birch bushes of the Mammoth Steppe. The descendants of these so-called Palaeo-Indians eventually spread across North America and south to Tierra del Fuego on the tip of South America.

There are three schools of thought about when this might have happened, two of which are based on terrestrial arrival and one, the most speculative, suggesting arrival by sea. On the basis of stone point evidence, that links finds of similarly aged bifacially flaked knives and weapon tips at places like Old Crow Flats and Bluefish Caves, in northwestern Yukon, Late Arrivalists argue that first peoples arrived in North America sometime around 12,000 years before present (B.P.), spreading rapidly and managing to wipe out the large animals by about 8,000 B.P. Moderates are of the opinion that initial entry may have begun as early as 20,000 B.P., spreading slowly and being affected by the eventual extinction of the megafauna due to climate change. Boldest of all because their claims are based on much slimmer evidence, Early Arrivalists contend that Amerinds may have moved across Beringia as early as 50,000–60,000 B.P. and that they did so by boat, the same way Polynesia, New Zealand and Australia were populated. Lithic artifacts, such as stone points and tools, in contrast, are much more durable, and it is largely on the basis of this type of evidence that patterns are drawn. Recent genetic evidence, from the DNA of plants, animals and people, shows quite clearly a link between North American and Asian populations.

If people did come on foot, hunting large game, and finally settling in various regions across North America, it would seem that canoe-building was a technology derived from available materials in response to local needs. To travel any distance, clearly water crossings must have been made. Speculation is that at first single logs were put to this purpose, followed by rafts, dugouts and other craft, like bark canoes, as transportation technology advanced. What is fascinating to see is the similarity in the bark canoes that emerged over time, as if First Nations across the country learned from the same master builder.

If, indeed, bark canoes evolved *in situ* across North America, how to account for the striking similarity between aboriginal craft in Europe and Asia with New World boats? Could it be that similarity between the Welsh coracle, that circular canoe-like craft made of a hide-covered willow-branch frame, and its North American cousin, the bullboat of the prairies, is a quirk of circumstance, a happy accident? And what about the striking similarity between the sturgeon-nosed Kootenay canoe of the central British Columbia plateau and the canoes of the Amur River valley that marks the northern border between China and the Soviet Union? Did these designs evolve independently, or was there at some point in prehistory some kind of technological transfer between the Old World and the New?

The funny, pointed triangular snoots of the Kootenay and Amur River canoes are, in fact, quite primitive in terms of boat design. I saw this demonstrated in the 1980s during a build-a-canoe-out-of-card-board competition at a canoe and kayak symposium on Vancouver's waterfront. The challenge offered to teams willing to cough up the entry fee was to construct a canoe out of one (or maybe two) 4- by 8-foot sheets of corrugated cardboard, using a roll of duct tape as adhesive. Similar to the pine and elm bark available in central BC and Northern China, the cardboard was stiff and tended to crimp rather than conform to fair curves. Although I'd been drafted into a team, as a visiting speaker from the East with pressed trousers and no real idea of what was going on, I'm afraid I wasn't much help to the cause. But there was much to see.

The design invariably explored by all first-time teams was ... the sturgeon-nose canoe. Some teams actually went with this as their final design, but most, especially teams with experience in the competition in other years, tended to move quickly to a more traditional bow curve and entry line. The attraction of the sturgeon-nose design was that this end called for the least amount of interior stiffening, and a relatively short, straight seam that had to be waterproofed. Teams simply rounded the cardboard into a trough on its longitudinal axis and then rolled the end corners over themselves, back from the end of the cardboard at the keel line, until a neat triangular end profile was achieved. Had this been done with birch or spruce bark, it was easy to see that one could likely achieve a serviceable end to a boat in this manner with very little wood on the inside to keep in in place.

The more the finished products looked like classic Canadian canoes, the more nuance of design seemed to be involved. Teams with more building experience tended to move away from the rudimentary sturgeon-nose to stems that curved up and away from the keel line. The craft that won that year—the final test being a race along False Creek in which paddlers actually had to get in the cardboard canoes—turned out be a very sophisticated canoe that had been designed by a team of engineers who had obviously been thinking about their entry for a long time. They had mapped the various cuts and seams on a paper template. Every triangular scrap of cardboard they cut to accommodate curvature of their finished canoe was incorporated into the design somewhere else, as stiffening element, decking or thwart material. The lesson I drew from this experience was about canoe evolution: I came to see that there was a possibility that different materials with similar bending properties could have given rise to similarly shaped canoes in different parts of the world. Canoe designer John Winters' theory of canoes conforming to the bending properties of available materials certainly makes it at least possible for this to occur. I wonder, though, about the switch from solid wood dugout-style canoes to canoes with skin. Why was it, for example, that these Palaeo-Indians or their descendants used bark and not the hides of the animals they they were killing anyway for bone and food? Was it that the bark was a better building material? Does hide get too sloppy when it's wet?[3]

The Early Arrivalists' idea that Palaeo-Indians came to North America in boats is even more intriguing. The gist of this argument comes from a theory that, even with the fluctuations of ocean levels around the world, Australia and New Zealand were never connected by land to Asia and, as such, had to be inhabited first by people who either swam or came by boat. Historian Robert McGhee links this process to the settlement of North America:

> There is continuing argument about the time of the first immigration to the New World. It was long thought that humans could not have reached the American continents until the end of the ice age, that prior to the last major ice advance, 25,000 to 15,000 years ago, human cultures in the Old World had developed neither technologies capable of living in the cold arctic conditions of northeast Asia nor water craft capable of crossing the open water of a flooded Bering Strait. Recent research indicates, however, that man had reached Australia across a wide stretch of open sea by at least 30,000 years ago, and that as long as 200,000 years ago the Paleolithic (Old Stone Age) occupants of Europe were living under extremely cold environmental conditions and may have had water craft capable of crossing the Strait of Gibraltar. It is theoretically possible, therefore, that humans could have reached North America from northeast Siberia at any time during the past 100,000 years.[4]

Other proponents of this more radical point of view about the populating of North America put forward the idea of a "voyaging nursery" that may have existed along the island chains of the South Pacific. The concept here is that particular types of craft, maybe even canoes, would be paddled or sailed from one island to the next, where the technology would grow and flourish before moving on, in a more evolved form, to the next island, and so on to the end of the line in Australia or New Zealand. A contemporary Maori chant celebrates the arrival of the "great canoe" bringing original inhabitants. It is recited nowadays to welcome guests to a Maori *marae*, a traditional communal gathering place, and is always accompanied by rhythmic hand and arm movements that mimic the pulling of a canoe onto land:

Leader	People	Translation
Toia mai,	te waka	Pull up, the canoe
Kumea mai,	te waka	Drag up, the canoe
Ki te uranga	te waka	To the resting place, the canoe

All

Ki to takotoranga i	To the place where it will lie
Takoto ai, te waka	At rest, the canoe[5]

Evidence supporting the claim that North America's first inhabitants came in similar fashion, through Japan, Sakhalin Island, Kamchatka, the Aleutians, in another "voyaging nursery," is, as yet, scanty at best. There is much stronger evidence pointing to a much later arrival from Asia, long after the arrival of the Amerinds, of early Inuit who came across the Bering Strait in skin-covered umiaks. Roberts and Shackleton, for example, point out that a wavy decorative line along the inwale of very early model of a Nootkan dugout canoe on the west coast is, in fact, a memory of the canoe's ancestor, the Arctic umiak, "reminiscent of the stretched edge of the umiak's skin cover where it was laced down to the frame of the boat."[6] George Dyson's work with baidarkas[7]—Russian sea-going kayaks—points to more or less the same conclusion, about relatively recent connections through the Aleutian chain of islands between Asia and North America. Thor Heyerdahl, through his experiential research, makes similar claims, but the open-ocean distances in his theories are much larger.

There are First Nations stories, of course, about the origin of the canoe that cannot be discounted. The most obvious of these link back to the legends of Dekanahwideh and Glooscap and their sudden arrival in the New World. Technologically, the paleontologists and archaeologists would agree, the people who arrived first in North America were of Stone Age culture. It would make perfect sense then that the first canoe was, in fact, made of stone. After all, they had the technology to fashion such a craft. As for what might have happened to these stone canoes, well who is to know? They were certainly more durable and rot-resistant than their wood-and-bark counterparts, but they were heavy and did tend to sink. Future imaging of the ocean floor and/or analysis of deep lake sediments will likely turn up evidence of these canoes, if it is there to be had.

There are other versions of these legends as well. There has been speculation about the blue-eyed, light-haired Mandan Indians of the central prairies (southern Saskatchewan/Manitoba, North Dakota), and their relationship to people of European stock, possibly of Viking or Celtic descent—the canoe-related conundrum being the verisimilitude between the round or oval Mandan bullboat, made of wooden frame with animal-hide cover and used for prairie river crossings, and the Welsh coracle. The notion of a possible race of white Europeans in central North America, predating Columbus, who may have brought with them the bullboat design and lived with North American First Nations was an object of investigation by the venerable American canoe-born explorers Lewis and Clark, who made their way from St. Louis to the Pacific in the early years of the nineteenth century. In spite of their desire to shed light on the situation, whether there was or is a relationship between the Mandan people, their canoe-like craft, and Europeans remains a matter of conjecture, as yet unfounded in the archaeological record.

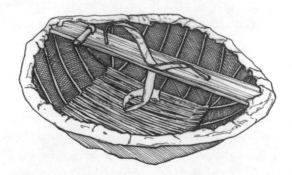

Mandan bullboat, sapling and buffalo hide, 6-foot diameter

Another sticky end in canoe cosmology is a story told by Tony Andre, a Gwichya Gwich'in elder from Tsiigehtchic in the Mackenzie River valley, about another legendary traveller, Atachuu kaii', who it is said "dreamed the birchbark canoe into existence."[8] As with most of the suppositions about how people and technology came to the New World—scientific and otherwise—this version of events is roundly endorsed by some and flatly rejected by others. It is interesting to note that other Dene stories from the Mackenzie valley feature huge beavers, very similar to ones that have turned up in the fossil record. Who is to say that a technology as venerable as the bark canoe did not come from a higher place via the dream of a great traveller?

Closer to home, Kirk Wipper carries with him the notion of cradle canoes, meaning designs from which whole lines of subsequent craft have evolved, based on the assumption that when people travelled, in canoes or on foot, the designs of their ancestors travelled with them. He explains:

Cradle boats are very ancient craft that gave rise to all kinds of others. It's my own expression. I don't think there are a great number of them. You'd have to go back to the beginning of humankind, and you'd have to say that the first cradle boat was probably a log floating by, and some enterprising human got on it and, much to his delight, he moved along the water, probably in the current. So in a sense that is *the* original cradle boat, and I just use the expression.

But I see the dragon boat that way, the idea of the beautiful, ornate character of the boat. Look at the Maori canoe—it's a lot like a dragon boat. And the artwork on this craft, like the dragon boat, represents a tribute to its builder's ancestors. The decorations are not there just for colour, they're there for this very fundamental notion, because the ancestors were important.

And the west-coast craft, like the Haida and Nootka canoes, I think they have a linkage to the Polynesian craft. I've always said that, and some of the ethnologists are tending to agree because many of the rituals surrounding the taking of the tree, the colour, the music, the construction modes, the paddling styles relate very much. Now that could be coincidence, but it may not be coincidence.[9]

As member of the Explorer's Club of New York, Wipper had a chance to compare notes with the great contemporary adventurer Thor Heyerdahl, and got in a bit of an argument on these matters:

> We discussed his book, *Kon-tiki*, and, you know, I told him I thought he was guilty of selective evidence, which is not uncommon in scientific research. He argued that there was a cache on Easter Island and that this was there as a result of migration of South Americans *out* into the Pacific. What he didn't say was that there were Polynesian artifacts in the same cache as well. I argued that what may have happened, and who knows the truth, is that Polynesians came across— which they were quite capable of doing—went to South America, picked up some artifacts, put them back on Easter Island with their own items, and then went back home again.
> And Thor said, "You know, if I had to write the book over again, that's the way I'd write it. I'd tell the whole story." But then he added, "I'm too old to do that now."[10]

Whatever its origins—and there is clearly much more study to be done on this topic—there can be little doubt about the place and significance of the canoe in Canadian experience. It is a device that crosses cultures and rivers of time, touching every aspect of Canadian life— eastern, western, northern, Aboriginal, French and English. Designed by First Nations, paddled by explorers, employed by industry, revered by recreationalists, the canoe has evolved from a simple conveyance to a complex symbol with deep, often spiritual, meaning. Some historians even go so far as to suggest that Canada exists because of the canoe. It might be slightly less emphatic to say simply that it would be impossible to tell even a small portion of the story of this nation without mentioning canoe again and again because, throughout Canadian history, the canoe has been a product of time, place and need. The magic of the canoe is that it is both timeless and a reflection of the changing culture around it.

Little wonder, then, that when the Government of Canada called for proposals for a sculpture to install outside its new embassy in Washington, DC, the central motif in the chosen entry was a canoe. Bill Reid's *The Spirit of Haida Gwaii* depicts an eclectic menagerie of mythological figures riding together in a giant dugout canoe. But so ingrained is the canoe in Canadian experience that in most interpretations of this sculpture the significance of all of the main characters is described in detail—all elements, that is, except the canoe. The canoe is just there, as womb or vessel, or as fact of the landscape from which it was derived, buoying the hopes and aspirations of the Bear Family, Frog, Eagle, Dogfish Woman, Raven, Mouse Woman, Chief and the Ancient Reluctant Conscript.

Known colloquially as "The Black Canoe"[11] (while he was working on it in his Granville Island studio in Vancouver, Reid referred jokingly to the work as "Sunday Afternoon on Lost Lagoon,"[12] and the "Ship of Fools"[13]), the canoe at the Canadian embassy in Washington confused some people. Among those was historian Daniel Francis, who worked through his befuddlement in *National Dreams*:

> Why are "we" always borrowing Aboriginal iconography, I
> muttered to no one in particular, "we" meaning mainstream,
> white, Euro-Canadian culture? Don't "we" have any stories of
> our own to tell? Clearly the government was attempting to
> merge Aboriginal mythology with a general mythology of
> relevance to all Canadians, Aboriginal and non-Aboriginal
> alike, but as I thought more about Reid's bronze canoe it
> became clear to me that the choice was a perfectly appropriate
> one after all. The canoe, and the story of transformation that
> it embodies, does not belong solely to the Aboriginal people.
> They are also central emblems of non-Native Canadian
> culture. Ever since the first European traders and colonists
> arrived in Canada, the canoe journey into the wilderness has
> been a consistent theme of our history and our culture ... The

canoe emerges as the mother image of our national dream life, the symbol of our oneness with a rugged northern landscape, the vessel in which we are recreated as Canadians. As much as the beaver or the Canada goose or the maple leaf, the canoe is presented as our link to the land, to the past, to our Aboriginal forebears, and to our spiritual roots.[14]

The Spirit of Haida Gwaii went on to become the subject of a ninety-cent stamp in the "Art Canada" series, issued in 1996 by the Canada Post Philatelic Service—about the thirtieth Canadian stamp since 1903[15] on which a canoe is featured—indicating that historian Daniel Francis has not been the only person to recognize the symbolic importance of the canoe in Canadian experience. As we have seen, there are canoes in music, literature, advertising, government, and in the experience of every place on every river and waterway in the land. And, while there are canoes throughout the northeastern United States and through the American heartland to the Gulf of Mexico, the prevailing historical experience south of the border is informed by a different set of symbols. Trent University historian John Wadland leans heavily on the canoe as a national symbol:

> As I see it, the central informing symbol of America is the horse, an imported domestic animal charged with the job of carrying cowboys, pulling wagons full of settlers, dispatching the cavalry against the Indians. The equivalent symbol for interior of Canada must surely be the canoe ... a domesticated tree.[16]

Masquerading as the famous canoe philosopher Kevlar Quarante-Neuf, Ottawa valley paddler and poet Philip Chester put a slightly finer tip on this point, saying: "When an American sees a canoe strapped to a car or float plane, he sees a canoe; a Canadian senses a way of life."[17] Historian John Jennings is of similar mind. He writes:

> Canada is short on unifying symbols. The maple leaf is not found universally and, in itself does not represent our history

or our qualities as a people. The Mounties and hockey are strong symbols, but the Mounties are not loved by significant numbers of Canadians and hockey, in an era of expansion franchises, is no longer particularly Canadian.

What is left? Certainly commitment to world order, as reflected in our peacekeeping role, and our belief in tolerance and diversity as represented in our policy of multiculturalism.

But the one unifying symbol unique to Canada, the Canadian parallel to the cowboy's horse, a symbol that links with our history, with adventure, with heroic deeds, with nation building and, most importantly, with a unique Canadian landscape is the canoe.[18]

But to suggest that any one canoe could represent the totality of Canadian experience with canoes in general is to deny the spectrum of craft and the significant differences in the ways in which canoe narratives have evolved in the various regions of the country. To consider the canoe as a Canadian cultural icon, one must embrace the bark canoe in all its variants along with the great dugouts of the West and the other permutations, like the Gander Bay boat, the York boat, or the Mandan bullboat, that are part of the Canadian canoe tradition.

The *idea* of canoe—the canoe as sacred text, perhaps—is a different thing altogether, and a much more pan-Canadian phenomenon. In this respect, the canoe unites Canadians from coast to coast to coast and girds us with the strength of common heritage. Arising from a riparian vessel made of local materials, by local people to meet local needs, the idea of canoe is, at its core, about relationships: between people and place, nature and technology, and among people who would pull together in common purpose. Canoe balances strength and vulnerability, old and new, regional differences and national interests, Aboriginal and Other, French and English. A durable idea, canoe reminds us of who we are, where we have been, as a nation, and where we might go— where we should go, and where we should not—in a world of shifting identities and fading political boundaries. The canoe grounds us through direct and accessible experience in our home landscapes. The canoe is Canada.

Another time, another sunny, summer day, still speculating about canoes and Canada, I've come down from Sheep Mountain, moved east to Northern Ontario, and I am sitting outside the Portage Store at Canoe Lake in Algonquin Park with my wife and daughters, eating ice cream and watching the dock where battered rental canoes come and go. An international parade makes its way from the parking lot to the kiosk, some folk in conventional summer dress like shorts, halter tops, T-shirts and bathing suits, but many in various types of flowing ethnic dress—silks, saffrons, vibrant floral prints—which are duly topped with personal flotation devices and settled onto the seats of Springbok aluminum canoes. Young staff, many of them alumni from the various nearby camps, are keen to provide instruction to help these visitors make way under their own steam. Many accept the lessons, some do not. Demonstration always works better than explanation. But all comers, sooner or later, and with plenty of lively discussion about improvisation and technique, make their way, however tentatively, out onto the waters that once floated Tom Thomson. I'm guessing that just about everyone in this location has come to the conclusion that to be part of the Canadian experience is to paddle a canoe. Between licks of ice cream, itching to embark on our own adventure in Algonquin Park, in this nation of rivers, I think they may be right.

EPILOGUE

WHERE CANOES RETIRE

CANOES IN TIME turn back to earth—paddles to ashes, gunwales to dust—to nurture new generations of bark, skin, and cedar. But they can be preserved. Most museums in North America (and a surprising number internationally) have canoes in their collections—notable among these being the Adirondack Museum at Blue Mountain Lake, New York (Web www.netheaven.com/~museum/index.html), which has in its collection 106 rowing craft, including 58 Adirondack guide-boats, and 59 canoes and kayaks, including 8 decked cruising canoes and 8 birchbark craft.

Two other superb canoe resources are the Canadian Recreational Canoeing Association, 446 Main Street West, Merrickville, Ontario, Canada, K0G 1N0—Tel (613) 269-2910, Fax (613) 269-2980, E-mail staff@crca.ca, and Web www.crca.ca (which publishes a lively journal and has the best catalogue of mail-order canoe books), and the Wooden Canoe Heritage Association, Box 226, Blue Mountain Lake, New York, USA 12812, Web www.wcha.org (which publishes the *Wooden Canoe Journal* and is the most engaging aggregation of canoe nuts anywhere on the planet).

However, the largest collection of canoes, kayaks and rowing craft in the world is in the Canadian Canoe Museum in Peterborough, Ontario, which opened its doors to the public in July 1997. Besides a collection more than 600 craft, including dozens of bark canoes, thousands of canoe-related artifacts, and a growing archive, the Canadian Canoe Museum has distinguished itself from the beginning by surrounding the craft with a robust culture of canoeing. Inside the main exhibit building, along side heritage craft of all kinds, there is a working shop overseen by a master canoe-builder where boats are constructed, repaired and restored and, in any given week, one will find educational programs of various kinds, re-enactments, guest speakers, hands-on workshops, or opportunities for more casual interaction with canoe people of all sizes and shapes. It's a national treasure. Contact:

The Canadian Canoe Museum,
910 Monaghan Road,
P.O. Box 1664,
Peterborough, Ontario,
Canada, K9J 7S4

Tel (705) 748-9153
Fax (705) 748-0616
E-mail canoemuseum@ptbo.igs.net
Web www.canoemuseum.net

NOTES

CHAPTER 1

[1] Rudy Wiebe, *Playing Dead: A Contemplation Concerning the Arctic* (Edmonton: NeWest Publishers, 1989), p. 12.

[2] Mason reiterated this point many times in print and in his public lectures and, having read and heard this many times over the last couple of decades, I am repeating it here as much from memory as from anywhere else. Those who would like a slightly more tangible source for this quotation can turn to Mason's books, where an actual written quotation goes as follows: "When you look at the face of Canada and study the geography carefully, you come away with the feeling that God could have designed the canoe first and then set about to conceive a land in which it could flourish": *Path of the Paddle* (Toronto: Van Nostrand Reinhold, 1980), p. 2. Mason's film *Paddle to the Sea* (Montreal: National Film Board of Canada, order number C 0166 061) is an adaptation of Holling Clancy Holling's classic children's story of the same title (Boston: Houghton Mifflin Company, 1941 & 1969). Although it was never eclipsed by other children's canoe stories, there are newer books for children and young people, ranging from an episode of the *Berenstain Bears* in which the family goes whitewater canoeing and illustrated volumes like *Little Beaver and the Echo*, written by Amy MacDonald and illustrated by Sarah Fox-Davies (London, Boston, Sydney: Walker Books, 1997); *Morning on the Lake*, written by Jan Bourdeau Waboose and illustrated by Karen Reczuch (Toronto: Kids Can Press, 1998); and *A Dog Came Too*, written by Ainslie Manson and illustrated by Ann Blades (Toronto/Vancouver: A Groundwood Book, Douglas & McIntyre, 1993).

[3] A Toronto event that began as a simple canoe-trip slide show in the living room of University of Toronto physics professor George J. Luste has become an international wilderness canoeing symposium, sponsored by the Wilderness Canoe Association, which takes place each year around the third weekend in January.

[4] John Winters, interview with author. Burks Falls, Ontario, February 19, 1997.

[5] Ibid.

246

[6] "The River Man." A segment in the Newfoundland-produced *Land and Sea* series (St. John's, NF: CBC Television, 1973).

[7] Gary Saunders, *Rattles and Steadies: Memoirs of a Gander River Man* (St. John's, NF: Breakwater Books, 1986), p. 171.

[8] John Winters, *The Shape of the Canoe* (Burks Falls, ON: Redwing Designs, 1996), p. 23. This highly readable (given the complex nature of the topic) booklet expands on a series of articles published in *Canoesport Journal* between 1988 and 1991. Says Winters about the content, "This book is written for the many paddlers and boat builders who would like to better understand how boats perform and should not be considered a comprehensive text on the topic."

[9] Saunders, *Rattles and Steadies*, pp. 174, 175.

[10] This reference to "man slaves" appears in an essay by ethnographer Lee Sultzman that draws on the original journals of Gaspar Corte-Real, entitled "Beothuk History," published on the World Wide Web at www.dickshovel.com/beo/html.

[11] Among these hazards were being hunted and shot (reputedly under bounty on occasion) for sport. The sorry story of the Beothuk has been treated by all manner of authors, from classical ethnographers like James Howley, in *The Beothucks or Red Indians* (Cambridge: Cambridge University Press, 1915) and Ingeborg Marshall, in standard ethnographic texts including his *A History and Ethnography of the Beothuk* (Montreal & Kingston: McGill-Queen's University Press, 1996) and *Beothuk Bark Canoes: An Analysis and Comparative Study* (Ottawa: National Museums of Canada, Canadian Ethnology Service Paper No. 102 in the National Museum of Man Mercury Series, 1985), and even historical books for young adults such as *The Beothuk of Newfoundland: A Vanished People* (St. John's, NF: Breakwater Books, 1989). And, like many historical events, the tragic demise of the Beothuk people has been considered in works of fiction and dramatic plays such as Geoffrey Ursell's *The Running of the Deer* (Toronto: Playwrights Canada, 1981).

[12] Howley, *The Beothucks or Red Indians*, p. 313.

[13] Edwin Tappan Adney and Howard I. Chapelle, *The Bark Canoes and Skin Boats of North America* (Washington, DC: Smithsonian Institution Press, 1983), p. 95.

[14] Kenneth Roberts and Phil Shackleton, *The Canoe: A History of the Craft from Panama to the Arctic* (Toronto: Macmillan, 1983).

[15] Marshall, *A History and Ethnography of the Beothuk*, p. 364.

[16] Ibid, p. 365.

[17] Marshall, *The Beothuk of Newfoundland: A Vanished People*, p. 14.

[18] Lloyd Seaward, interview with author, Bishop's Falls, Newfoundland, October 15, 1998.

[19] Ibid.

[20] Ibid.

CHAPTER 2

1 Roderick A. Macdonald, Canexus: *The Canoe in Canadian Culture* (Toronto: Betelgeuse Books, 1988), pp. 167, 170.

2 Arthur Ray, *I Have Lived Here Since the World Began: An Illustrated History of Canada's Native Peoples* (Toronto: Lester Publishing/Key Porter Books, 1996), p. 48. "Contact" in this context means in the broad Canadian sense, not including encounters between the Beothuk and Cabot and any of the European fishers. What is intriguing about this account is that it is the first time in the Canadian historical record that canoes and ships on the same horizon are described.

3 Ibid, pp. 49–50.

4 Also called the Iroquois League, or Haudenosaunee, this early seventeenth-century confederation of indigenous peoples included the Mohawk, Oneida, Onondaga, Cayuga and Seneca, and spanned a geographic range from the Hudson River (New York City) north to the St. Lawrence River and west to the Genesee River.

5 Zoltan E. Szabo is a member of the Mohawk Nation of Akwesasne. His research article entitled "Origin of the Two-Row Wampum Belt, or Kahswentha" is published on the Web (http://vs1.ws4.u-net.net/www.peacetree.com/akwesasne/wampum.htm), p. 1.

6 In *Iroquois Indians: A Documentary History of the Diplomacy of the Six Nations and Their League* edited by Francis Jennings (Woodbridge, CT: Research Publications, 1984, microfilm, Z no. 024, Reel #50, information-reference no. 27), this covenant wampum is described as "representing early treaty with the English, the agreement being that both parties should travel by separate but parallel paths (the two stripes of purple beads), the Indians by canoe and the white man by his boat, neither interfering with the other except in cases of murder or robbery."

7 This particular rendition comes from an Oneida version of the story (http://one-web.org/oneida/wampum.html).

8 Jennings, *Iroquois Indians.*

9 This version of the Great Law comes from the text of a paper entitled "The Influence of the Great Law of Peace on the United States Constitution: An Haudenosaunee (Iroquois) Perspective," written by Kanatiyosh, a Mohawk from Akwesasne (also known as the St. Regis Mohawk Indian Reservation), located on an island in the St. Lawrence River between Ontario and New York State, opposite the city of Cornwall, Ontario. The paper was written in the mid-1990s when Kanatiyosh was a third-year law student at Arizona State University and has since been published on the Web (http://www.tuscaroras.com/graydeer/influenc/page1.htm). A different

version of the Mohawk Prayer of Thanksgiving is in a poem "Prayer for the Great Family" by Gary Snyder, in *The Sacred Landscape*, edited by Fredric Lehrman (Berkeley, CA: Celestial Arts), p. 1.

[10] Kanatiyosh, "The Influence of the Great Law of Peace on the United States Constitution: An Haudenosaunee (Iroquois) Perspective," p. 3.

[11] Pauline Joly de Lotbinière, "Of Wampum and Little People: Historical Narratives Regarding the Algonquin Wampum Record," in *The Algonquins*, edited by Daniel Clement (Hull, PQ: Museum of Civilization, 1996), p. 93.

[12] Ibid, p. 94.

[13] Ethnologist David Gidmark, who did an apprenticeship with William and Mary Commanda, has become something of a phenomenon with publications about his bark canoe learning. His books include: *Building a Birchbark Canoe: The Algonquin Wananaki Tciman* (St. Catharines, ON: Vanwell Publishing, 1994); *Birchbark Canoe: The Story of an Apprenticeship with the Indians* (Burnstown, ON: General Store Publishing, 1989); *The Algonquin Birchbark Canoe* (Princess Risborough: Shire Publications, 1988); *The Indian Crafts of William and Mary Commanda* (New York: McGraw-Hill Ryerson, 1980). A personal favourite book about bark-canoe building remains John McPhee's story about a trip into the Maine woods with canoe builder Henri Vaillancourt as described in *The Survival of the Bark Canoe* (New York: Farrar, Straus & Giroux, 1975).

[14] David Finch, interview with author, Calgary, Alberta, October 1997, and by phone October 1998.

[15] From Archibald Lampman's poem "Morning on the Lièvre," as published in *100 Poems of Nineteenth-Century Canada* (Toronto: Macmillan, 1974), p. 140.

[16] J.B. Sykes, *The Pocket Oxford Dictionary of Current English (Sixth Edition)* (Oxford: Oxford University Press, 1978), p. 172.

CHAPTER 3

[1] From a story told by Fred Pine in *Spirits on Stone: The Agawa Pictographs* by Thor and Julie Conway (San Luis Obispo, CA: Heritage Discoveries, 1990), p. 64.

[2] There are many excellent sources of Micmac creation stories and other legendry, including: Albert D. DeBlois, *Micmac Texts* (Hull, PQ: Canadian Museum of Civilization, 1991), and a classic older volume by Silas T. Rand, *Legends of the Micmacs* (London: Longmans, Green, and Co., 1894).

[3] Garrick Mallery, *Picture-Writing of the American Indians* (New York: Dover Publications, 1972), p. 40.

[4] Wilson D. Wallis and Ruth O.S. Wallis, *The Micmac Indians of Eastern Canada* (Minneapolis: University of Minnesota Press, 1955), p. 330.

[5] John Murray Gibbon, *The Romance of the Canadian Canoe* (Toronto: Ryerson Press, 1951), pp. 4–5.

[6] Http://www.capitalnet.com/~jason/content/legends.html

[7] Ella Elizabeth Clark, *Indian Legends of Canada* (Toronto: McClelland & Stewart, 1960), pp. 115, 117.

[8] Michael A. Bradley, *Holy Grail Across the Atlantic: The Secret History of Canadian Discovery and Exploration* (Willowdale, ON: Hounslow Press, 1988), p. 88.

[9] Frederick J. Pohl, *Prince Henry Sinclair: His Expedition to the New World in 1398* (New York: Clarkson Potter, 1974).

[10] Green's comments are published on the Web at: http://marlowe.wimsey.com/~rshand/streams/masons/glooscap.html.

[11] There are other interesting parallels and overlaps between ancient European and Micmac cultures discussed in "A Fur Trade Emblem," *Pathways: The Ontario Journal of Outdoor Education* 10/3 (August 1998): 15–16. Author Bob Henderson points out that the Micmac word for friend is *adesquidex*, while in an archaic Basque dialect the word for friend is *adeskide*, which raises the question: Did the Basque learn this from the Micmac or vice versa?

[12] James D. Edgar, *The White Stone Canoe: A Legend of the Ottawas* (Toronto: The Toronto News Company/Canadian Institute for Historic Microreproductions, microfiche no. 02883, 1885).

[13] Gibbon, *The Romance of the Canadian Canoe*, p. 5.

[14] Roberts and Shackleton, *The Canoe*, p. 30.

[15] Donald Burry, "The Canoe in Canadian Art" (Edmonton, AB: University of Alberta, Department of Physical Education and Sport Studies, unpublished doctoral dissertation, 1993).

[16] *Spirits on Stone* is an excellent interpretive guide to Agawa Rock.

[17] Clark, *Indian Legends of Canada*, pp. 87–88.

[18] John B. Mansfield, *History of the Great Lakes, Volume 1* (Cleveland, OH: Freshwater Press, 1972), p. 56.

[19] Edith Fowke, *Folktales of French Canada* (Toronto: NC Press, 1972), pp. 116–17.

[20] Ibid, p. 124.

[21] William H. Drummond, *The Habitant, and Other French-Canadian Poems* (New York and London: G.P. Putnam's Sons, 1897). Excerpting Drummond's work in the 1990s, one must acknowledge the different cultural sensibilities and the spirit of fun in which they were written. Politically correct, Drummond is not.

[22] Rheostatics, *The Blue Hysteria* (Raise A Little Elf/Warner Chappel Music, 1996).

[23] Nora Stewart's comments are in an article by Stuart Clark, "The Boat that Shouldn't Float," in *Like It Is* 1/4 (1975): 55.

[24] Found on-line at http://www.masterbuilders.com/canoe/mbt.htm.

[25] From the National Concrete Canoe Championship, 1999 Rules and Regulations (http://www.masterbuilders.com/canoe/Ccrule99.htm).

[26] A 1998 example of this phenomenon was a bulletin board that was part of the McMichael Gallery's "In the Wilds: Canoeing and Canadian art" exhibit in Kleinburg, Ontario. People were asked to create a collage of memorable canoeing moments on chits of paper, a surprising number of which included stories of canoes and weddings, a couple of which came documented with photos.

[27] James Raffan, *Summer North of 60: By Paddle and Portage across the Barren Lands* (Toronto: Key Porter Books, 1990).

[28] Alan Sullivan, "The White Canoe," published originally in *Our Canadian Literature: Representative Verse, English and French*, edited by Bliss Carman and Lorne Pierce (Toronto: Ryerson Press, 1935) and excerpted by John Murray Gibbon in *The Romance of the Canadian Canoe*, p. 143.

CHAPTER 4

[1] Song of Cree canoe-builder Miitaaskoonaanicaa, as recorded in J.Garth Taylor's monograph *Canoe Construction in a Cree Cultural Tradition* (Ottawa: National Museum of Man Mercury Series, Canadian Ethnology Service Paper No. 64, 1980), p. 25.

[2] James Raffan, *Fire in the Bones: Bill Mason and the Canadian Canoeing Tradition* (Toronto: HarperCollins, 1996).

[3] This phrase evokes an aural as well as olfactory response that brings to mind a superb tune written by folksinger Ian Tamblyn. My favourite version of it is by the Ottawa-based *a capella* trio Three Sheets to the Wind, on their album *Grace Under Pressure* (Ottawa: Canal Records, 1994).

[4] Jack wax is a term used in Eastern Ontario (and maybe elsewhere) to describe the gooey taffy created when overboiled maple syrup is poured on spring snow.

[5] There is another lovely portfolio of the sketches and models of Edwin Adney (most of them not published in *Bark and Skin Boats of North America*), tucked away in the back of John McPhee's classic *The Survival of the Bark Canoe* (New York: Farrar, Straus & Giroux, 1975).

[6] Stephen Greenlees, "Indian Canoe Makers," *The Beaver* (June 1954), pp. 47–48.

[7] Jerry Stelmok and Rollin Thurlow, *The Wood & Canvas Canoe: A Complete Guide to its*

History, Construction, Restoration, and Maintenance (Camden East, ON: Old Bridge Press, 1987), p. 18.

[8] Kenneth Grahame, *Wind in the Willows* (New York: Scribner's, 1933).

[9] Richard Sparkman, "The Venerable Chestnut Canoe," *Wooden Canoe Journal*, 86/ 21(2) (April 1998): 6.

[10] Kenneth Solway, *The Story of the Chestnut Canoe: 150 Years of Canadian Canoe Building* (Halifax, NS: Nimbus Publishing, 1997).

[11] Quoted in Roger MacGregor's book, *Chestnut Canoe: Catalogue F (February 1950): A Reprint* (Lansdowne, ON: Plumsweep Press, 1994), p. i.

[12] Ibid, p. ii.

[13] Susanna Moodie, *Roughing It in the Bush, or, Forest Life in Canada* (Toronto: Hunter, 1871), pp. 154–55.

[14] The Canadian Canoe Museum Archive (housed at Trent University) and the Peterborough Centennial Museum and Archive have a lively collection of ephemera, unpublished essays and other useful tidbits, including notes to the Centennial Museum exhibit, entitled "Peterborough: The Canoe Capital of Canada," mounted in the 1980s by archivist Andrew McDonald; Donald Cameron's essay "The Peterborough Canoe" (read at the Peterborough Historical Society, March 18, 1975); an essay entitled "Selected Insights into the Peterborough Area Canoe Building Industry," by Roger Tilden, dated March 1982 (Centennial Museum Archive, no accession detail); Gerald F. Stephenson's interesting little book about his grandfather entitled *John Stephenson and the Famous "Peterborough" Canoes* (Peterborough: Peterborough Historical Society, 1987); and a remarkable complete term paper by Trent University student Sheila Rutledge, entitled "The Canoe Industry in the Otonabee Valley, 1858–1978," written for Professor John Wadland, Canadian Studies 200, March 31, 1978. These of course only supplement more available historical accounts of canoe building in the Peterborough area such as John Marsh's essay "The Heritage of Peterborough Canoes," in *Nastawgan: The Canadian North by Canoe and Snowshoe*, edited by Bruce W. Hodgins and Margaret Hobbs (Toronto: Betelgeuse Books, 1985), pp. 211–22; and *Canoecraft: A Harrowsmith Illustrated Guide to Fine Woodstrip Construction* by Ted Moores and Merilyn Mohr (Camden East, ON: Camden House, 1983).

[15] This research was described at a conference in England and then reported in "Studying Historic Canoes and Kayaks," *Canoeist* (British Canoeing Union, April 1986), pp. 27–28. A much more complete account of C. Fred Johnston's findings are contained in an as-yet-unpublished manuscript entitled "In Search of the Canadian Canoe: The Columbia Canoe and Its Place in the Evolution of the Canadian Canoe."

[16] *Chestnut Canoe: Catalogue F*, p. iii.

[17] This text is taken from a reprinting of what might be the 1936 Chestnut Canoe Company catalogue in Solway's *The Story of the Chestnut Canoe* (p. 79) but the exact same passage is also present in Roger MacGregor's reprinting of the 1950 catalogue, *Chestnut Canoe: Catalogue F*, p. 13.

[18] Don Cayo, "You Can't Hurry a Hand-Crafted Canoe," *This Country Canada*, Summer 1996, p. 34.

[19] One of the most entertaining parts of Ken Solway's story of the Chestnut Canoe Company is "Who Bought What," pp. 134–37, which indicates that Don Fraser purchased forms for the 16-, 18-, 20-, and 22-foot Ogilvy canoes. The 26-foot Ogilvy form went to another long-time Chestnut employee, Carl Jones, who did his best to reincarnate the Chestnut spirit in a new company called Cedarwood Canoes. See Stephen Branch, "Continuing the Chestnut (Canoe) Tradition," *The Atlantic Advocate*, August 1988, pp. 12–14.

[20] Ibid, p. 35.

[21] John Marsh, "The Heritage of Peterborough Canoes," in *Nastawgan: The Canadian North by Canoe and Snowshoe*, edited by Bruce W. Hodgins and Margaret Hobbs (Toronto: Betelgeuse Books, 1985), p. 217.

[22] Solway adds that although the original business may be no longer in operation, bickering over the Chestnut company name and trademarks continues: see *The Story of the Chestnut Canoe*, pp. 147–48.

[23] *Chestnut Canoe: Catalogue F*, p. 18.

[24] Jamie Benidickson, "'Idleness, Water and a Canoe': Canadian Recreational Paddling between the Wars," in *Nastawgan*, p. 163. Benidickson expanded his research on this theme, publishing a comprehensive book, *Idleness, Water and a Canoe: Reflections on Paddling for Pleasure* (Toronto: University of Toronto Press, 1997).

[25] *Chestnut Canoe: Catalogue F*, p. 8.

[26] Advertisement for the "Rice Lake Canoe Company Limited, Cobourg, Ont." in *The Beaver*, January 1924, pp. 144–45.

CHAPTER 5

[1] From a poem "Coureurs de Bois" by Douglas LePan, originally published in *The Wounded Prince* (1948), as compiled in *Weathering It: Complete Poems, 1948–1987* (Toronto: McClelland & Stewart, 1987), p. 74.

[2] Lachine Rapids is a popular recreational destination for kayakers and has become a small

industry in the Montreal tourist scene, supporting a variety of outfitters offering tours on jet skis, jet boats, and various propeller-driven craft. In 1998, the firm Saute Moutons was offering, with daily departures every two hours, jet boat rides "through the wildest stretches of the Lachine Rapids [that will] leave you wet and wanting more," and thirty-minute speedboat outings described as follows in promotional literature: "Faster than a speeding bullet? Take a ride on the wild side. Rodeo style jet boating with enough twists and turns to resemble a chase scene in a James Bond movie."

[3] From Cartier's "A short and briefe narration," in Richard Hakluyt's *The principall navigations, voiages, traffiques, and discoveries of the English* (originally published 1589, republished Cambridge, MA: Hakluyt Society and the Peabody Museum of Salem, 1965).

[4] Timothy J. Kent, *Birchbark Canoes of the Fur Trade* (Ossineke, MI: Silver Fox Enterprises, 1997), p. 101.

[5] This is an entry from William T. Boutwell's journal dated September 12, 1835, as quoted in Grace Lee Nute's classic volume *The Voyageur* (St. Paul: Minnesota Historical Society, 1955), pp. 48–49.

[6] Ibid, p. 30.

[7] Clifford P. Wilson, "The Beaver Club," *The Beaver*, March 1936, p. 21.

[8] *Sail and Paddle* 7/1 (January 1889): 12.

[9] Ibid, p. 13.

[10] Nute, *The Voyageur*, p. 52.

[11] Peter C. Newman, *Caesars of the Wilderness* (Markham, ON: Penguin Books Canada, 1988), pp. 304–5.

[12] As published by Malcolm McLeod in "Canot du Nord: Canoes One Hundred Years Ago," in *The Beaver*, March 1931, p. 173.

[13] Newman, *Caesars of the Wilderness*, p. 304.

[14] Samuel H. Scudder, *The Winnipeg Country, or, Roughing It with an Eclipse Party* (Boston: Cupples, Upham and Company, 1886), p. 44.

[15] Germaine Warkentin, *Canadian Exploration Literature* (Toronto: Oxford University Press, 1993), pp. 175–6.

[16] This story comes from Clifford P. Wilson, "The Emperor's Last Days," *The Beaver*, December 1934, p. 50.

[17] Ibid, p. 51.

[18] Ibid, p. 53.

[19] These gestures began what has become a tradition of Canadians giving canoes to royals; in 1947, the City of Peterborough gave another lovely Canadian boat, a patented cedar rib canoe, to Princess Elizabeth on the occasion of her marriage to Philip Mountbatten, Duke of

Edinburgh. The Government of Canada got in the business of giving canoes to royalty during Pierre Trudeau's reign as prime minister, with the gift to Charles and Diana, on the occasion of their wedding, of a Bear Mountain "stripper," another immaculately constructed wooden canoe with mirror finish. In 1976, the Town of Lakefield, Ontario, showed its respect to Prince Andrew with the gift of a cedar strip canoe made by Walter Walker, one of the last of the original canoe builders in the Otonabee River valley. And, having whetted her appetite for canoes on their much-celebrated "secret" honeymoon on the Thelon River, Andrew's bride, Sarah, the Duchess of York, when in Canada to promote her book *My Story*, on *The Dini Petty Show*, was presented with a canoe stuffed with gifts, including Roots jackets for the little princesses, Beatrice and Eugenie. Royals traditionally bestow gifts such as these on worthy causes, but in this case the worthy cause was Fergie herself, who sent the canoe to her hotel and told the concierge to ship it home, charging the $1,600 transatlantic freight bill to her suite, which was paid for by her publisher, Simon & Schuster.

[20] John MacGregor, *A Thousand Miles in the Rob Roy Canoe on the Lakes and Rivers of Europe*, 7th ed. (Boston: Roberts Brothers, 1867).

[21] *Wooden Canoe*, 69 (June 1995), front cover.

[22] This account of the life and times of the voyageurs by Eric W. Morse appeared first in a series of three articles in the May, July and August 1961 issues of the *Canadian Geographical Journal* under the title "Voyageur Highway." They were reprinted in Ottawa as the volume *Canoe Routes of the Voyageurs : The Geography and Logistics of the Canadian Fur Trade* expressly for the Quetico Foundation of Ontario and the Minnesota Historical Society, 1962.

[23] Eric W. Morse, *Fur Trade Canoe Routes of Canada/ Then and Now* (Ottawa: National and Historic Parks Branch, 1971).

[24] Canada Centennial Commission, *Athletics and Voyageur Canoe Pageant, Centennial Facts Volume 5* (Ottawa: Canada Centennial Commission, 1965), p. 59.

[25] Ibid, p. 60.

[26] From an unpublished booklet entitled "Voyageur Soul," produced as a course handout for participants in Bill Peruniak's canoe-based graduate courses and management seminars conducted under the auspices of Queen's University Faculty of Education in cooperation with St. Lawrence College in Kingston, Ontario.

[27] Promotional brochure: "River Seminar for Educators and Managers: 'Leading High-Performance Teams,' July 25–31, 1993, French River, Ontario" (Kingston: Queen's University Faculty of Education and St. Lawrence College).

[28] From the brochure advertising the Nineteenth Annual Voyageur Seminar, "Revisiting Canada at the Millenium, July 17–23, 1998, French River Estuary" (Kingston: Queen's University Faculty of Education), p. 1.

[29] Harold A. Innis, *The Fur Trade in Canada: An Introduction to Canadian Economic History* (Toronto: University of Toronto Press [1930] 1956).

[30] Donald Creighton, *The Commercial Empire of the St. Lawrence* (Toronto: Macmillan of Canada [1937] 1956).

[31] CBC Radio's flagship A.M. program "Morningside" conducted a listener poll in 1997 which nominated "Northwest Passage" as the unofficial Canadian national anthem.

[32] Stan Rogers, "Northwest Passage," from the album *Northwest Passage* (Dundas, ON: Fogarty's Cove & Cole Harbour Music Ltd., FCM 004D, 1981).

CHAPTER 6

[1] Ken Roberts, *Maclean's*, July 30, 1979, p. 7.

[2] Dorothy Collins (*née* McMichael), interview with author, Guelph, Ontario, September 12, 1997.

[3] "Northway Lodge: A Summer Camp for Girls Conducted by Miss Case, Algonquin Park, Canada." Annual camp brochure, 1929, pp. 10–11.

[4] Ibid, p. 11.

[5] Joyce Plumptre Tyrrell, "Among Ourselves," a memorial tribute to Fannie L. Case, originally published in *Canadian Camping*, reprinted *The Story of Northway Lodge, 1906–1942*, p. 15.

[6] Dorothy Collins interview.

[7] S. Bernard Shaw, *Canoe Lake, Algonquin Park: Tom Thomson and other mysteries* (Burnstown, ON: General Store Publishing House, 1996).

[8] Ibid, p. 75.

[9] Alex Bryans and Edward Thring, interview with author, Kingston, Ontario, January 17, 1997.

[10] Ibid, Alex Bryans.

[11] John Turner, interview with author, Toronto, Ontario, March 24, 1997.

[12] John Turner, unpublished notes for a Canadian Club speech delivered on December 2, 1996.

[13] Bruce W. Hodgins, interview with author, Peterborough, Ontario, December 10, 1997.

[14] Http://www/tamakwa.com/noframes/Lou_and_Omer.htm. Used by permission of Camp Tamakwa.

[15] Kent, *Birchbark Canoes of the Fur Trade*, p. 320.

[16] Ibid, p. 323.

[17] Ibid.

[18] Marsh's poem with this final stanza by Kirk A.W. Wipper was published in *The Kanawa Journal*, January 1985, p. 1. The original version of "The Old Canoe" by George T. Marsh was published in *Scribner's Magazine*, vol 44 (October 1908), p. 52.

[19] These conversations with Wipper about the canoes in the original Kanawa Canoe Collection were part of a research project funded in part by the Wooden Canoe Heritage Association. Tapes and transcripts are destined for the archives of the Canadian Canoe Museum, currently housed at Trent University. Interviews were conducted on March 7, 1995, December 9, 1996, February 20 and September 18, 1997, and September 24, 1998.

[20] Excerpted from the Canadian Canoe Museum current mission statement, October 27, 1998, p. 1.

CHAPTER 7

[1] From a compendium titled "Vessel Types on Minnesota's Inland Waters," published online at (www.dted.state.mn.us/ebranch/mhs/prepast/mnshpo/ship/mpdf/incraft.html).

[2] Arthur J. Ray and Donald Freeman, *"Give Us Good Measure": An Economic Analysis of Relations between the Indians and the Hudson's Bay Company before 1763* (Toronto: University of Toronto Press, 1978), p. 24.

[3] It should be noted that the French took great interest in the HBC posts on the bay and, in fact, at various times, through various skirmishes and pitched battles, had possession of these installations, the principal draw in a business sense being that they were easier and quicker to access from the west than was the port at Montreal.

[4] Bruce W. Hodgins and Gwyneth Hoyle, *Canoeing North into the Unknown* (Toronto: Natural Heritage Books, 1994), p. 83.

[5] Ray and Freeman, *"Give Us Good Measure"*, pp. 45–46.

[6] Dennis F. Johnson, "The York Boats of the Hudson's Bay Company," in *WoodenBoat* 144, (September/October 1998): 50.

[7] Ibid, p. 51.

[8] Dennis Johnson indicates that one of the "most vital pieces of equipment" carried in the spartan appointments of an HBC York boat was a medicine chest containing the following items: 2 pounds of Epsom salts, one dozen purgative powders, one dozen vomits, one small spirits smelling salts, one half-dozen bottles painkiller (laudanum), one or two rolls of sticking plaster, a lancet and a pair of forceps.

[9] W. Kaye Lamb, ed., *Sixteen Years in Indian Country: The Journal of Daniel Williams Harmon, 1800–1816* (Toronto: Macmillan of Canada, 1957), pp. 197–98.

[10] This characterization of Orkney boatmen by Murdoch Mackenzie is taken from a

History of Saskatchewan Waterways published on-line
(www.lights.com/waterways/history.htm). The original source is unconfirmed.

[11] It is only fair to acknowledge that, after the amalgamation of the HBC and the NWC, men of French, aboriginal and Métis blood took up the oars of York boats. Recent evidence of this is in a June 19, 1998, wire story in the *Ottawa Citizen* (p. A10) describing how the the team of Solomon Carrière, a forty-one-year-old Métis trapper and fisherman from northern Saskatchewan, and Steve Landick, a long-distance paddler from Marquette, Michigan, won the gruelling 1,000-kilometre Dyea to Dawson hike/canoe race (over the Chilkoot Pass from Skagway, Alaska, on foot and down the Yukon River by canoe to Dawson City). Interviewed upon finishing the race in four days, one hour and fifty-two minutes, Carrière credited his incredible endurance to his Québécois grandfather, who "rowed York freighters around Saskatchewan."

[12] Neil Ray, "William Sinclair of Orkney" (http://pas1.erols.com/sinclair/wmsinclair.html-ssi). A resident of Goulais River, on Lake Superior north of Sault Ste. Marie, Ontario, Ray is the great-, great-, great-, great-grandson of HBC employee William Sinclair.

[13] This replica was part of a York boat building program at Fort Edmonton headed by self-styled boatwright Joseph Isserlis, who had himself built another replica some years earlier and travelled in it from Edmonton to Lower Fort Garry on the old fur-trade route. The boat that was used for the bicentennial celebration was actually one that had been built at Fort Edmonton for an exhibit at Expo 86 in Vancouver. This boat, made completely of western white pine, was 44 feet from "tip to tip" built on a 32-foot straight keel timber.

[14] Builder Joseph Isserlis estimated that this pine York boat absorbed something in the order of 500 pounds of water before its wood was saturated.

[15] Tim Marriott, interview with author, Edmonton, Alberta., October 30, 1998.

[16] Ibid.

[17] Newman, *Caesars of the Wilderness* (Markham, ON: Penguin Books), p. 302.

[18] Johnson, "The York Boats of the Hudson's Bay Company," p. 51.

[19] As cited in Jerry Stelmok and Rollin Thurlow, *The Wood and Canvas Canoe: A Complete Guide to Its History, Construction, Restoration, and Maintenance* (Camden East, ON: Old Bridge Press, 1987), p. 17.

[20] Ibid.

[21] "The Canoe Pastime," *New York Times*, 1872, contained in the documents in the Canadian Canoe Museum Archive, Trent University, accession number 93-016-2-113.

[22] Ken Cupery, "A Short History of Paper Boats" (http://home.eznet.net/~kcupery/SH.html, 1997), p. 1.

[23] As mentioned in chapter five, "Lachine," MacGregor came to Canada in 1859 and very

likely experienced the hospitality of Sir George Simpson, which included a constellation of opportunities to try out birchbark canoes. From central Canada, MacGregor continued on to Kamchatka and the Siberian peninsula before returning home to the United Kingdom, where he developed a decked, lapstrake, canoe he called "Rob Roy" that became the prototype of recreational canoes through Europe and into North America.

[24] Nathaniel H. Bishop, *Voyage of the Paper Canoe: A Geographical Journey of 2500 Miles from Quebec to the Gulf of Mexico, during the Years 1874–5* (Boston: Lee and Shepard Publishers, 1878). Like Samuel Hearne's journal and a growing number of difficult-to-access historical texts, *Voyage of the Paper Canoe* has been mounted in its entirety on the World Wide Web (http://eldred. ne.medianone. net/nhb/paperc/intro.html). This quoted text is taken from the electronic version of the book, Chapter V, p. 1.

[25] There is a slight resemblance to the lines of the Dogrib bark canoe in the Mackenzie Valley, but this is too far removed geographically to have had any likely effect on boat design at the E. Waters Company.

[26] This is from a catalogue, *Rushton's Portable Boats* (year unknown), as scanned and published on-line (http://web0.tiac.net/users/eldred/nhb/JPG/B6A.JPG), 14.

[27] Ibid.

[28] Canadian Canoe Museum Archive, Trent University, accession number 93-016-2-152.

[29] Paul Mason, interview with author, Chelsea, Quebec. February 14, 1997. Mason has since published the story on the Web of how he cut a foot out of the middle of his off-the-rack ABS plastic canoe. See "Short Cuts to Advance Canoeing," at (http://www/nowr.org/tech/cano_cut.htm).

[30] On-line advertisement for Escape Canoe at (http:///www.escapecanoe.com/canoe.htm).

CHAPTER 8

[1] Note from a cairn on the shore of Hoare Lake on the Hanbury River erected in 1978 to commemorate William "Billy" Hoare, first game warden of the Thelon Game Sanctuary. On a trip to commemorate the fiftieth anniversary of Hoare's achievement, his son built this cairn and put in it a reproduction of Hoare's journal with blank pages for visiting paddlers to add their comments.

[2] Details of this situation are nicely laid out in Margaret Hobbs's essay "Purposeful Wanderers: Late Nineteenth Century Travellers to the Barren Lands," in *Nastawgan*, edited by Bruce W. Hodgins and Margaret Hobbs (Toronto: Betelgeuse Books, 1985), pp. 56–81.

[3] J.W. Tyrrell, *Across the Sub-Arctics of Canada: A Journey of 3,200 Miles by Canoe and*

Snowshoe through the Barren Lands (London: T. Fisher Unwin, 1898: Facsimilie edition published by Coles Publishing Company, Toronto, 1973).

[4] Hobbs, "Purposeful Wanderers," p. 64.

[5] Tyrrell, *Across the Sub-Arctics of Canada*, p. 7.

[6] David T. Hanbury, "Through the Barren Ground of North-Eastern Canada to the Arctic Coast," *Geographical Journal* 22 (August 1903): 78–91. Also *Sport and Travel in the Northland of Canada* (London: Edward Arnold, 1904).

[7] Shelagh D. Grant, "George M. Douglas and the Lure of the Coppermine," in *Nastawgan*, edited by Bruce W. Hodgins and Margaret Hobbs, p. 102.

[8] George M. Douglas, *Lands Forlorn: A Story of an Expedition to Hearne's Coppermine River* (New York: G.P. Putnam's Sons, 1914).

[9] George Whalley, *The Legend of John Hornby* (Toronto: Macmillan of Canada, 1962), p. 54.

[10] From James Critchell-Bullock's journal, as cited in ibid, p. 210.

[11] Ibid, p. 239.

[12] Ibid, pp. 239–40.

[13] By quirk of topography and climate, the Thelon River valley supports an island of tree growth well beyond the conventional treeline. This so-called boreal oasis is home to all manner of plant, bird and animals life, so much so that the Chipewyan and Dogrib Dene who have hunted in this area for centuries call the Thelon valley "the place where God began." Futher detail on this can be found in "Where God Began," *Equinox* 71 (October 1993): 44–57.

[14] Whalley, *The Legend of John Hornby*, pp. 246–47.

[15] Ibid, p. 250.

[16] Text taken from Christian's diary as rendered in *Who Look in Stove & The Edgar Christian Diary*, a dramatic play by Lawrence Jeffery (Don Mills, ON: Exile Editions, 1993), p. 141.

[17] Ibid, p. 309.

[18] K.M. Dewar, "I Found the Bodies of the Hornby Party," *Canadian Geographic* 97/1 (1978): 18–23.

[19] Edgar Christian's diary was first published in Canada by Oberon Press in 1980, entitled, *Death in the Barren Ground*, with an introduction by Queen's University historian and Hornby *aficionado*, George Whalley.

[20] With some notable exceptions like P.G. Downes, who, in 1939, canoed north from Reindeer Lake in Saskatchewan to Nuelton Lake and the HBC post at Windy Lake, subsequently producing the classic canoe-tripping book, *Sleeping Island* (New York: Coward-McCann, 1943).

[21] Arthur R. Moffatt, "Man against the Barren Grounds, Part I," *Sports Illustrated*, March 9, 1959, p. 71. The story was actually published in two parts, the second entitled "Man against the Barren Grounds, Part II: Danger and Sacrifice" (March 16, 1959, pp. 80–88).

[22] George J. Grinnell, "Art Moffatt's Wilderness Way to Enlightenment," *Canoe*, July 1988, p. 20.

[23] Ibid.

[24] George J. Grinnell, *A Death on the Barrens* (Toronto: Northern Books, 1996), pp. 224–25.

[25] Ibid, pp. 219–20.

[26] Grinnell, "Art Moffatt's Wilderness Way to Enlightenment," p. 56.

[27] Grinnell, from a transcript of the *Ideas* series "Perfect Machines: The Canoe," Seth Feldman, producer (Toronto: Canadian Broadcasting Corporation, 1995, ID 9536), pp. 10–11.

[28] William C. James, "The Quest Pattern and the Canoe Trip," in *Nastawgan*, pp. 9–23. The original version of this classic essay was published as "The Canoe Trip as Religious Quest," in *Studies in Religion* 10(2) (Spring 1981): 151–66.

[29] Rudy Wiebe, *Playing Dead: A Contemplation Concerning the Arctic* (Edmonton: NeWest Publishers, 1989), p. 33.

[30] This is a story that has been given much play in the canoeing literature. Best among these versions is a book by authors of the classic canoe-tripping book *The Complete Wilderness Paddler*, James West Davidson and John Rugge. Their book about Leonidas Hubbard is *Great Heart: The History of Labrador Adventure* (New York: Viking Penguin, 1988).

[31] Margaret Atwood, "True North," *Saturday Night* 102/1 (January 1987): 146.

[32] Eric W. Morse, *Freshwater Saga: Memoirs of a Lifetime of Wilderness Canoeing in Canada* (Toronto: University of Toronto Press, 1987), p. 81.

[33] A superb contrast of perspectives that arise from tragic versus comic views of human enterprise is contained in Joseph W. Meeker's thought-provoking book *The Comedy of Survival: In Search of an Environmental Ethic* (Los Angeles, CA: Guild of Tutors Press, 1972).

[34] Christopher Norment, *In the North of Our Lives: A Year in the Wilderness of Northern Canada* (Camden, ME: Down East Books, 1989), p. vii.

[35] Yellowknife writer Bruce Valpy has written a play (as yet unpublished) entitled *Hornby* (1984) and Vancouver-born playwright Lawrence Jeffery published his dramatic play *Who Look in Stove* (Toronto: Exile Editions) in 1993.

[36] CBC Radio play written by George Whalley, date unknown.

[37] M.T. Kelly, *Out of the Whirlwind* (Toronto: Stoddart, 1995).

[38] The most current translation of this essay, originally published in French, is "The Ascetic in a Canoe," in *Against the Current: Selected Writings of Pierre Elliott Trudeau, 1939–1996*, edited by Gérard Pelletier (Toronto: McClelland & Stewart, 1996), p. 11.

[39] More on this can be found in "A Child of Nature: Trudeau and the Canoe," in *Trudeau's Shadow: The Life and Legacy of Pierre Elliott Trudeau*, edited by Andrew Cohen and J.L. Granatstein (Toronto: Random House of Canada, 1998), pp. 63–78.

[40] Roy MacGregor, "Like His Father, He Tested His Country," *National Post*, November 16, 1998, p. 1.

[41] Bruce Hodgins, interview with author, Peterborough, Ontario, December 10, 1997.

[42] W.R. Bocking, "A Canoe Trip," *Rod and Gun in Canada* (Woodstock, ON: W.J. Taylor Limited, November 1915 issue), p. 580.

[43] Grinnell, *A Death on the Barrens*, p. 303.

CHAPTER 9

[1] Mark Solby, interview with author, Toronto, Ontario, January 27, 1997.

[2] Glenn Lewis, interview with author, Gibsons, BC, July 7, 1998.

[3] In response to the assertion (often attributed to Pierre Berton) that a Canadian knows how to make love in a canoe, Ottawa Valley poet Philip Cluster has remarked that *anyone* can make love in a canoe—it is a Canadian who knows enough to take out the centre thwart.

[4] Citizen X, *Who Are the People of Canada Anyway?* (Toronto: eastendbooks, 1997).

[5] Will Ferguson, *Why I Hate Canadians* (Vancouver: Douglas & McIntyre, 1997). In a section of this book about the "evolution of nice," there is a chapter, "Voyageurs and Habitants," that touches in an interesting way on canoes and their effect on the movement of French surnames across Canada.

[6] John Murray Gibbon, *Steel of Empire: The Romantic History of the Canadian Pacific, the Northwest Passage of Today*, (New York: Bobbs-Merrill, 1935), p. 44.

[7] Daniel Francis, *National Dreams: Myth, Memory and Canadian History* (Vancouver: Arsenal Pulp Press, 1997) p. 25. This book also has a very thoughtful chapter that examines the place of the canoe in Canadian culture, entitled "The Ideology of the Canoe: The Myth of Wilderness."

[8] John Murray Gibbon, *The Romance of the Canadian Canoe* (Toronto: Ryerson Press, 1951), pp. v–vi.

[9] John Murray Gibbon, *New World Ballads* (Toronto: Ryerson Press, 1939), p. 82.

[10] Ibid, p. 79.

[11] This term is explored in a chapter of the same name in Jamie Benidickson's book

Idleness, Water and a Canoe: Reflections on Paddling for Pleasure (Toronto: University of Toronto Press, 1997).

[12] Gibbon, *New World Ballads*, p. 167.

[13] Ibid, p. 173.

[14] Disks 130845 and 130846.

[15] Disk 216587.

[16] Connie Kaldor, "Canoe Song," on her album *Wood River* (Coyote Entertainment Group/Word of Mouth Music, 1992).

[17] Gibbon, *The Romance of the Canadian Canoe*, p. vii.

[18] Benedickson, *Idleness, Water and a Canoe*, p. 16f.

[19] *Maclean's*, June 1, 1921, p. 39.

[20] Canadian National Railways, *Canoe Trips and Nature Photography* (1934), p. 3.

[21] Mark Solby interview.

CHAPTER 10

[1] Peggy Ahvakana, in *Our Chiefs and Elders* by David Neel (Vancouver: University of British Columbia Press, 1992), p. 54

[2] Kenneth Roberts and Phil Shackleton, *The Canoe: A History of the Craft from Panama to the Arctic* (Toronto: Macmillan of Canada, 1983), p. 98.

[3] Donald Burry, "The Canoe in Canadian Art" (Edmonton: University of Alberta, Department of Physical Education and Sport Studies, unpublished doctoral dissertation, 1993), p. 250.

[4] What is interesting about descriptions and didactic interpretations of the work, on billboards and in books, is that the presence and significance of all of the characters in this canoe are described in some detail—all elements, that is, except the canoe itself.

[5] David Neel, *The Great Canoes: Reviving a Northwest Coast Tradition* (Vancouver: Douglas & McIntyre, 1995), p. 23.

[6] The *Globe and Mail*, March 29, 1986.

[7] In its final and most appropriate service and traditional tribute to its builder, *LooTaas* carried Bill Reid's ashes to their final resting place in a solemn funeral ceremony to convey a spirit from one world to the next. See "The Raven's Last Journey" by Moira Johnston, *Saturday Night* November 1998, pp. 72–84.

[8] Neel, *The Great Canoes*, p. 4.

[9] Kirk Wipper, interview with author, Keene, Ontario, February 20, 1996.

[10] Claude Cousineau, interview with author, Ottawa, Ontario, July 5, 1998. Cousineau

remembers paddling for hours to a planned rendezvous with a stationary fishing boat, getting mixed up with the tides, arriving at the wrong anchored trawler and having to paddle back to Masset in darkness.

[11] Hugh MacMillan, interview with author, Guelph, Ontario, June 28, 1998.

[12] John Fallis, interview with author, Mono Centre, Ontario, June 27, 1998.

[13] Neel, *The Great Canoes*, pp. 133–4.

[14] Damon Vis-Dunbar, "The Year of the Dragon Boat," *The Peak* (Simon Fraser University's student newspaper), July 2, 1996, p. 1.

[15] Jennifer Hunter, "Enter the Dragon Women," *Chatelaine*, October 1997, p. 53.

CHAPTER 11

[1] William C. James, "The Quest Pattern and the Canoe Trip," in *Nastawgan: The Canadian North by Canoe and Snowshoe*, edited by Bruce W. Hodgins and Margaret Hobbs (Toronto: Betelguese Books, 1985), pp. 9–10.

[2] Robert W. Service, *Songs of a Sourdough* (Toronto: William Briggs, 1909), p. 58.

[3] Since that competition in Vancouver, I have become quite attached to one of Kirk Wipper's favourite craft in the Canadian Canoe Museum in Peterborough. It's a Loucheaux-style birch-bark canoe from the Mackenzie River delta, almost kayak-form with slender, decked bow and stern, but along its gunwale are Chinese trade beads. No one, including Wipper, seems to know how these beads might have found their way onto this canoe, whether they came separately and were attached after to a domestically constructed canoe, or whether the whole boat had some connection in its genesis to Asia, but these beads and the boat to which they are fixed also speak to the mysterious synergy between canoes of North America and the Orient.

[4] Robert McGhee, *Canadian Arctic Prehistory* (Hull, PQ: Canadian Museum of Civilization, 1990), p. 81.

[5] This Maori chant was sent to me by a student who went to teach in New Zealand. She writes in a letter that the lyrics refer to the great canoe which in Maori myth brought the original inhabitants of other places to Aoteroa, the Land of the Long White Cloud (reference unknown).

[6] Kenneth Roberts and Phil Shackleton, *The Canoe: A History of the Craft from Panama to the Arctic* (Toronto: Macmillan of Canada, 1983), p. 105.

[7] George Dyson, *Baidarka* (Edmonds, WA: Alaska Northwest Publishing Company, 1986).

[8] From *Gwichya Gwich'in Googwandak: The History of the Gwichya Gwich'in and of*

Tsiigehtchic by the Elders of Tsiigehtchic (Tsiigehtchic and Yellowknife: Gwich'in Social and Cultural Institute, March 1996), p. 363.

[9] Kirk Wipper, interview with author, Keene, Ontario, March 7, 1995.

[10] Ibid.

[11] A second and final bronze casting of *The Spirit of Haida Gwaii* was given a greenish finish and dubbed "The Jade Canoe." This sculpture now rests in the Vancouver International Airport, welcoming visitors from around the world.

[12] Ulli Steltzer, *The Spirit of Haida Gwaii: Bill Reid's Masterpiece* (Vancouver: Douglas & McIntyre, 1997), p. 20.

[13] Ibid, p. 18.

[14] Daniel Francis, *National Dreams: Myth, Memory, and Canadian History* (Vancouver: Arsenal Pulp Press, 1997), pp. 128–29.

[15] Lyse Rousseau-Darnell and Emanuel Darnell, *Stamps of Canada Catalogue* (Montreal: Darnell Publishing, 1994) is an excellent full-colour resource to the iconography of Canadian stamps.

[16] John Wadland, "Great Rivers, Small Boats: Landscape and Canadian Historical Culture." An unpublished paper presented at the annual meeting of the Canadian Historical Association (June 1994), pp. 20–21.

[17] Philip Chester, "Motives for Mr. Canoehead," in Canexus: *The Canoe in Canadian Culture*, edited by James Raffan and Bert Horwood (Toronto: Betelgeuse Books, 1988), p. 100.

[18] John Jennings, "The Canoe: The Boat that Built a Nation," in a prospectus entitled *The Case [for] The Canadian Canoe Museum* (Peterborough: The Canadian Canoe Museum, 1996), p. 6.

INDEX

*"n" preceding a number indicates the
number of the note*

ACKNOWLEDGEMENTS

My thanks to Brenda Allen of Kingston, whose archival and library research left no stone unturned; to my one-of-a-kind friend the Dragon, Jan Carrick, of Kingston, who transcribed miles of audio tape, read drafts and helped balance teaching and writing; to Kirk Wipper of Keene, whose patience in helping me understand the collection in the Canadian Canoe Museum was invaluable; to Bill Byrick, Dawn McColl and the staff at the Canadian Canoe Museum, who were always helpful; to my friend and retired colleague Bert Horwood, who always seems to come along at the right time with new ways to look a things; to my sister Helen Batten, her husband, Doug, and daughter, Elsa, of Lakefield, who never seemed to mind visitors at all hours of the day and night when at the museum in Peterborough; to Don and Willy Morgan, of Winnipeg, whose gift of a red Chestnut canoe continues to inspire in so many ways; to Joyce Mason, of Old Chelsea, Quebec, always a cheerful voice; to Albert and Tina Angenent, who teach and support and continue to laugh at their neighbours' peripatetic ways; to Don Kilby for his fine illustrations and Sue Thomas for her maps with just the right feel; to Phyllis Bruce and the staff at HarperCollins in Toronto, who treat each book as if it were their own; and finally, to our daughters Molly Claire and Laurel Cole, who run toward the dawn every day with infectious delight. Your generosity has enriched these pages.

Many others have supported this project in substantial ways over the last few years: Joseph Agnew at the CRCA in Merrickville, Justine

ACKNOWLEDGEMENTS

Allan from *Voyageur* magazine, Tom Andrews at the Prince of Wales
Northern Heritage Centre in Yellowknife, Alex Bryans in Kingston, Jim
Burant at the National Archives in Ottawa, Don Burry in Edmonton,
Kevin Callen in Peterborough, Dorothy Collins in Guelph, Claude
Cousineau in Ottawa, Bernadine Dodge at Trent University, John Fallis
in Mono Centre, David Finch in Calgary, Ned Franks in Kingston,
Doug Gifford in Toronto, Mike Greco in Ottawa, George Grinnell in
Ottawa, Chris and Nancy Hanks in Yellowknife, Bob Henderson at
McMaster University, Bruce and Carol Hodgins of Wanapitei, Gwyneth
and Alex Hoyle in Peterborough, Ted Johnson in Montreal, Fred
Johnston in Odessa, Ingrid Kritsch of the Gwich'in Social and Cultural
Institute, Peter and Sandra Labor near Wawa, Jack LaPointe in
Westport, Glenn Lewis in Kelowna, Carl Lawrence in Seeley's Bay,
George Luste of the Wilderness Canoe Symposium, Grant Linney in
Georgetown, Craig Macdonald in Dwight, Hugh MacMillan in
Guelph, Tim Marriott in Edmonton, Paul and Becky Mason in Chelsea,
Mary McCreadie on Joliffe Island in Great Slave Lake, Jane Mock in
Colombia, Pamela Morse in the Gatineau Hills, Craig Oliver in Ottawa,
Suzie Patterson in Toronto, Hamish and Betty Raffan in Guelph, Drew
Ridpath on Stoney Lake, Gary Saunders in Truro, Matt Saunders in
Seeley's Bay, Joan Schwartz at the National Archives in Ottawa, Angus
Scott in Toronto, Lloyd Seaward in Bishop's Falls, Mark Solby at
Labatt's, Hugh Stewart in Wakefield, Ted Thring in Kingston, John
Turner in Toronto, John Winters in Burks Falls, Rick Wolfe in Toronto,
and Bob Wolfe in Kingston. Appreciation to all of you.